# SIGNIFICATIONS

*Signs, Symbols, and Images
in the Interpretation of Religion*

### Charles H. Long

*The Charles E. Winquist Series
in
Philosophical and Cultural Studies in Religion*

*The Davies Group, Publishers*  *Aurora, Colorado*

*SIGNIFICATIONS: Signs, Symbols and Images in the Interpretation of Religion.*
©1986, Fortress Press, ©1995, Charles H. Long.

All rights reserved. No part of the contents of this book may be reproduced, stored in an information retrieval system, or transcribed, in any form or by any means — electronic, digital, mechanical, photocopying, recording, or otherwise — without the express written permission of the publisher, and the holder of copyright. Submit all inquiries and requests to the publisher.

Address all requests to:
  The Davies Group, Publishers
  PO Box 440140
  Aurora, CO  80044-0140
  USA

*Library of Congress Cataloging-in-Publication Data.*

Long, Charles H.
  Significations: Signs, Symbols, and Images in the Interpretation of Religion

  Includes index.

  ISBN 1-888570-51-2

  1. Religion.  2. Afro-Americans — Religion.
  Title

  Library of Congress Catalog Card Number:  98-89387

Most of the material in *SIGNIFICATIONS: Signs, Symbols, and Images in the Interpretation of Religion* appeared in a book by the same title published in 1986 by the Fortress Press.

Printed in the United States of America
Published 1999. The Davies Group Publishers, Aurora CO  80044-0140

Cover design by The Davies Group

23456789

# Contents

Foreword..........v

Proem..........ix

Acknowledgments..........xxi

Introduction..........1

Part I: Religion and the Study of Religion..........11
    Chapter 1    The Study of Religion: Its Nature and Its Discourse..........15
    Chapter 2    Prolegomenon to a Religious Hermeneutic..........31
    Chapter 3    Archaism and Hermeneutics..........43
    Chapter 4    Silence and Signification..........61

Part II: Religion and Cultural Contact..........71
    Chapter 5    Human Centers: An Essay on Method in the History of Religions..........75
    Chapter 6    Primitive/Civilized: The Locus of a Problem..........89
    Chapter 7    Conquest and Cultural Contact in the New World..........107
    Chapter 8    Cargo Cults as Cultural Historical Phenomena..........125

Part III: Shadow and Symbols of American Religion..........139
    Chapter 9    Interpretations of Black Religion in America..........145
        A:  The Black Reality: Toward a Theology of Freedom
        B:  The Ambiguities of Innocence
        C:  Civil Rights — Civil Religion: Visible People and Invisible Religion
    Chapter 10    The Oppressive Elements in Religion and the Religions of the Oppressed..........171
    Chapter 11    Perspectives for a Study of Afro-American Religion in the United States..........187
    Chapter 12    Freedom, Otherness, and Religion: Theologies Opaque..........199

Index..........215

TO MY TEACHERS
in the Public Schools of Little Rock, Arkansas,
and at The University of Chicago

*Foreword*

---

Charles H. Long opens *Significations* with two epigraphs. The first is an African-American colloquialism: "Signifying is worse than lying." The second is a quotation from Ferdinand de Saussure: "The bond between the signifier and the signified is arbitrary." The first of these epigraphs marks the thickness of experience incorporated within the African-American community and the second is emblematic of the profound philosophical interrogations that characterize all of Long's work. The lived meaning of these epigraphs intercalate in the thinking of Charles Long and pressure the creation of a vision of the understanding of religion that is both postmodern and American.

Long defines religion as orientation in the ultimate sense. "That is, [religion is] how one comes to terms with the ultimate significance of one's place in the world." What appears to be a simple and yet comprehensive definition is actually very complex. The logic of thinking about religion is a logic of ultimate sense. His sense of *sense* is deeply implicated in his opening epigraphs. There is no thinking outside of the specificities of a historical moment and cultural location; and, there is no thinking that is not afflicted by the arbitrariness of the relationship between the signifier and the signified. Long brings semiotics into the discipline of the history of religions and develops what might be called a *contact epistemology* that respects the materiality of culture and the ideality of thinking processes.

The disciplinary consciousness of the history of religions in Long's work is traced back through Joachim Wach, Rudolph Otto, Friedrich Heiler, and Max Müller to an Enlightenment consciousness. At the core of the history of religions is epistemological theory. It would never be enough for the history of religions to understand itself as area or topical studies. Long writes that "[t]he issue at stake is the mode of discourse one uses to make sense of one's data." There is a merger of epistemology and hermeneutics in his thinking that has relevance for an understanding of thinking itself that is much larger than the range of any specific discipline or special problem. The combination of *materiality* and *ideality* in thinking processes mark a *cultural contact* and the possibilities for *complex signification* that can both disclose and obscure realities of which we seek understanding. The cultural contact forces a thickness in description but the signifying that is "worse than lying" can produce elaborations of culture that are non-identical with the cultures they purport to describe. The hermeneutical problem that complicates epistemology is that interpretive cultural constructions can be *other* than the *otherness* of material cultural practices and experience.

Long is not simply imposing a hermeneutical problem on epistemology. He deepens an epistemological sensibility that is implicated in the realities of contact and exchange. If we follow the lead of physicist Murray Gell-Mann and note that there is a continuum of interrogation, analysis, description and understanding from coarse-grained to fine-grained experience, we can also note that Charles Long interrogates and theorizes religion along this continuum. He, for example, investigates the material expressions of religion in Melanesian Cargo cults and also investigates the meaning of *thinking* in Enlightenment epistemology, American Pragmatism, and the Whiteheadian philosophy of organism. Implicated within the interstices of his textual production, notions such as Charles Sanders Pierce's *thirdness* or Alfred North Whitehead's *relationality* inform, interrogate and are interrogated by the data of material expressions of religion and culture. He is not just a collector of religious data. He is a thinker of the coarse- and fine- grained complexity of religious and cultural meanings.

There is a strong affirmation that philosophical analysis should arise from historical understanding if it is to serve the history of religions. There is also an understanding that the data of religion is the *stuff* of human experience. Human presence within the world is what needs to be understood. Long quotes Georges Dumezil that "it is under the sign of *logos* and not *mana* that we place our research today." There is neither a retreat from rationality nor a simplification of the experience of *reason* in Long's understanding. Rationality seeks to unlock the enigma of experiences even when rationality is not fully identical with the experiences to which it attends. Thinking, in this sense, is a deconstructive supplement that adds to the production of an important knowledge.

The task of the historian of religions is to reveal a structure, a language of the *sacred*, "that describes human immersion in life." This language is a supplement that is also a medium for insertion into the historical being of others. The study of religion is never simple description. There is an emergent *thirdness* that is an inevitable product of the contact and exchange that is the work of understanding. This is an achievement and not a fault of thinking.

Thinking the "other" is always also a thinking of ourselves. It is impossible to configure what it would mean to think the "wholly other" or a "pure" otherness. Thinking is always contact and exchange. Long recognizes that there is an existential weight to thinking the history of religions even when one uses the phenomenological *epoché* to bracket the data under investigation. He understands the *epoché* as a meditation on our own existence; a meditation linking to us to our existence in the world; "a meditation possible through the appearance of the 'other'." In the history of religions the *epoché* is not a tool for phenomenological reduction. It is a tool for meditation and mediation of the "otherness" of the experience of "others." It is a tool for understanding and expressing the "otherness" within our own experience. The positive and negative ambiguity of the *mysterium tremendum* of religious experience is given a place to be thought.

In a certain way, *Significations* is a deconstructive theology of the history of religions. This is not because Long specifically writes of *theologies opaque* and *theologies of oppression*. The opacity and silence of reality marks the human condition, and the affirmations that "God is red" or "black is beautiful" elaborate the importance of the complex opacity of the real. The theological importance of his thinking is that there is a *primordium* and it is secular. It is implicated in the everydayness of life. The "otherness" of experience within the everyday does not violate the Wittgensteinian sense that "[t]he world is all that is the case." Long's thinking of the extraordinary within the ordinary is a coming to terms with the ultimate significance of one's place in the world. His work is a discernment of meaning, and to advance his vision he makes common cause with the many voices of artists, folklorists, poets, and anthropologists as well as philosophers and theologians. His thinking says *no* to traditional theological authority and *yes* to a thinking that is commensurate with the beauty of life as we can come to know it if we choose to care.

*Syracuse University*                             Charles E. Winquist
*Thomas J. Watson Professor*
*of Religion*

## *Proem*

In his essay "Why Read the Classics", Italo Calvino urges us, in this time of critical confusion, to invent our own ideal libraries of classic works to read and be read. One of his definitions of a classic is that it "…is a book that has never finished saying what it has to say." Another definition of Calvino's classic is "…something that tends to relegate the concerns of the moment to the status of background noise…"

I first became aware of a living classic as a student in the Divinity School at the University of Chicago when I accidentally walked into one of Charles H. Long's classes. Long's teachings on religious symbolisms, millenarian movements, cargo cults, and creative hermeneutics have become for generations of students a profound and constant fountain of ideas, challenges, insights and questions that reflect Calvino's first definition of the classic — Long never stops speaking to us, and his ideas continue to have a powerful relevance to the changing interpretive landscape. His teachings, many of which are represented in this collection, worked the intellectual magic, amidst the highly charged social and political concerns of the 60's and 70's, of placing those feverish concerns, and much of what was at stake, in the rich and paradoxical context of the history of religions. Those concerns became the background noises — the counterpoint — to Long's ability to demonstrate how all of the furious significations of our awful century were expressions of another background, the background of the arche and the new arche, about which he writes so persuasively in this book.

Long's *Significations*, as the following review essay I wrote of the Fortress Press edition will show, is the work of a creative, insightful mind that produces another kind of work that is characteristic of a classic. It disturbs and nurtures our own thinking. It is a signification from the background and *must* be included in the new millennial list of classic works in religious studies. *Significations* has not finished saying what it has to say. Nor has Charles H. Long finished reordering our concerns or disturbing and nurturing our thinking.

## Insight/Signification

*Significations: Signs, Symbols, and Images in the Interpretation of Religion.*
By Charles H. Long. Philadelphia: Fortress Press, 1986. Pp. 207.

At the beginning of the film *The Never-ending Story* a ten-year-old child takes refuge from a group of bullies in an old bookstore, where he is challenged by the crusty owner to go waste his time in a video arcade. The boy protests that he loves and reads books like the classics surrounding him and asks about a book with unusual symbols on it which the old man is guarding; but he is told, "This book? This is something special. The books you read are *safe.* This one isn't. This book isn't for you. It is an unsafe book. It will change you." When the owner is distracted, the boy takes the book, leaving a note promising to return it, goes to the attic of his school and reads it in one long night. During the ordeal his view of the world is radically changed.

In a number of ways, Charles Long's *Significations: Signs, Symbols, and Images in the Interpretation of Religion* is just such an unsafe book that has the potential to change or at least enlarge the mind and practice of the history of religions in America. Long's study of the "cultural language" and the "stylistics ... the emerging shape of thought" of disciplines in the West is hazardous, not because it is menacing, but because, in the spirit of the works of Harold Cruse and Ashis Nandy, it is a sustained criticism of several major approaches (phenomenological, historical, theological) and pre-suppositions ("shadows of the discipline") which make up some of the work of religious studies in the United States. Within this critical spirit, Long attempts (1) a reevaluation of some of the basic issues forming the study of religion in America, (2) an outline of a hermeneutics of conquest and colonialism generated during the formation of the social and symbolic order called the "New World," and (3) a critique of the categories of civil religion, innocence, and theology from the perspective of the black experience and the experience of colonized peoples. Along the way, Long displays what is perhaps his greatest gift, namely, insight. He sees and shows us how to see into the moral condition of the interpreter of "empirical others" as well as into the richness and complexity of religious symbols, "the sacred things" of others. If we attend to the substance of *Significations,* say as seriously as we have attended Mircea Eliade's *The Quest* or Jonathan Z. Smith's

---

I want to thank Reginald Ray for assistance with this review article.

©1991 by The University of Chicago. All rights reserved.
0018-2710/92/3101-0004 $01.00

*Map Is Not Territory*, or Wendy Doniger's *Other People's Myths*, the practice of the discipline of history of religions will be equally enriched and have to change in several aspects.

First, the formative history of the disciplines of religious studies will have to be reconsidered and rewritten. One of the official litanies of this history is that our disciplines are "children of the enlightenment." From Cassirer to Eliade to Kitagawa to Long himself, scholars in the field proceed in their interpretive work and form their judgments with the mighty tools and categories of the *Aufklärung*. But according to Long there is another, equally powerful, formative awakening at the root of *Religionswissenschaft:* "The other critical element in the discussion of religion in the modern world is related to the Western exploration of the world that is symbolized by the voyages of Christopher Columbus in the late fifteenth century. From that time until the twentieth century, the Western world, through conquest, trade, and colonialism, made contact with every part of the globe" (p. 3). But the combination of Enlightenment methods and epistemologies with the opening of a New World led not so much to better understanding of "others" as to intellectual strategies which "paved the ground for historical evolutionary thinking, racial theories and forms of color symbolism that made the economic and military conquest of various cultures and peoples justifiable and defensible. In this movement both religion and cultures and peoples throughout the world were created anew through academic disciplinary orientations — they were signified" (p. 4).

We must be very careful, however, not to think of Long as merely a scholar of protest. In his earlier work, partly expressed in the first section of *Significations*, "Religion and the Study of Religion," he carried out a sustained reflection on epistemological styles of the Enlightenment. As his articles "Prolegomenon to a Religious Hermeneutic" and "Archaism and Hermeneutics" show, this included reading projects on Immanuel Kant, René Descartes, and Blaise Pascal, as well as focused work on Chantepie de la Saussaye, Rudolph Otto, Gerardus van der Leeuw, and Raffaele Pettazoni. Summarizing both his admiration for the philosophical achievements of some of these thinkers as well as his discomfort, he concludes his decade-long exercise troubled that two crucial epistemological errors remain uncorrected. They are the (1) use of exterior norms, in fact an ontology, to draw meaning from data which, while being gathered, constituted, and systematized, failed to (2) deal with the "interrelation of the subject to the world," that is, the human fabric, especially the symbols and symbolic fabric, woven and experienced by the "others."

This led to Long's work of elucidating a "historical ontology" (p. 50) which demands a series of hard reflections (he invokes Hegel's "lithic imagination") on religious symbolism. He writes, "Through religious symbolism we may find a new and authentic basis for reflection. Reflection proceeding from religious symbolism has the merit of correlating the interpreter on a search for the inner being of self and humanity with a level of historical expression commensurate with this intention. As the interpreter moves from symbolism to rationality, another movement will become necessary — a movement back into the shadows of one's ego and history" (p. 57).

As he shows in "Conquest and Cultural Contact in the New World" and "The Black Reality: Toward a Theology of Freedom," the reflection on symbols and the movement back into one's history reveal both the "inner dynamics of religious consciousness" and the pervasive tie between the hermeneutics of Conquest and the hermeneutics of Enlightenment in the study of religion and culture. In this sense, I am reminded of Ashis Nandy's honest assessment: "Let us not forget that the most violent denunciation of the West produced by Frantz Fanon is written in the elegant style of a Jean-Paul Sartre. The West has not merely produced modern colonialism, it informs most interpretations of colonialism. It colours even this interpretation of interpretation" (Ashis Nandy, *The Intimate Enemy: Loss and Recovery of Self under Colonialism* [Delhi: Oxford University Press, 1983, p. *xii*]).

Another change urged by Long's approach relates to what Mircea Eliade called the "historical moment" scholars face as they attempt to "improve the hermeneutics of religious data" (*The Quest* [Chicago: University of Chicago Press, 1969], pp. 1-2). What constitutes our historical moment for Long is not primarily the encounter with Asian spiritualities or the appearance of so-called primitives as subjects "on the horizon of greater history" or new opportunities to imagine religion but rather *"the dynamics of concealment,"* that is, history of "significations" reflected in the delayed and distorted appearance of the colonized, the signified, the "others" in our epistemology. As he shows in "Silence and Signification" there is a real connection between this masking of the oppressed in scholarship and the history of slavery, Buchenwald, Hiroshima, the black freedom movement, colonialism in Latin America and the "monstrosities . . . of the Western world" (p. 66). In Long's view Western hermeneutics has never been primarily about understanding and meaning. It has also always been about meanings which transform the objects of hermeneutics from strangers into intimate enemies. Today, historians of religions must begin to deal with this history as well as the fact that the "intimate others" have always articulated their own meanings and understandings of this intimacy. Long feels that this is a very difficult task.

Long's work also rearranges our view of the territories and conversation partners that historians of religions must work in and with. On the one hand, he is kin to the "Chicago School" of the history of religions and its precursors, including the influential voices of Soderblöm, Müller, Otto, van der Leeuw, Wach, and Eliade. On the other hand, he is close to the concerns of Tzvetan Todorov, Albert Memmi, Frantz Fanon, Michael Taussig, and especially Ashis Nandy, who see the terror or Western colonial history as a conceptual *and* corporeal reality, as Nandy says, in "bodies . . . in structures and in minds" (Nandy, p. *xi*). A new hermeneutical action is demanded. In Long's view it appears that this action is not so much interdisciplinary as a disciplined discourse between thinkers alert to the philosophical, political, and symbolic powers of colonialism and signification.

This double kinship is what is rare and fresh, challenging scholars of religions to think in a different way. In what follows I want to explore parts of his work by summarizing aspects of his critical orientation and focus on specific essays which carry his dual interpretive program forward.

## *Openings and Indices*

Long opens his book with two revealing juxtapositions about education and language. The book is dedicated to "My teachers in the public schools of Little Rock, Arkansas, and at the University of Chicago." The social and symbolic distance between these two educational systems (one legally segregated, the other seemingly integrated) is large, painful, even immense. As one reads on in the book, especially where Long writes about how people who have undergone master-slave significations combat them with symbols of transformation and truth, we reflect back on the symbolic strategy of this dedication. Long is pointing out the distance and overcoming it at the same time. Yet as we read on it becomes clear that this ability to be in two places at once is a personal achievement and not a collective one. Religious studies as a collection of disciplines does not cover this kind of distance well. In fact, it has hardly acknowledged it.

This juxtaposition (or to use his symbol appearing in the essay "Primitive/ Civilized: The Locus of a Problem") this slash (/) which joins two apparently opposed worlds is repeated in the opening quotations of the introduction. First, we are given "Signifying is worse than lying," an Afro-American colloquial expression associated with, among other things, the street chant about the signifying monkey. Then, we are taken into the prose of Ferdinand de Saussure, "The bond between the signifier and the signified is arbitrary" (p. 1). To be arbitrary, especially from the position of powerful privilege, Long is telling us, is worse than lying, and it is no street game. It is an obfuscation of human communication, and it is just this arbitrariness and its powers to distort that have filtered into the structures of discourse that constitute much of the landscape of cultural hermeneutics in the United States.

We learn something of Long's journey across this terrain by perusing the book's index, which forms a lively mirror of the text. Consider these names and terms from the index which I arrange as juxtapositions, reflecting something of the playful, even sly spirit of his discourse:

Thomas Altizer/Brer Rabbit
Karl Barth/James Baldwin
Calvin/Cargo Cults
William Clebsch/Eldridge Cleaver
Concealment/University of Chicago
Wilhelm Dilthey/W. E. B. Dubois
Freud/Terror of History
Hysteria/Human Sciences
Herder/Flotsam and Jetsam of Bits and Pieces of a Reality that was once thought to be an order
Innocence of America/Jabberwocky of Loose Ends and Bad Fits
Kitagawa/New World
Language/Mexico
Octavio Paz/Plato
Other/Oppenheimer
Religious Studies/Patchwork of Potpourri
Theologians/Vailala Madness
Wheatley/Pascal

### *The Potency of Latency*

These terms and juxtapositions are placed, as explained in his introduction, within the context of the art of "significations" defined as the "verbal art ... which obscures and obfuscates a discourse without taking responsibility for doing so" (p. 1). This art is a power game, a game of setting up power relationships in which language is the instrument of subordination of people we study. But the process of subordination in academia is often subtle and latent. Significations, the obscuring of the "others" in the discourse, seep into the theories and methods guiding the study of other people's cultures and are not just limited to individual monographs of interpretation. The really potent relationships and terms of superiority and subordination emerged from the Western exploration of the world, the European encounters with the natives of other lands, and the masked discourse on religion, race, and territory. "Significations constitute the texture and network of various relationships between and among the relations of cultures and peoples in the modern world" (p. 4). This signified texture keeps historians and historians of religions from seeing the real situation of cultural contact and thereby from including the character and consequences of social anguish in their intellectual formulations about other people's myths, symbols, rituals, histories, and imaginations. The problem of hermeneutics is, in part, the problem of understanding the experience of colonialism which created, in part, the ground for some of our ambitions to interpret the sacred things of others.

One important area of concern for Long is the recent movement in comparative studies to emphasize differences rather than similarities. The move to employ differences out of a reaction to previous generalities can also be a signification unless it is made clear "what leads one to locate the difference within what is common" (p. 5). The indexing of differences does so much more than reveal an array of experiences, a diversity of manners, a wealth of local knowledge. An overemphasis on difference can also lead to a new exoticism wherein we may lose access to the ways the "others" used their alienation as a resourceful and critical otherness which "allowed these communities to undertake a radical internal criticism of themselves, their situation and the situation of the majority culture" (p. *xxiii*).

## *Hermeneutics and Colonialism as Shared Culture*

Some of Long's later work is based on the insistence that we develop an understanding that the intimacy of the religious symbols of the colonizer and the colonized is an intimacy of not just mind, but of body and mind. It is Long's insight that scholar and informant/text share in this intimacy. This demands not just new strategies of self-reflection but an act of liberation within the attitudes of the signifier. His own study of the religious symbols linking signifier/signified, colonizer/colonized, primitive/civilized leads to an illumination about three kinds of religious creativity which challenges the hermeneut: (1) a primordial creativity in all humans which first constituted mind and body, (2) a colonizing creativity or the experience of signification which inflated the mind and body of the colonizer and reduced the mind and body of the signified persons, and (3) the creativity of the oppressed which discovers the fictive character of colonial significations. A complete hermeneutics and historical understanding will be based, in part, on the investigation of these three types of creativity.

The shift from phenomenology to a historical understanding of religious creativity and significations sets the stage for the four essays in the second section, "Religion and Cultural Contact." Long is at work demasking a series of metaphors of subordination — including "center," "civilized," "primitive," "conquest," "others" — in order to see the methods used to inhibit reciprocity of language between the signifiers and the signified. The arbitrariness of this inhibition can be monstrous. It can take life away from the "sacred things" of others. The essay "Primitive/Civilized: The Locus of a Problem" honed out of an intense period of reflection while directing several NEH summer seminars on the topic reveals some of Long's work of demasking.

Long's critique of these metaphors of subordination is mounted on his category of the "empirical other" defined as "a cultural phenomenon in which the extraordinariness and uniqueness of a person or culture is first recognized negatively" (p. 90). Covering this negativity are "various stratagems of description and diagnosis employed to represent the other in the relationship" (p. 91). European society, a great inventor of cultural masks, utilized the ideology of hysteria in relation to women and the motif of the wild man in relation to strangers and illness to build a basis for "symbolic and mythological languages used to describe and interpret the new worlds" of America (p. 92). These diagnoses led to metaphors of confinement, and in particular to the devastating slash metaphor of "primitive/civilized." There is a will to power and a symbolic hierarchy in this masked relationship and no objectivity whatsoever. "The self conscious realization of the Western European rise to the level of civilization must be seen simultaneously in its relationship to the discovery of the new world which must necessarily be perceived as inhabited by savages and primitives who constitute the lowest rung on the ladder of cultural reality" (p. 94).

Several ramifications of Long's insistence on a historical mode of analysis of symbols come clearer in the final section of the essay when he states that the peoples and cultures named "primitive" were not just imaginary structures but human beings, part of a universal human condition. That his sense of history is not a liberal concern for diversity but a concern for a radical hermeneutics is indicated in the two questions which emerge from the insistence that the study of other people's symbols always be attached to the voices and conditions of empirical others. "If the symbol of civilization is demythologized, if this symbol no longer possesses an ontological prestige among the other symbols of human culture, in what manner do the others appear?" (p. 104). Long's answer is something like *we will be touched and gain insight and a new conception of human community may emerge.* This question leads to another, which is what would happen if "we demythologized in turn our own discipline?" The answer to that question is hardly being formed.

## *"Hey Man, There's Real People Down Here:" Ralph Ellison to Irving Howe*

The discussion of "empirical others" and a new community leads into the four essays in the third section of the book "Shadow and Symbols of American Religion." The focus is on the black experience in America "demonstrating the dynamics of the creation of a discourse of power that prevents the meaning of what really happened from becoming a part of the cultural language of the nation" (p. 142).

Long's sense of the dynamics of concealment which blocks the realization of the meaning of community as a religious experience of inclusion is partly stated in his Harvard lecture, "Oppression in Religion and Religions of the Oppressed." He compares the interpretations of powerful emotional experiences undergone by William James and W. E. B. Dubois in order to ask the question, "How radical was James' radical empiricism?" Another way of asking this question is, "How did James and Dubois interpret the appearance of uncanny otherness in their lives?" Both Henry and William James had unnerving emotional experiences that left them quivering in fear and terror, and which they interpreted within "neurological-biological and individualistic categories" without significant reference to family, social or historical events and relations. This "psychologically oriented rhetoric of that which is totally unrelated to existence" is compared with the approach of William James's student Dubois whose first encounter with a Southern Negro revival led to feelings of a "pythian madness, a demonic possession that lent terrible reality to song and word" (quoted in Long, p. 177). While Dubois had similar feelings as the James had, his interpretation focused on the historical community which was the source and meaning of these feelings and not primarily on theories of mind. In fact, these kinds of experiences within the black community led Dubois to perceive the nature of the shared but fractured Soul of Blacks/Whites in America as well as the double consciousness of the Black Soul. Dubois is quoted by Long: "A Double consciousness . . . this sense of always looking at one's self through the eyes of another, measuring one's soul by the type of a world that looks on in amused contempt and pity . . . two souls, two thoughts, two unreconciled strivings, two warring ideals in one dark body, whose dogged strength alone keeps it from being torn asunder" (p. 178).

Out of this strength to maintain a double consciousness of mind and history comes the awareness that the hermeneutical circle of the signifiers can be broken, the hierarchy can be rearranged by the community of interpreters who have been signified. You must be in two places at once to have insight!

There are other significant sections of *Significations,* including Long's sustained debate with Thomas Altizer concerning innocence and history, a criticism of white and black "theologies opaque" alongside of his appreciation for James Cone's "new mode of theological writing," a meditation on Blaise Pascal's ("man with a double vision") view of the modern world, a sensible application of Stephan Greenblatt's *Renaissance Self Fashioning* to the problem of myth, insightful glosses on Hegel, Kant, and Eliade and remarkable sections on cargo cults and their social and symbolic creativity. Exceptional is Long's seminal essay "Perspectives for a Study of Afro-American Religions in the United States," in which he elucidates the symbolic images of (1) Africa as historical reality and religious image, (2) the involuntary presence of the black community in America, and (3) the experience and symbol of God in the religious experience of blacks.

### *Innovator*

Whether you agree with Long or not, it is necessary to acknowledge his genius and the message to the discipline. Historians of religions have to transform their understanding of their hermeneutical situation and find "new grounds and new terms" to renew the study of religious realities. The boldness of this message recalls Victor Turner's discovery of the "capacity of individuals to stand at times aside from models, patterns, paradigms for behavior and thinking . . . and, in rare cases, to innovate new patterns themselves or to assent to innovations" (Victor Turner, *Dramas, Fields and Metaphors* [Ithaca, N.Y.: Cornell University Press, 1974], p. 15). While it is not clear that Long has innovated a new pattern, it is clear that he is one of the most creative thinkers in the discipline and has stood at times aside from models and patterns of thought and seen the problem of "hermeneutics as signification" and that he assents to, insists upon, and inspires, out of pain and hope, innovation in the study of religion in America.

*Princeton University*                                                      Davíd Carrasco

# *Acknowledgments*

I wish to gratefully acknowledge the following publishers who have generously allowed me permission to republish materials originally published by them in this form.

"The Study of Religion: Its Nature and Its Discourse" was originally given in 1980 by Charles H. Long as the inaugural lecture of the Department of Religious Studies, University of Colorado, Boulder, Colorado.

"Prolegomenon to a Religious Hermeneutic" appeared in *History of Religions* 6, no. 3 (February 1967), and is reprinted by permission of the University of Chicago Press.

"Archaism and Hermeneutics" appeared in *The History of Religions: Essays on the Problem of Understanding* (1967), edited by Joseph M. Kitagawa, Mircea Eliade, and Charles H. Long, and is reprinted by permission of the University of Chicago Press.

"Silence and Signification" appeared in *Myths and Symbols: Studies in Honor of Mircea Eliade* (1969), edited by Joseph M. Kitagawa and Charles H. Long, and is reprinted by permission of the University of Chicago Press.

"Human Centers: An Essay on Method in the History of Religions" appeared in *Soundings* 61, no. 3, copyright© 1978 by *Soundings*, and is reprinted by permission.

"Primitive/Civilized: The Locus of a Problem" appeared in *History of Religions* 20, nos. 1 and 2 (August and November 1980) and is reprinted by permission of the University of Chicago Press.

"Conquest and Cultural Contact in the New World" was presented by the author at the University of Queensland, Brisbane, Australia, Summer 1983.

"Freedom, Otherness and Religion: Theologies Opaque" was originally published in the *Chicago Theological Seminary Register* 73, 1 (Winter 1983).

"Cargo Cults as Cultural Historical Phenomena" was originally delivered by Charles H. Long as the 1973 Presidential Address of the American Academy of Religion in Chicago. It subsequently appeared in the *Journal of the American Academy of Religion* 42, no. 3 (1974) and is reprinted by permission.

"The Oppressive Elements in Religion and the Religions of the Oppressed" was originally given by Charles H. Long as the William James Lecture on Religious Experience at Harvard Divinity School. It was subsequently published in the *Harvard Theological Review* 69, nos. 3-4, copyright© 1976 by the President and Fellows of Harvard College. Reprinted by permission.

"Perspectives for a Study of Afro–American Religion in the United States" originally appeared in *History of Religions* 11, no. 1 (August 1971), and is reprinted by permission of the University of Chicago Press.

Portions of chapter 9 "Interpretations of Black Religion in America" appeared in "The Black Reality: Toward a Theology of Freedom," *Criterion* 8, 2 (Spring-Summer 1969); "The Ambiguities of Innocence," from *America and the Future of Theology*, ed. by William A. Beardslee, copyright© MCMLXVII The Westminster Press; and, "Assessment and New Departures for a Study of Black Religion in the United States," *The Chicago Theological Seminary Register* 21, 1 (Winter 1981): 4-16, and are reprinted by permission.

The lyrics by James Weldon Johnson of the song "Lift Every Voice and Sing" are reprinted by permission of Edward B. Marks Music Company.

I should also like to express my gratitude to all my colleagues, students, friends, who have over the years urged me to publish in this form. They include Joseph Sittler, Jay Kim (deceased), J. Geller, S. Churchill, Irene Vasquez, Davíd Carrasco, and C. Shelby Rooks. Ms. Julia Hardy saw me through the first publication of this project, through editing, proofreading, and all the little emergencies involved in every stage. She also prepared the index for the 1986 edition.

# Introduction

*Signifying is worse than lying.*
— Afro-American colloquial expression

*The bond between the signifier and the signified is arbitrary.*
— Ferdinand de Saussure

A long personal history lies between these two epigraphs. The first one I learned as a boy growing up in Little Rock, Arkansas; I became acquainted with the work of Saussure in 1957. By that time I was teaching in one of the distinguished universities in America. But though the statements at first glance appear paradoxical or juxtaposed in terms of their origin, I think my community of origin and Saussure have much in common.

From the colloquial and slang expressions of my youth I learned something about the forms of linguistic expression. Signifying is worse than lying because it obscures and obfuscates a discourse without taking responsibility for so doing. This verbal misdirection parallels the real argument but gains its power of meaning from the structure of the discourse itself without the signification being subjected to the rules of the discourse.

As a matter of fact, the signifier may speak in agreement with a point of view, while the tone of voice creates doubt in the very act and words of agreement. Or the signifier may simply add comments that move the conversation in another direction. Or the signifier will simply say a word or make a comment that has nothing to do with the context of the discourse, but immediately the conversation must be formulated at another level because of that word or phrase. Signifying is a very clever language game, and one has to be adept in the verbal arts either to signify or to keep from being signified upon.

It is precisely the arbitrariness of signification that makes it so frustrating. As Saussure put it, "The bond between the signifier and the signified is arbitrary." The signifiers of my community knew this and thus through tone of voice, and the injection of new words and phrases, attempted to form new and different relationships within a discourse that was already taking place.

But on another level, my community was a community that knew that one of the important meanings about it was the fact that it was a community signified by another community. This signification constituted a subordinate relationship of power expressed through custom and legal structures. While aware of this fact, the community undercut this legitimated signification with a signification upon this legitimated signifying. On the one hand, the fact that signification represented an arbitrary relationship between the signifier and the signified meant that the relationship could be changed, while on the other hand, the very fact that the relationship was arbitrary was the source of its terror.

But all is not signification. There is a long tradition in the interpretation of symbol that defines the symbol as an intrinsic relationship between the symbol and that which is symbolized. Even Saussure affirms this interpretation of symbol. "One characteristic of the symbol is that it is never wholly arbitrary; it is not empty, for there is a rudiment of a natural bond between the signifier and the signified."(Saussure, *Course in General Linguistics,* ed. Charles Bally and Albert Sechehaye in collaboration with Albert Reidlinger, trans. Wade Baskin [New York: Philosophical Library, 1959]).

As a historian of religions I affirm this general meaning of the symbol and especially the religious symbol. However, religious symbols, precisely because of their intrinsic power, radiate and deploy meanings; the spread of these meanings creates an arena and field of power relationships which, though having their origin in symbols and symbolic clusters, are best defined in terms of significations and signs. On a methodological level this tendency is expressed in the range of disciplines such as the sociology, psychology, and anthropology of religion. My essay "Prolegomenon to a Religious Hermeneutic" is an indication of this tendency.

The power of signification is equally present when one places various methodological theories within the various cultural milieux in which they arose. This enables one to see the different forces and valences that come into play when the tools of method are being fashioned and to see that it is quite possible that methodological theories could have been otherwise, but also it enables one to understand why they were not. I am not suggesting that all methodology should be reduced to a problem of the sociology of knowledge. I am, rather, stating that a total hermeneutical discussion cannot overlook the role of signification in the creation of theoretical formulations.

The essays published here were written over a period of some two decades. They were originally written for other occasions, and almost all have been published in journals and other books. There is of course a kind of unity that stems from a single author working self-consciously within the resources and restraints of a particular academic discipline. As I read them over again for publication as a single text I noted other sorts of unities and threads of common meaning.

All of the essays have a methodological tone and intent. To be more precise, all of the essays are hermeneutical attempts to make sense of the phenomenon of religion on the most general level and of the problematic meaning of religion in the United States in particular. The reality, status, meaning, and proper methods for the study of religion are issues that are grist for the mill for one who has chosen to be a historian of religion. This disciplinary orientation begins with the problematical nature of religion in the post-Enlightenment world of the West. While continuities between religion in the modern world and the meaning of this phenomenon in premodern cultures are attested to in theories and methods for the study of religion, the problematical status of religion itself as an authentic and even necessary mode of human experience and expression is an acute issue of the modern period. Two critical issues brought about this ambiguity regarding the nature of religion.

The Enlightenment as a critical orientation sought new and different modes of understanding that were both universal and communal in humankind, thus displacing various normative meanings of religion in human societies, especially in the societies of the Western world. Obviously, religion did not vanish from Western societies, but it did have to compete with other realities for the role of normativity regarding the nature and destiny of the human being. The struggle over the meaning and nature of religion in the modern world is a long and varied chapter in the history of theological apologetics in the modern West — and it continues.

The other critical element in the discussion of religion in the modern world is related to the Western exploration of the world that is symbolized by the voyages of Christopher Columbus in the late fifteenth century. From that time until the twentieth century, the Western world, through conquest, trade, and colonialism, made contact with every part of the globe. These encounters and confrontations with other cultures raised again the issue of religion. Did all peoples possess religion or were there cultures that were devoid of the religious sentiment? If religion was a form of human meaning that might be dispensed with, what status should one allow the religions of these other cultures? Is there a continuity of some sort between the religions of other cultures and the religions that are part of the Western meaning of religion? Is it possible that there can be a general category of religion, given the many varieties of this phenomenon? These are some of the issues that have confronted the modern student of religion. As these kinds of questions have been dealt with, the notion of religion has taken on a new life. In seeking to give a unitary meaning to this phenomenon, religion has been almost created anew within the categories of the disciplines of the human sciences that undertook a study of this phenomenon.

On the one hand, these disciplines were practically and rhetorically devoted to an empirical approach derivative from historical and philological studies and also from the new "field work" and research methods of the anthropologists and sociologists. On the other hand, these disciplines inherited the existential and philosophical cultural issues surrounding the meaning and nature of religion that had formed the discussions of religion since the Enlightenment. For the most part, those discussions served to distantiate religion. Either religion was authentic to the extent that it constituted the past of Western culture or human culture at large or it was relegated to the peripheries of human existence, for example, the contemporary Western lower classes or women or in the peripheral areas of the world, among "primitive" peoples or other cultures that were technologically inferior to the West.

There is a complex relationship between the meaning and nature of religion as a subject of academic study and the reality of the peoples and cultures who were conquered and colonized during this same period. Both meanings — religion as an authentic mode of the human and the situation of those cultures that were overcome by the West, the enslaved, colonized, and conquered — constituted something of a scandal. While the reformist structure of the Enlightenment had mounted a polemic against the divisive meaning of religion in Western culture and set forth alternate meanings for the understanding of the human, the same ideological structures through various intellectual strategies paved the ground for historical evolutionary thinking, racial theories, and forms of color symbolism that made the economic and military conquest of various cultures and peoples justifiable and defensible. In this movement both religion and cultures and peoples throughout the world were created anew through academic disciplinary orientations — *they were signified.*

By signification I am pointing to one of the ways in which names are given to realities and peoples during this period of conquest; this naming is at the same time an objectification through categories and concepts of those realities which appear as novel and "other" to the cultures of conquest. There is of course the element of power in this process of naming and objectification. This power is both latent and manifest. It is manifest in the intellectual operations that exhibit the ability of the human mind to come to terms with that which is novel, and it is manifest in the manner of passivity that is expressed in the process wherein the active existential and self-identifying *notae* through which a people know themselves is almost completely bypassed for the sake of the conceptual and categorial forms of classification. The latency of the power is obscured and the political, economic, and military situation that forms the context of the confrontation is masked by the intellectual desire for knowledge of the other. The actual situation of cultural contact itself is never brought to the fore within the context of intellectual formulations.

The authenticity of the intellectual power is expressed through those categories and procedures which strive for the clarity of description and in the search for those structures in the lived world of the others which are both common and different in the worlds of the signified and the signifier. However, the latency of the power of the context itself, the situation of cultural contact, filters through the categorial and intellectual structures. The descriptive and analytical categories and taxonomies form the basis for an accusatory or compensational order of meaning. For example, on the descriptive level, one cannot deny that there are peoples and cultures of dark-skinned, kinky-haired human beings who do not wear clothing in the manner of the cultures of the investigators, and, in addition, they express very different meanings regarding their orientations in their worlds. While this may be true on the descriptive and analytical levels, the fact that these characteristics were noted as the basis for significant differences is often unexplored. In other words, what leads one to locate the differences within what is the common? More often than not, the differences that bring a culture or a people to the attention of the investigator are not simply formed from the point of view of the intellectual problematic; they are more often than not the nuances and latencies of that power which is part of the structure of the cultural contact itself manifesting itself as intellectual curiosity. In this manner the cultures of non-Western peoples were created as products of a complex signification.

The nature of this signification is at once a structure of experience and an intellectual problem for both the signified and the signifier. It constitutes the texture and network of various relationships between and among the relationships of cultures and peoples in the modern world. Various protest movements among peoples who were confronted by the West since the fifteenth century attest to the tenacity of this structure. On the one hand, some of these protests demand a continuity of the Western ideals in dealing with them. To some extent, some of these protest movements see a certain normativeness in Western values and are surprised that the Western investigators were not able to discover the primordial structures of these values in their own cultures. In other cases, the protest represents disavowals of all that is associated with the West and idealizes the authenticity of their cultures prior to the contact situation. In still other cases, the attempt is made to come to terms with the contact situation itself as a new form of human creativity.

But the response is not simply and only from the situation of those signified. The situation of cultural contact brought about changes in the cultures of the signifiers. This is, to be sure, often overlooked, for the signifiers tend to hide these changes through rhetorical recourse to historical and cultural continuities internal to their own cultures that tends to explain all changes as modes of development and evolution of ideational and historical clusters of meaning that have come to fruition in the modern period. However, especially since the end of the Second World War, we are able to see more serious studies that move toward the hermeneutical problem of the making of the modern Western culture and thus the formation of the modern human being in the West in relationship to the situation and confrontation of the cultures of the world.

In some cases this is simply an appreciative response to the diffusion of certain non-Western values into the Western world — for example, Picasso's use of artistic techniques from certain forms of West African art forms. That is well and good, but the issue is much deeper than the appreciation of cultural diffusion; it is an acute intellectual problem. One does not have the option of finding another place outside the structure of these relationships. The intellectual issue has to do with a critical language that recognizes the situation and is able to undercut the very structures of cultural languages that undergird the problematical situation itself.

These essays adumbrate various critical responses to the situation of cultural contact in the modern world. As an Afro-American, the situation to which I have alluded is an issue of experience and the locus of an intellectual critique. The religion of those who have had to bear the weight of this confrontation in the modern world should generate forms of critical languages capable of creating the proper disjunctions for a restatement of the reality of the human in worlds to come.

At another level, I have been concerned in these essays with the issue of the religion of Afro-Americans as the source for new modes of thought.

Many of the recent works dealing with issues of black culture in America are encompassed within the cultural categories of the American reality. This is to be expected. The civil rights movement is a case in point. It has become clear to many of us that that movement itself invites a deeper and more radical critique of the American cultural categories. I have not engaged in the project of black theology, not because of its black connotation, but because I did not wish to assume even this categorial structure as a mode of thought and expression. The religion of Afro-Americans afforded another opportunity.

As a historian of religions I have not defined religion in conventional terms. To be sure, the church is one place one looks for religion. Given the situation of Americans of African descent, their churches were always somewhat different from the other churches of the United States. But even more than this, the church was not the only context for the meaning of religion. For my purposes, religion will mean orientation — orientation in the ultimate sense, that is, how one comes to terms with the ultimate significance of one's place in the world. The Christian faith provided a language for the meaning of religion, but not all the religious meanings of the black communities were encompassed by the Christian forms of religion. I have been as interested in other forms of religion in the history of black communities — as those forms are contained in their folklore, music, style of life, and so on. Some tensions have existed between these forms of orientation and those of the Christian churches, but some of these extra-church orientations have had great critical and creative power. They have often touched deeper religious issues regarding the true situation of black communities than those of the church leaders of their time.

The religion of any people is more than a structure of thought; it is experience, expression, motivations, intentions, behaviors, styles, and rhythms. Its first and fundamental expression is not on the level of thought. It gives rise to thought, but a form of thought that embodies the precision and nuances of its source. This is especially true of Afro-American religion. Americans of African descent have been forced to deal with several heritages — those of Africa, those of the New World in the form of the cultural and political situation of the United States, and the heritage of a distinctive culture created in this country from this amalgam. And they have had to deal with these realities always under a situation of oppression and duress.

For the majority culture of this country, blacks have always been signified. By this I mean that they have always been a part of a cultural code whose euphemisms and stereotypes have indicated their meaning within the larger framework of American cultural languages. The cultural reality of blacks in the United States has been created by those who have the power of cultural signification — and the range of this power in the language of political, social, and cultural reality is enormous. In this regard, blacks are a part of the same structures of cultural categories that create the categories of the primitives and colonized peoples of the contemporary world. The first official language about such peoples in the modern world is not a language which they have created, but a language of signification created by others about them. It is for reasons of this kind that a most extensive literature exists *about* them, most of it written and presided over by others.

If one is oppressed, unable to mold a meaning about oneself that can become cultural coin, one must nevertheless deal critically with the language about oneself. This language is itself contradictory, and many of the struggles of Afro-Americans have taken place within this language game. It has been an attempt to verify, act upon, and come to terms with a language created *about* them. More often than not this is a losing battle, for the arbiters of this language have a very different conception of language than those defined by it. For the arbiters, this language expresses a wide semantic range whose internal coherency is constituted by power valences. It exists primarily to keep the others in their place, and that place is always defined by the others.

My concern for the meaning of the religious reality of black Americans is obviously part and parcel of my scholarly discipline, the history of religions. This academic choice itself was probably rooted in a deeper, unconscious desire to make sense of my life as a black person in the United States. I was attracted to this scholarly orientation, for it was the only discipline that responded to the religious experience and expressions of my origins in the black community of this country. This in itself was illuminating. A note was struck when I felt a recognition of reality from my community of origins in the religious experiences and expressions of others far and near. There was, I felt, a mode of making sense of the experiences of my tradition that did not begin with a methodology of pathology, one of the primary American cultural and social scientific languages about blacks. I perceived that there was a structure for the universal in the human world that, though created from Enlightenment understandings of the human venture, expressed an opening for the authentic expression of others. Religion thus became the locus for a meaning that carried an archaic form; it was a root meaning and could thus become the basis for radical critical thought.

The essays presented in this volume explore the possibilities of a form of thought that is rooted in the religious experience of black traditions. In one sense, these essays are, in Rudolf Otto's language, ideograms — those forms of meaning which lie between experience and category. This is the exploratory range. In another sense, the essays may be seen as exercises in stylistics. I mean by this to indicate the *shape* of thought, or better, the emerging *shape* of thought. The concern represented by this geometric metaphor has to do with the change in the structure of thought itself.

Thought, or even changes of thought, do not occur *de novo*. One must always deal with the given situation. From this perspective, the tradition of black religious experience has had its passive and critical moments. Blacks have undergone the *rise of the West,* in the most intense manner, and the very subjection to the hegemony of the modern West has been affirmative and critical. In many respects, the West has been severely criticized by this community for not *being* the West, for not living up to its cultural ideals, and this critique could not have taken place if the black traditions had not themselves internalized the meanings and possible meanings of this cultural formation. But there were other moments. The situation of the cultures of black peoples in the United States afforded a religious experience of radical *otherness,* a resourceful and critical moment that allowed these communities to undertake radical internal criticisms of themselves, their situation, and the situation of the majority culture. In religious terms, this was an experience of a kind of *mysterium tremendum,* or the experience of a *deus otiosus.* "And I couldn't hear nobody pray, O Lord/And I couldn't hear nobody pray."

The religious experience forces us to come to terms with these modalities, affirmative and critical. My project on the critical level is a form of the archaic critique, or, if you will, a kind of crawling back through the history that evoked these experiences. In other words, for the sake of thought blacks must now freely accept for themselves that which in a previous history they were forced to undergo. This critical *recursus* is a vital resource for critical thinking. But this time the return is in the form of a critique. I am attracted to Jacques Derrida's *deconstruction,* because it seems to be a philosophical mode akin to what I mean by "crawling back" through one's history. The languages and experiences of signification can be seen for what they are and were, and one might also be able to see a new and counter-creative signification and expressive deployment of new meanings expressed in styles and rhythms of dissimulation. The religious experience is the locus for this resource.

I hope that these essays might provide an opportunity for the renewal of a conversation between those of us interested in religion and other scholars in the human sciences, as well as poets, novelists, and creative artists. Black scholars have more often than not thought of their scholarship as a "reformers' discipline," to use E. B. Tylor's apt phrase. Generations of black scholars within the social and human sciences expressed a religious and ethical concern in their work. If these essays serve to renew that older conversation on new grounds and in new terms, I shall be grateful.

Charles H. Long

*Part One*

*Religion and the Study of Religion*

———————— ◆ ————————

*Part One*

*Religion and the Study of Religion*

---

In several ways the essays in this section explore the backgrounds, moments, and methodological nuances of the study of religion. From these perspectives they take us "back into the shadows" of the disciplinary orientations of the study of religion. Attention to problems raised in the history of the study of religion does not necessarily imply a return to the solutions of other scholars in past generations; however, such attentiveness could alert the contemporary student to basic issues that informed the study at its beginnings.

We are also able to observe how the cultural milieu feeds into the way issues are put and how they are resolved. The first essay, "The Study of Religion: Its Nature and Its Discourse," discusses how members of the several departments of religious studies, "the new kid on the block" in academic divisions of arts and sciences of several state universities, must come to terms with their interpretive communities. Several members of departments of this kind have come from either doctoral programs in theological studies or area studies. Departments of religion are neither theological schools nor area study programs. What are they? In many cases the notions "multidisciplinary" or "interdisciplinary" are used to describe departments of religion. Too often this description in terms of the plurality of disciplines involved in the study of religion is a way of skirting the problem of constitutive and systematic questions in the study of religion. The failure to deal with the history of interpretive communities in the study of religion leads to facile solutions and resolutions in the study of religion. No common language of discourse or argumentation is forthcoming, and thus what could be an important meaning in our academic and cultural lives is in danger of being trivialized.

When the history of interpretive communities in the study of religion is seen within the context of their several cultural milieux, one is able to observe the situation of interpretation, the ideological and cultural meaning of interpretation and the ideological and cultural meaning of the study at particular times and places. This might prompt contemporary interpreters to reflect upon similar issues involved in their own work.

In "Prolegomenon to a Religious Hermeneutic," the possibility of some rapprochement between the study of religion as a social science and as a hermeneutical enterprise as represented in the history of religions is addressed. I turned to Charles Sanders Peirce's logic as a philosophical approach to this issue. The issue addressed in this essay may not be as difficult to discuss as when this essay was first published. The popularity of Claude Lévi-Strauss among various social scientists and the hermeneutical writings of such scholars as Paul Ricoeur and Hans-Georg Gadamer have convinced many of our colleagues in the social sciences that the problem of interpretation is a crucial one.

The essay "Archaism and Hermeneutics" represents efforts to evoke certain styles and moods surrounding methodological discussions of religion. I suggest that there is a reciprocity between the constitution of the data of religion and the methodological procedures of the interpreter. This reciprocity, though specific in the case of each interpreter, is at the same time a procedure that reveals and/or obscures a form of cultural subjectivity.

In "Silence and Signification," attention is directed to the meaning of the study of religion within a culture which expresses one of its fundamental modes of creativity in the forms of a scientific technology. The implied objective methodology consonant with this mode of creativity raised the issue of the a priori on the level of history, moving beyond that of the internal constitution of consciousness as we saw it in the case of Rudolf Otto. Another form of the *a priori* is constituted; silent and unexpressed in itself but opening up a wide range of significations. I suggest several issues in the study of religion and theology which must come to terms with these implications.

# Chapter 1

## *The Study of Religion: Its Nature and Its Discourse*

The study of religion within separate departments of religion or religious studies is a comparatively recent innovation in the world of the university. Though European universities have for a longer time been engaged in the study of religion in faculties outside those of theology, the growth of departments of religion in America has surpassed those of Europe, if not in quality, at least in quantity. It is not hyperbolic to speak of the establishment and growth of such departments in American universities as phenomenal.

This phenomenon is at once a mixed blessing and the source of ambiguity. Over the last twenty years the proliferation of departments of religion in American universities, the expansion of the professional society of the American Academy of Religion with its journal and publication series, the new intellectual climate brought into being by these factors — neither all of these together nor any one of them alone enables us to define an essential meaning, goal, or purpose for the establishment of departments so dedicated and consecrated to such a study. To be sure, scholars at particular universities have been able to convince their academic colleagues and administrators of the practical and theoretical reasons for the establishment of departments of this kind; this is well, good, and proper. Novelty in the academic life is seldom accompanied by initial explicit order but more often than not emerges from embryonic structures which only later are seen as mature, ordered form. This is therefore not the source of ambiguity nor the locus of mixed blessing.

The ambiguity and mixed blessing arise from another observation. It is my observation that in the midst of this activity in the study of religion, we are not able to discern any specific structure, embryonic or otherwise, that might constitute the membrane of meaning for the development of mature form. It is possible to make the argument that the entire area of religious studies is a confused patchwork of potpourri, a jabberwocky of loose ends and bad fits, an unserious clown within the arena of academic disciplines.

---

Originally published as the Inaugural Lecture of the Department of Religious Studies, University of Colorado, Boulder, 7 October 1980.

The history of the establishment of departments of religion in the universities and colleges of this country over the last two decades should have by this time produced meanings that might orient us to those structures of essential order which would define serious positions. I am afraid that this has not been the case. It is therefore incumbent upon any such new establishment that it take unto itself a difficult task — namely, to set forth those meanings, structures, and methods which will enable faculties to define their data and the discourse appropriate for its study. This department will be important to the extent that it undertakes this task; it will be mediocre to the extent that it avoids it. As the inaugural lecturer on the occasion of the establishment of this department, I propose, with your indulgence, to open this discussion.

## *The Study of Religion: The Roots*

What constitutes the *study* of religion and why has it taken so long for the academic community to define its disciplinary structures? One reason for this quandary is related to the history of the study of religion in institutions of higher education prior to the establishment of departments of religion or religious studies. For the most part, these departments were offshoots of theological faculties, and the early leaders in this movement were trained as theologians or biblical scholars. This kind of background should not count against such scholars; as a matter of fact, in many cases the presence of scholars of this type prevented these early departments from succumbing to various and sundry positivist, reductionist orientations; this background nevertheless raised its own set of problems. More often than not, serious attention to the constitutive issues involved in the *study* of religion as a humanistic discipline was smothered under the moral, political, and theoretical concerns that had their origins in theological and biblical studies.

All too often the study of religion was understood as the study of "world religions" or of non-Christian religions, as a way of broadening the awareness of students to a wider world of cultures and meanings. There was, and still is, great value in this intention, but the essential meaning of religion in the life of humankind was seldom broached. Seldom was there reference to the fact that there was, in fact, a discipline that understood its task as the comprehensive study of the meaning and nature of religion in the life of humankind. This discipline dates from the writings and scholarly activities of F. Max Müller, who symbolizes the methodological orientation and style of discourse appropriate to the study as a cultural and humanistic discipline.

Müller, though a German national, spent his entire scholarly career in England. He would come to be known as the founder of the discipline, *Religionswissenschaft* ("history of religions"). Müller was born in 1823 in Dessau in the east of Germany. He attended the University of Leipzig, receiving his doctorate in 1843 at the age of twenty. He later studied at the University of Berlin, attending the lectures of Franz Bopp and Friedrich Schelling. By this time he was enamored with the study of Sanskrit, and when an opportunity arose he traveled to Paris to continue studies with Émile Bournouf. Through the good offices of Bournouf and Baron Bunsen, the Prussian minister in London, he was invited to Oxford to undertake the translation and editing of Sanskrit religious texts. This project resulted in the monumental *Sacred Books of the East*.

From 1848 until his death in 1900, Müller spent his life in Oxford, though he made frequent visits to Germany. He held a professorship in the Taylorian Institute; this institute, devoted though it was to modern European languages, was not one of the regular Oxford colleges and Müller was never to become a regular Oxford professor. When the Boden chair of Sanskrit was left vacant by the death of Professor H. H. Wilson in 1860, Müller hoped to be appointed. His rival for this position was a French Sanskritist, Monier-Williams. Monier-Williams got the chair, but allow me to discuss the "politicking" that went on for it, which will explain why Max Müller is called the founder of *Religionswissenschaft* and why, though he was one of the most eminent Sanskritists of his day, except for his translations he is hardly consulted today. Monier-Williams is still known as editor of the English-Sanskrit dictionary.

When notice of the position was made, Müller circulated a manifesto that stated in a straightforward manner his intentions regarding the chair. He said that the professor of Sanskrit ought to lecture on (1) the history and literature of India; (2) the religion and philosophy of the Hindus; and (3) comparative philology. Of course his first statement in the manifesto had already made it clear that it would be his obvious duty to give daily and practical instruction to those who wished to learn and study Sanskrit.

Monier-Williams's political rejoinder to the Müller declaration was to concede defeat in the terms stated by Max Müller but, simultaneously with this concession, to appeal to a higher authority — the bequest and requirements of the donor, one Lieutenant-Colonel Joseph Boden of the East India Company, who had retired in 1807 and died in 1811. Monier-Williams's political strategy was to take literally the bequest of the donor. In his manifesto for the chair he stated the following:

Had I found plain instructions that the electors of the University were to search throughout Europe for the man most likely to secure a world-wide reputation for the Sanskrit Chair, I confess that I should have hesitated to prosecute my design. But Colonel Boden thought more of aiding, by means of Sanskrit, the diffusion of Christianity in India than of promoting in all parts of the globe the fame of the Professorship.... The establishment of a school of European comparative philology and Indian history and mythology and philosophy would doubtless be attractive, but such a departure from the object of the Founder and strict province of the Professorship would not in my opinion be justifiable.

Monier-Williams had played his cards well; he won the chair. But more than political strategy is revealed by this contest. Monier-Williams in his manifesto had made clear the difference between the German regard for Sanskrit and Indian culture and the English orientation to this same area of scholarship. This difference in regard has been noted by many careful observers. Sir Henry Maine in the Rede Lectures of 1875 commented on the subject as follows:

> No one can observe the course of modern thought and enquiry on the Continent and especially Germany, without seeing that India, so far from being regarded as the least attractive of subjects, is rather looked upon as the most exciting, as the freshest, as the fullest of new problems and of the promise of new discoveries. The fervour of enthusiasm which glows in the lines of German poets when the dramatic genius of the Hindoos first became known to them through the translations of the Sakuntala seems to have scarcely abated in the scholars of our day who follow philological studies.... No one can avoid seeing their view of India affects in some degree their view of England ... as a nation of shopkeepers [with] a halo of romance spread around it by its great possessions.

Max Müller a few years later made the same kind of observation. He said:

> In France, Germany, and Italy, even in Denmark, Sweden and Russia, there is a vague charm connected with the name of India.... A scholar who studies Sanskrit in Germany is supposed to be initiated into the deep and dark mysteries of ancient wisdom, and a man who has traveled in India, even if he has only discovered Calcutta or Bombay, or Madras, is listened to like another Marco Polo. In England a student of Sanskrit is generally considered a bore, and an Old Indian Civil Servant, if he begins to describe the marvels of Elephanta or the Towers of Silence, runs the risk of producing a count-out.[3]

This difference between the English and the Germans might be attributed to the rather vague notion of national character. Though there might be something to this, it is possible to be more precise, for this precision is related not simply to a description of two cultural types but to one of the dominant issues of modernity — the relationship between the German ideology and the meaning of modernity, especially as this problem is related to the humanities and the human sciences.

At this point we might do well to look at the intellectual climate that surrounded the humanistic education of the young Müller; he reaped the harvest of the German Enlightenment and Romanticism. Let us note the following dates: Immanuel Kant (1724-1804); Johann Gottfried Herder (1744-1803); August Wilhelm von Schlegel (1767-1845); Friedrich Schlegel (1772-1829); Franz Bopp (1791-1867); and Leopold von Ranke (1795–1886). Müller had come under the direct influence of some of these scholars or their students, but German academic life was permeated with a specific intellectual orientation — which is characteristic of this nation of scholars — to the novelty and innovation represented by the symbols Enlightenment and Romanticism.

Unlike England, France, and other European powers that had embarked upon missions of colonization since the end of the fifteenth century, Germany had not acquired colonies or, for that matter, national identity during this same period. A specific ideology was nevertheless developing in its intellectual life. I am using the term "ideology" in a nonpejorative and descriptive sense. I am, as a matter of fact, using the term in the manner defined by Louis Dumont, the French sociologist. Dumont's definition is as follows:

> Our definition of ideology thus rests on a distinction that is not a distinction of matter but one of point of view. We do not take as ideological what is left out when everything true, rational or scientific has been preempted. We take everything that is socially thought, believed, acted upon, on the assumption that it is a living whole, the interrelatedness and interdependence of whose parts would be blocked out by the *a priori* introduction of our current dichotomies. The ideology is not a residue; it is the unity of it all — a unity that does not exclude contradictions or conflicts.[4]

I don't know whether I wish to go as far as Max Müller's latest biographer in his characterization of German Romanticism, but there is a great deal of truth in what he says.[5] For him, the Romantic movement everywhere was a reassertion of the Germanic element in European civilization after its relative suppression in the age of the Enlightenment. Therefore, says Nirad Chaudhuri, the German Romantic movement *is the* Romantic movement, just as the Italian Renaissance *is the* Renaissance. In any case, Romanticism had a profound impact on Müller and it can be noted in his scholarly life and publications.

## A New Language

I shall be speaking of a "new" language in two related senses. In the first sense, I shall be speaking of the discovery of the Indo-European language family, and second, I shall be speaking of the modes of discourse developed in relationship to the analysis and meaning of this discovery. In the case of the Germans, it was the Sanskrit language, its origins and traditions. With the French, a similar discussion took place in regard to the primitives, who were distant in space. In both cases the problems of continuities and discontinuities emerge, and in both cases discussion surrounding these new data led to new disciplinary orientations.

Holger Pedersen remarked that the discovery of Sanskrit was a genuine revelation. It had a profound effect on philology and linguistics from that time to the present. The Englishman William Jones had discovered the affinities between Sanskrit and European languages in 1788, but the philological and cultural implications were to be stated by the Germans. First of all, Franz Bopp in 1808 had made clear the similarity of grammars, and later the implied relationship between race and language was made by Friedrich Schlegel in his *Essay on the Language and Wisdom of the Indians*. While linguistic and philological studies of this new language family continued apace in Western Europe, in Germany this study was more often than not allied with theories concerning the first language, or the origin of language, and/or the relationship between the origin of language and the origin of religion. The Aryan myth develops directly out of this cultural ferment. Many of these orientations were to be taken up by Müller, and while he was not a proponent of the Aryan myth, and though he offered scientific methods for his analysis and investigations, he was not free from the German cultural ideology regarding the Indo-Europeans. In his *Introduction to a Science of Religions,* in speaking of the authors of the Vedas, he states quite explicitly:

> Those men were the true ancestors of our race; and the Veda is the oldest book we have in which to study the first beginnings of our language, and of all that is embodied in language. *We are by nature Aryan, Indo-European, not Semitic*: our spiritual kith and kin are to be found in India, Persia, Greece, Italy and Germany; not in Mesopotamia, Egypt

or Palestine. This is a fact that ought to be kept clearly in view, in order to understand the importance which the Veda has for us, after the lapse of more than three thousand years, and after so many changes in our language, thought and religion.[6]

We might well be reminded here of the structure of Giambattista Vico's *New Science* of a century earlier. Vico's method was also philological, and he too sought through linguistic analysis to divine the origins of the earliest institutions and forms of languages. And, indeed, he eliminated the people of revelation, the Jews, from his analysis. How strongly this was a methodological principle or a political strategy designed to prevent problems with the papacy is a matter of dispute. But even if Vico's method and discourse seem similar to the method and discourse of the German cultural nationalist, it is clear that Vico did not have cultural ambitions for his study; it is just as well, for he was all but ignored by his contemporaries.

Apart from the issue of the origin of language and the relationship of Sanskrit to the Germanic languages, the Brothers Grimm had undertaken a historical research of the German language. This research had involved them in the study and analysis of nursery tales, household tales, and myths. In his rather long introduction to his four-volume work *Teutonic Mythology*, Jacob Grimm traced the history of Christianity across Western Europe, and while he praised the Christian message, he gave equal honor to the old pagan religions of the Teutons.

The Grimm brothers rather early in their student careers had met Friedrich Karl von Savigny, the brilliant historian of law. He had taught them scientific method and introduced them to Ludwig Tieck's collection of the Minnelieder. Savigny's studies in the history of law were not formed by ratiocination but grew out of a natural evolution from within society itself. The relationship between the Brothers Grimm and the legal scholar Savigny continued throughout their lifetimes and gave rise to a body of scholarly historical-linguistic data and methods.

### *Sensus Communis and Sensus Numinus*

It is clear that in the work of the Grimms, Savigny, Bopp, and other German scholars, a new sense of the German people was developing; this sense was, on the one hand, chauvinistic and excessive, and on the other, part and parcel of new modes of research, scholarship, and methods stemming from the

Enlightenment. If the Enlightenment, in the words of Ernst Cassirer, "caused an exchange of index symbols," creating a situation wherein that which had established other concepts (God, truth, morality, and law) moves into and now finds itself in the position of a concept that requires justification, the Romantic tendency is to found the older concept in new soil, and from this soil the concept will sprout new branches pointing in several directions.

In the first instance, there will be a branch in the direction of historical and empirical specificity. Whatever the notion — God, law, language — the data must be close at hand; in the case of language, there is the Indo-European language of which German is a branch, and there is the more immediate case of Teutonic mythology. One is secondly able to discern a universal intent. Universality may be seen in terms of origins and history or in method of study. Thus Indo-European languages are imputed to be the original or the oldest languages, and in the history of their spread to almost all the countries of Western Europe a universal intent is expressed. The methods of study of this language, whether as comparative philology, comparative mythology, or oral literature, are valid for the study of any similar data. The intuitive and empirical nature of experience does not give knowledge in combination with the *a priori* ideal forms of Kantian epistemology. In the case of the Romantics, the prior historical and empirical forms of languages, institutions, and history take over the role of ideal forms. In this move, Romanticism approximates Wilhelm Dilthey's statement, "There is no pure reason, there is only historical reason."

There is a pervasive religiousness endemic to these movements; in their seriousness and soberness, in the studies of law and languages, something akin to a religious empirical mood is present. I am not speaking of the specific areas of the study of religion and mythology; rather, I am referring to a kind of Romantic *sensus communis* of language and style that leads to a *sensus numinous*.

Müller attracted large audiences throughout the United Kingdom when he went on the lecture circuit — which was often. His lectures on mythology, Indian religions, and the origins of religion and languages were a part of the intellectual climate of Victorian England. He was a spirited debater, taking on E. B. Tylor and Andrew Lang on the problem of myth, and Darwin on the problem of the evolution of language. He was indeed a major figure among Victorian men of letters, but he was never quite convincing to the British academic community; while charming, intelligent, scholarly, and persuasive, he was never quite able to convince them of that *sensus communis* which informed the background of his thoughts and ideas. The British had an empire and the mysteries of India were more nearly defined for them in economic, political, and military terms than those of philosophical religious speculation.

Müller's fruits were reaped on the Continent. The first chairs in the history of religions, following the Müllerian model, were established in the Netherlands at Leiden in 1873 (C. P. Tiele) and at Amsterdam in 1877 (Chantepie de la Saussaye); these chairs were followed in 1879 with a chair at the Collège de France first occupied by Albert Réville.

Interestingly enough, the German universities were reluctant to establish chairs in the history of religions. Several reasons may be given for this strange situation. In the first place, German universities were organized along confessional church lines and the kind of study indicated by a discipline such as the history of religions might be inimical to certain theological positions. Though several of the theories and methods that had gone into the intellectual background of Müller had their origins in the German academy, they were represented in Germany by a variety of separate academic subjects and disciplines. And again, some of the highly speculative philosophical theories regarding religion fell more into conflict with philologists and historians. In 1901, Adolf Harnack, the great historian of Christian dogma, made a famous speech at the University of Berlin attacking the proposal for a history of religions chair at the university. He felt that such study would lead to dilettantism and that those who wished to study other religions should study them through Christianity. Christianity was the absolute religion and anyone who knew one religion knew them all! Müller's efforts had related the study of religion to the study of languages, and in this connection he had put forth speculative theories regarding the origins of language and religion. In the case of the Indo-European languages, he thought that he had discovered a new primordium for Western culture — a primordium different from that of the Hebraic tradition.

This linkage of religion to philology and to the speculative problem of origins was a part of the discourse of his time, reflected in other ways in the studies of Charles Darwin and E. B. Tylor. It was the speculative dimension that would survive as the distinctive ingredient for the future study of religion. The continuation of this tradition after the First World War would take place in the work of Nathan Söderblom, Rudolf Otto, and Joachim Wach. The First World War destroyed the optimistic euphoria that surrounded the Müller generation. The primordium was no longer sought for in the quest for the origin of language and religion within historical time. Attention was turned to the nature of experience itself as expressive of a primordium of human consciousness. Söderblom, Gerardus van der Leeuw, Otto, and Wach were theologians on the one hand and proponents of *Religionswissenschaft* on the other; they kept speculative meaning alive in the interpretation of religion and created a language for the expression of this element of uniqueness in the experience of religion. The discourse from Müller through Wach was one that moved from a *sensus communis* to a *sensus numinous*.

In 1911, Nathan Söderblom from Uppsala was invited to fill the new chair of history of religions at Leipzig, his way having been prepared by Rudolf Kittell, the Old Testament scholar, and Wilhelm Wundt, the psychologist of religion. Subsequently, Marburg established a chair in the history of religions, and it is from Marburg that the German tradition in the twentieth century has been renewed. I refer to the careers of Rudolf Otto, Friedrich Heiler, and Joachim Wach. In Otto's *The Idea of the Holy,* Heiler's *Prayer (Das Gebet),* and Wach's *Sociology of Religion,* a new tradition of history of religions begins. Gone are the pseudo-problems of the original language, the Aryan myth and mythology as a disease of language. If there is a problem of origins, it is related to the primordial sense of the religious faculty in the consciousness of every human being. The phenomenological turn cleared the air for sound historical scholarship. The *sensus communis* was indeed, for Otto and Wach, found in the *sensus numinous,* that capacity for the experience of the sacred that has always been the same for every human being.

But if the discipline of history of religions did finally emerge as an academic discipline, it too had to face the problem of every modern discipline in the human sciences. Religion could no longer be defined in its traditional manner. The mode of analysis became almost identical with the definition of the datum. And this is not unique to the area of religion. Joseph Schumpeter's monumental *History of Economic Analysis,* for example, nowhere gives us a definition of economics. And if you peruse books in the history of religions, a similar problem is evident. The issue at stake is the mode of discourse one uses to make sense of one's data, and thus the problem of hermeneutics becomes a central issue.

While the expatriate Max Müller may have laid the ground for the discipline of the history of religions, it is doubtful whether he could have accomplished this task if he had remained in Germany. It was he who brought Germanic roots to England — and to a primarily English audience he presented his theories and methods for the study of religion, theories and methods that fell all too often on hard academic ground. But he did accomplish one thing; he opened up the area of religion for hermeneutical reflection. The vestiges of this tradition may not be represented in Germany by the proliferation of chairs in the history of religions, but rather in the rich tradition of hermeneutical theories from Wilhelm Dilthey through Erich Auerbach to Hans-Georg Gadamer.

"Though ideas are not born in a vacuum nor by a process of parthenogenesis, knowledge of social history, of the interplay and impact of social forces at work in particular times and places, and the problems that they generate, is needed for assessing the full significance of all but the strictly technical disciplines." We agree with Sir Isaiah Berlin,[8] who made that statement, but there must be a meaning and significance beyond simply these social forces if the idea is to survive as an intellectual meaning. Müller had such an idea and it has survived. It is this tradition in the study of religion that made its mark in America with the coming of Joachim Wach to this country in 1943.

### *Excursus*

At this juncture I must relate a personal experience. Two years ago I experienced a mild intellectual trauma. While browsing through a used-book store I spied a title on the shelf; the spine of the book read *The Study of Religion*. I took the book off the shelf and thumbed through the pages. The book was written by Morris Jastrow, Jr., and was published in New York in 1902. In addition to this, the book is dedicated to Cornelius P. Tiele, who held one of the first chairs in the history of religions in the Netherlands. The book is composed of fifteen chapters divided into three sections: General Aspects, which covers chapters entitled "The Study of Religion — Its History and Character," "The Classification of Religions," "The Character and Definition of Religion," and "The Origin of Religion." The second part, Special Aspects, contains chapters dealing with factors involved in the study of religion — for example, religion and ethics, religion and philosophy, religion and mythology, religion and culture, religion and history, and so on. The third part, the practical aspect, deals with general attitudes in the study of religion such as the study of religion in colleges and universities and seminaries, and museums as aids in the study of religion. The text concludes with two appendixes that discuss the program of the Section for History of Religions at the École des Hautes Études in Paris and the arrangement of the Musée Gurmet.

The reason for my mild trauma was the realization that my graduate training in the history of religions under Joachim Wach had followed almost to the letter the same structure as Jastrow's text; second, that Joachim Wach never referred this text to any of us (did he know of its existence?); and third, this book was written by an American scholar in 1902! 1 have not been able to trace the history of this book since its publication seventy-eight years ago, but it is clear that our situation would be quite different today if the scholarly community had understood and followed our scholarly colleague and compatriot.

It is a mark of the cogency and perspicacity of Morris Jastrow that his work can still be recommended as a guide after almost eight decades. We are left to ponder why his work received so little attention over the ensuing years. While all the intellectual ingredients are present in his study, what was lacking, in my estimation, was the intellectual and ideological (in Dumont's sense) ferment for the expression of this new meaning of the study of religion on the American scene. Joachim Wach, who came to America in the 1940s, would definitely have approved of Jastrow's manual. But there were other ingredients in Wach's intellectual background. His very presence in America was an index to a critical issue of Western civilization. This fact should remind us that Jastrow's work was published before the great wars, and Korea and Vietnam, and before the bomb. It is a work without benefit of Edmund Husserl's *The Crisis of European Sciences and Transcendental Phenomenology,* Rudolf Otto's *The Idea of the Holy,* or Mircea Eliade's *The Myth of the Eternal Return.* I don't mean to suggest here that Jastrow was unaware of methodological issues. He states quite explicitly:

> Method may be said to constitute three-fourths of any science. Discoveries may occasionally be due to accident, or to what appears to be such, but a genuine advance in any science is always accompanied by a change in method, and new results are but the application of improved methods of investigation.

Jastrow himself seems to have relied upon the methods of history of philology, and though he is aware of the philosophies of Hegel, Kant, and Hartmann, what is most lacking in his methodological approach is a hermeneutical orientation. Hermeneutics in the modern sense is a response to intellectual crisis, and in our case this crisis is one regarding the very nature and being of the human.[10]

The chaotic situation to which I referred at the beginning of this essay is analogous to the kind of ferment that characterized the era of Max Müller and it is against this situation that we must understand his work. Müller's work can be seen as part of the context of the Aryan myth with its expression in forms of the Indo-European languages and myths. In America we are confronted with the demystification of the American myth and the myths of origin in the histories of the Greeks, Romans, and Italians of the academic disciplines of the humanities.

The myth of America as a land of innocent immigrants from Europe who came to a virgin land no longer has the power to state the reality of the human case for us. The rise of other orientations regarding the peopling of this land and the appearance of new structures and sources of power within the ethnic communities of this land, though seen as political realities, are more often than not religious statements about the nature of human reality.

At least since the time of Husserl, the proper epistemology for the perception and expression of authentic and distinct meaning of human reality has posed a problem for all of the human sciences. The problem has grown more acute since the *others,* whether in the form of the disciplines of Orientalism or primitivism, have fallen under increasing critical pressure. The religious critique of history as an absolute norm for human authenticity by Eliade in his *The Myth of the Eternal Return* is matched by the historiography of the Annales school on the one hand and by the structuralists on the other.

Discourse concerning the meaning of the study of religion must take place within this context. It should be a discourse that is aware of the ambiguity of our situation, but this ambiguity should not stifle us. In the last analysis, we are attempting to find those existential structures of the life of human communities across space and time which concretely gave and give expression to who and what we are in the scheme of things.

Within the history of hermeneutical theories since the time of Friedrich Schleiermacher, who changed the meaning of hermeneutics from the interpretation of biblical texts to a general theory of interpretation and understanding of human existence, hermeneutics always found a relationship with the interpretation of religion. Its theories always constituted part of the web, or at least a thread of intelligibility within the reigning culture ideology.

Rudolf Otto's *The Idea of the Holy is* the most explicit example of this relationship, and this history was continued by Joachim Wach, Mircea Eliade, and the Chicago School. But the play of hermeneutics is at the same time a critique of the web of ideology of which it is a thread. Let me explain in this manner: At one period a few years ago, the history of religions field at Chicago was composed of Mircea Eliade, Joseph Kitagawa, Jonathan Smith, and Charles Long. In one sense we shared the same scholarly history of hermeneutical interpretation; in another sense we were, in an obverse manner, the negativity of cultural ideology: Eliade, a Rumanian, the cultural heir of a country that was Slavic in its origins and Latin in its culture, a country subjected to necessitudes of Balkan history, a pawn in the historical destinies of the great powers; Joseph Kitagawa, a Japanese native, who was interned in concentration camps during the Second World War; Jonathan Smith, a Jewish scholar of Hellenistic religions and culture; and myself, an American black. Our very being in many cases was problematic as far as the norms of the prevailing ideology were concerned. We were all historians of religion. We were, simultaneously, the other, and the others. Our methodologies and theories about the "others" were challenges to the same kinds of theories developed during Western colonialism. The negotiation of the hermeneutical issue when the others are on both sides is a tricky issue; it called forth a peculiar and different form of discourse concerning method in the study of religion. This can be seen, for example, in Eliade's *Patterns in Comparative Religion,* where in an implicit way he overcomes the "Myth of the Given," an epistemology of the privileged status of the perceiver. In this work, Eliade shows that the originary being and nature of the human is based upon the imagination of matter, of the forms of the world as they are apprehended in human consciousness, not as abstract categories but as concrete modalities of meaning, whether in the form of sky, stone, water, or plants. We are constituted concretely by the specific mode. And of course, mention has already been made of his attack of the veracity of historicity.

But one does not need to become like us, or imitate us, for this discourse to proceed. One need only ponder the meaning of the *other* in the interpretation, description, and understanding of our data. And this could be the "wholly other" in Rudolf Otto's work or the "vague somewhat" that opposes us as "something other" in the words of Gerardus van der Leeuw, or that "other" which constitutes the world of the Orientals and the primitives. In every case, for ideological and methodological reasons, the "other" has become another kind of other.

In my presidential address to the American Academy of Religion[11] in 1973, I spoke to this issue in the same manner as my opening comments in this essay. New discourse concerning the meaning of religion — a discourse whose possibility is present in America in its departments of religion — will occur when Americans experience the "otherness" of America; only then will the scholars in religion be able to understand that human intercourse with the world of sacred realities is, hermeneutically speaking, one way, and probably the most profound way, of meeting and greeting our brothers and sisters who form and have formed our species for these several millennia.

## Notes

1. Nirad C. Chaudhuri, *Scholar Extraordinary: The Life of Professor the Rt. Hon. Friedrich Max Müller* (London: Chatto & Windus, 1974), 223.
2. Ibid., 124.
3. Ibid., 125.
4. Louis Dumont, *From Mandeville to Marx: The Genesis and Triumph of Economic Ideology* (Chicago: University of Chicago Press, 1977), 27.
5. Chaudhuri, *Scholar Extraordinary*, 86.
6. F. Max Müller *Introduction to the Science of Religion* (New York: Arno Press, 1978), 1.
7. At the end of Max Müller's preface to his translation of Kant's *Critique of Pure Reason*, we read: "I do not venture to give the right and full explanation of what Kant has said or has meant to say. I myself have learnt from him all that I cared to learn, and I now give to the world the text of his principal work, critically restored, and so translated that the translation itself may serve as an explanation, and in some places even as a commentary of the original. The materials are now accessible, and the English-speaking race, the race of the future, will have in Kant's *Critique* another Aryan heirloom, as precious as the Veda — a work that may be criticised, but can never be ignored" (Max Müller, translation of Immanuel Kant's *Critique of Pure* Reason [London: Macmillan Co., 1922], lxxviii and lxxix).
8. Sir Isaiah Berlin, *Vico and Herder: Two Studies in the History of Ideas* (New York: Viking Press, 1976), xv.
9. Morris Jastrow, Jr., *The Study of Religion* (New York: Charles Scribner & Sons, 1902), 4.
10. I was quite surprised when I learned that my late colleague, Professor William A. Clebsch, had discovered this work by Jastrow the same year as I. The volume has been reprinted by Scholars Press, Chico, California, 1981. The reprinted edition contains an introduction by Professor Clebsch and myself. The book had gone through four previous reprintings; 1902, 1904, 1911, and 1914.
11. Charles H. Long, "Cargo Cults as Cultural Historical Phenomena," *Journal of the American Academy of Religion* 42, no. 3 (September 1974): 403-14; chap. 8 in this volume.

# Chapter 2

## Prolegomenon to a Religious Hermeneutic

One of the central problems posed by contemporary studies of religion results from the tension between the interpretations and descriptions of religion by phenomenologists and morphologists and descriptions of the dynamic, historical, and practical sides of religious activity by sociologists, ethnologists, and anthropologists. The problem cannot be solved by simply forcing these two kinds of interpretations and descriptions together, for basic methodological principles are at stake in both points of view. If, for example, one takes the point of view that religion is simply an expression of a practical existential response to the world, such expression might then be discussed in economic, social, or psychological terms, leaving the term "religion" devoid of any referent. If, on the other hand, one is satisfied with the position of the morphologists and phenomenologists of religion, the practical-existential activity of religious communities too often does not receive adequate explanation. This tension between two interpretations of religion has often forced students of religion to make a choice between them. If, however, we are to achieve a unified approach to religion encompassing not only the phenomenology and morphology of religion but equally the existential, social, and practical dimensions of religion, some logical framework which does justice to all of these ingredients must be articulated. I propose to reexamine this problem from a position that might enable us to resolve the tension.

### Manifestation, Mystery, and the Logic of Discovery

All religions acknowledge that their orientation is predicated on the manifestation of some new form of reality. This manifestation has a double meaning; it makes itself known through some concrete form of cultural life, and its showing testifies to the reality of a mode of being that is prior to and different from the ordinary cultural categories. This is another way of referring to the nonhomogeneous, arbitrary, and anomalous character of the manifestation. That which shows itself is the sacred, or, to be more precise, the showing constitutes the quality of sacredness, a quality that permeates the object through which it is apprehended. The qualities of sacredness may be described as those of power and ultimacy. The object through which it appears is revealed for the first time as a fundamental datum to the human consciousness.

Religious experience is that mode of experience which apprehends and discovers the sacredness of the forms of the world. The expression of this type of experience in myth and symbol enables us to see that there is present here a logic or a set of axioms peculiar to this specific mode of manifestation. W. E. H. Stanner in describing the religion of the Australian aborigines states this point when he says:

> There were no Aboriginal philosophers and one can thus speak of "philosophy" only metaphorically. But there is ground for saying that they lived — and therefore thought — by axioms, which were "objective" in that they related to a supposed nature of man and condition of human life. Myths presented the axioms in an intuitive-contemplative aspect.... No Aboriginal put axioms into words but the existence and efficacy of anything — including intuitional awareness and insight — do not depend on someone's formal affirmation of them in words. Myths would not be stories, and rites would not have an invariant structure if axioms could not subsist by other than formalized means.[1]

The axioms of logic that are revealed in symbols and myths are of different kinds. The symbol expresses the imaginative experience through which a new form of the world is discovered by the human consciousness. In this experience the subject and the object are so inextricably interwoven that they seem identical. We are reminded of Gerardus van der Leeuw's definition of the term "phenomenon." He says that "the phenomenon as such, therefore, is an object related to a subject, and a subject related to an object; although this does not imply that the subject deals with or modifies the object in any way whatever, nor (conversely) that the object is somehow or other affected by the subject."[2] But even on this level of experience we discern a religious imagination that expresses both a qualitative modality of the experience and an intention. It is the quality of the experience as sacred that differentiates it from other experiences, and the form of the world through which this experience gains expression — for example, sky, tree, stone, agriculture — clarifies and provides a basis for the ordering of this experience in a more explicit manner. The myth is the expression of this more specific order, for in the myth a definite structure may be discerned. In the myth we see a "logic of symbols" — an ordering of symbolic experience in such a manner that it refers to the primordial immediate experience of the sacred and simultaneously expresses an intentionality toward action.

The initial showing reveals the possibility for the realization of a new qualitative order in culture. The beings and acts of the myth possess reality, but a reality different from that of culture. The myth is often replete with the bizarre and the paradoxical when compared with the ordinary categories of culture; assent is given to the myth, however, because one is able, in spite of its bizarre character, to decipher the new order of meaning which has been revealed in it.

The actions of the beings in the myth are usually described as having their locus in another time and space — in primordial time and space. Their actions, while revealing, remain mysterious, for they possess a superabundance of power and being. It is this essential revealing-in-mystery that sustains the religious mode of apprehension, for even when the myth becomes the model and sanction for action, its mystery and power as an inexhaustible resource remain.

In symbol and myth, primacy is given to the forms of the world as they reveal themselves to the human consciousness.[3] This is the basis for the notion of the *a priori* status of the religious object and for the conception of the time of the myth as primordial. The temporal sense of the myth carries with it the idea of permanence. It is from a consideration of these elements in the myth that ontological status is attributed to it.

I have attempted to summarize some of the salient points in the work of phenomenologists and morphologists of religion. Several of the points are thoroughly elaborated in works of this type from Rudolf Otto to Mircea Eliade.[4] They have all in their own ways insisted on the *sui generis* and ontological status of religious experience and expression. By doing so, they have provided an interpretive schema that enables the investigator to study religion as religion. None of them has simply left the problem at this stage. Otto, for example, shows how religious experience articulates its meaning in theological concepts; van der Leeuw and Eliade describe the religious apprehension of the world of nature, humanity, and spirits; and Joachim Wach in his *Sociology of Religion*[5] delineates the relationship of religion to different types of social groups. Their studies, however, do not constitute a resolution of the initial tension that defined our problem; rather, they tend to state the problem more clearly, for, while each one in his own way envisages a step beyond the initial experience and behavior of *Homo religiosus*, the articulation of the relationship of religion to the other categories and dimensions of cultural life is stated abstractly and does not match their careful and refined analysis of the ontological structure of religious experience and expression. Thus, the practical side of the religious life, even when it is admitted to exist, does not seem to follow logically from their initial analysis.

## The Rupture of the Myth

The myth emphasizes the primordial and *a priori* forms of the world. But myth at the same time defines the locus of the rupture between humanity and the world. The recitation of the basis for the human condition through the language of myth is a sign that the first step toward human autonomy has already taken place, not simply because the myth tells the story of a rupture but equally because language itself, even the language of myth, is a premonition of human autonomy.

It is difficult to know from an internal analysis why the rupture takes place. In those cases where an explanation is given in the myth, the consequences of a particular act seem incommensurate to the act itself. We have only to think of the Genesis myth in this connection, but the theme is well-documented in cosmo-gonic myths from several cultures. In Africa, Marcel Griaule reports a myth that tells how the intent of the creator-god, Amma, is thwarted because the egg that had been prepared as a model for creation is destroyed by one of the beings maturing within it. Pemba, the malevolent twin, leaves the egg before his maturity, tearing a portion of the egg as he comes out.[6] A similar example may be seen in the Hainuwele myth recorded by A. E. Jensen. In this myth it is difficult to understand the jealousy that caused the death of Hainuwele and subsequently the end of humanity's paradisiacal condition.[7] Other examples are not necessary, for the theme is a familiar one in the history of religion. What intention lies behind this meaning in the myth? I take the position that these ruptures are mythic ways of expressing the intentionality toward action as a structure of the human consciousness. The compulsion, the dynamic, the desire to stand over against the imagination of nature happens simultaneously with the first imagination of nature. The action that brings about the rupture is unexplainable, for no rules for conduct have as yet been established. The fact that there are no rules as yet has reference again to the bizarre and fantastic imagination which is present in intense religious experience and which results in the expressions of the mythic imagination. The tendency toward existence is at the same time a reaction to the passive consciousness of nature.[8] I am emphasizing the fact that there is a compulsion in experience to seek expression. For the religious person this rupture from the ground of creativity elicits a response of intimacy and nostalgia. Stanner describes this attitude among Australian aborigines.

> The idea that living men are lesser beings than the ancestors, and dependent on them, is strongly held. It is justified by a mythology which uses a simple but vivid imagery to show how great were the powers which men have lost. The ancestors stocked the land with rivers, springs, food, weapons and other means of life, raised up hills and mountains, put spirit-children into the waters, used the wind and songs as agencies of will, went up into the sky, provided dreams as a means of communicating with the living, and performed a host of similar marvels.[9]

In like manner, Godfrey Lienhardt describes the meaning of this rupture in the religion of the Dinka.

> The total situation represented in the myths is one of conjoined opposition between man and the Divinity, a relationship in which it is a part of the function of religious rites to regulate and maintain.... It is to be noted that the separation is represented as accidental, not essential. The stories do not begin with a state of affairs now known, but assume (or create) an original conjunction for which there is no basis in the simple observation of earth and sky as they now are.[10]

The paradoxical perspective on the nature of human existence is at once an expression of the nostalgia for wholeness and completeness and the drive toward human autonomy. The world from this perspective of the human consciousness will reflect the meaning issuing from the rupture in the myth. To be sure, humanity has lost paradise and is subject to suffering, death, and all the vicissitudes of life, but at the same time the possibility for communication with a reality prior to this state of life is opened to humanity.[11] The human world of experience is defined now in dependence on ontological reality, and human creativity takes place within this context. All aspects of culture, or, rather, the manner in which culture is experienced through the forms of language, social structure, work, dance, and so on, convey a sense of creativity and dependence on an ontological dimension. The symbols expressed by the rupture in the myth affirm the human experience of nature and culture as ontological dimensions of existence.

## Community and Conduct

I alluded above to the fact that the rupture in myth is directly related to the availability of the ontological dimension in human existence. This rupture may entail a sacrifice of a divine being or it may be described as the winning of some favor from the deity. In any case, the ontological dimension as the modality of the sacred may show itself through certain forms of the natural environment, in social structure, language, and so forth. If the showing takes place through the natural environment, the form of the natural object — tree, cattle, and such — will serve as the ordering principle of the sacred, thus preventing the sacred reality from remaining merely the fantastic and the bizarre. The manifestation of the sacred on the level of the social is expressed ceremonially in rites and morally in the relationships obtaining between individuals and social groups. I shall return to this point later. The meaning of the sacred as social or the ontological dimension of social reality does not exhaust the manifestations of sacrality. Lienhardt, for example, in his discussion of free divinities, describes persons possessed by spirits, religious specialists such as seers, diviners, and prophets. These instances are examples of the bizarre and fantastic sacred power, and thus a norm for human conduct is not expressed. There is a permissiveness regarding manifestations of power in this manner, but since this type of manifestation is not regularized, it appears somewhat out of the ordinary, and in the case of spirit possession may be treated as a sickness.[12]

But the expression of the ontological dimension in individuals is not the only nonritual showing of the sacred. It makes itself known as an imaginative lure and as a basis for speculative thought. Stanner gives us a fun account of a riteless myth in the religion of the Australian aborigines. "Each myth," he remarks, "has something to say — something significant, said beautifully and tragically — about the first and last formula of things, the ultimate conditions of human beings, the instituted ways in which things exist, and the continuity between the primal instituting and the experiential here-and-now."[13] Stanner suggests the possibility that the mythic imagination might not be contrived for effect but might in fact have effect simply as a work of passion and imagination.

The ontological dimension as sacred reality reveals two interrelated cultural modes of experience and behavior. These modes may be referred to as those of objectivity and intimacy. V. W. Turner seems to have reference to something like this when, in his analysis of the exegetical meaning of symbolism among the Ndembu, he speaks of oretic and normative poles of symbolism. He describes his meaning in discussing the symbolism of the milk tree among the

Ndembu: "We find that the milk tree stands at one and the same time for the physiological aspect of breast — feeding with its associated affectual patterns, and for the normative order governed by matriliny. In brief, a single symbol represents both the desirable and the obligatory."[14]

The experience of the sacred reveals the social structure as an arena in which intimacy and obligation, actualities and potentials, and habits and conduct are defined and clarified. It is within the social structure that the dynamic relationships between groups and persons express a generality of conduct and behavior that becomes normative for the society, thus defining the events of social life.

As over against the bizarre and paradoxical imagination expressed in the initial presentation of reality to humankind and the specificity and unexplainable rupture of the primal, the consciousness of the social emphasizes generality, rules, and transactions. The sheer otherness of persons and groups qualifies and produces a sense of oppugnancy to the mythic imagination, and the consequences of action as it impinges on the environment and other persons require that the mythic imagination be clarified in order that it may become the basis for a more general moral order. The sacred as obligation is the definition of the objective pole on the level of social reality. I do not mean to imply by taking this position that the mythic imagination cannot be objectified in other ways. Eliade has spoken of the "transconsciousness" as another way of stating the objectivity of the religious consciousness.[15] In this orientation, the human being moves beyond the fantastic images of the gods and the obligations of the social to a consciousness free of both fantasy and obligation. In the Indian tradition this position must be seen in opposition to the orientation presented in the Bhagavad-Gita — an orientation that justified social action as the mode of revelation of the Lord Krishna. The position described by the transconsciousness is that of the religious genius and takes account of religion as a total system by giving a negative evaluation to the social. While it can be encompassed within the general scheme I am proposing, I do not consider it normative in relationship to the social meaning of religion. Another point is illustrated here, and I shall return to it later in the text.

The essential issue at stake in a discussion of the social is communication — communication predicated on the understanding of reality as objective and cognitive and at the same time oretic and mysterious. I shall discuss this issue in terms of language, using language in the strict sense of verbal communication and in the metaphorical sense to designate any mode of behavior that has as its purpose the communication of sacred meaning to the social group.

Dominique Zahan's analysis of the mythic structure of an African language illustrates both the cognitive-objective and the oretic-mysterious; characteristics of this cultural form.[16] It is the dialectical movement in the use of language among the Bambara that enables it to exemplify both characteristics. The Bambara have three words to designate language. The general phoneme *kuma* has affinity with the word *ku,* which means the tail of an animal. Language as *kuma* expresses the idea of an instrumentality or tool; language is an instrument for taking hold of the world. Language as *ka* is sound before it has become a particular word; it is the primordial sound expressing an elementary simplicity and is used to refer to the ancestors and to the ancient words which are normative for the tradition. The term *ko* characterizes a subtle interiority of language; it refers to the "parent" of the word, the speech that precedes all language. This is the language of God before the world was created. "Par lui, la parole reçoit l'empreinte de la person et lui imprime sa propre marque. Privé de lui, le processus liant l'homme à son acte perd de son importance."[17]

In the thought of the Bambara the word proceeds from the silence of the deity. Because of the rupture in the myth, the word begins its articulation in the forms of *ka* and *kuma* and finally returns to the silence of the deity. Through its articulation, the natural environment and the relationships and things of humankind are made known. The articulation of the word defines the cosmos. The naming of things requires all three meanings of language either directly or through homologies. Naming also implies a characteristic form of behavior toward things and relationships. This behavior is expressed by the acceptance of the thing named as given in creation and implies that human beings possess the capacity to use it creatively in controlling human existence. The names of things exhibit the ontological model or laws of the cosmos. But, we must remember, for the Bambara the articulation of the cosmos by the word was accomplished in order that the word might return to its original silence. Zahan states: "La grande réalité n'est pas le verbe, mais son défaut. Au coeur du silence, la parole est comme un point lumineux environné des toutes parts par les profondeurs de la nuit."[18]

Stanner's work, *On Aboriginal Religion,* which I have quoted liberally throughout this essay, is a masterful handling of the rules, operations, and transactions that occur in Murinbata religion. From a description and analysis of these transactions in myths and rites, he demonstrates how the transactions — the religious actions — which are expressed symbolically describe in fact the social structure and cosmos of the Murinbata. The "language of religious transactions" is the basic element in his method, and by using it he constructs a model for the study of religion that does justice to the religion as religion, while at the same time his analysis elaborates the invariant and speculative levels of thought and action. It is through a description of the conduct and rules of transactions, myths, rites, and symbols that he is able to decipher the religious meaning in all of its dimensions.

## *Conclusion*

I have tried to explicate three logical moments of the religious consciousness and to show how they account for the ontological and existential dimensions of religious experience and behavior. Each of these moments is necessary for the others, but none of them is reducible to the other. On the one hand, religion may be seen as an opening to and discovery of a new order of reality, and, on the other hand, it may be seen as a serious exercise in the control of human experience. Both meanings are true and both are necessary.

Religion is a practical social concern, and the reality of its objective pole must in some sense be validated by communal consensus. But, at the same time, it is a mode of release from the entanglements of the social, and it is the awareness of an objectivity that lies beyond the social and the existential. Again, these positions presuppose each other, for both must be accounted for as intentional forms of the human consciousness. The Indian mystic must experience the vicissitudes of existential existence before realizing a state beyond it, and the word of the Bambara must articulate the forms of the cosmos before returning to silence. The ontology of the sacred is manifested on all levels of the human consciousness and colors all experience and expression with its peculiar qualities.

## Notes

1. W. E. H. Stanner, "Religion, Totemism, and Symbolism," in *Aboriginal Man in Australia,* ed. C. H. Berndt and R. M. Berndt (London: Angus & Robertson, 1965), 219-20.
2. Gerardus van der Leeuw, *Religion in Essence and Manifestation,* trans. J. E. Turner (London: George Allen & Unwin, 1938), 671. This general characteristic of immediate experience has been described by Charles Sanders Peirce in his discussion of "phaneron," by which he means "the collective total of all that is in any way or in any sense present to the mind, quite regardless of whether it corresponds to any real thing or not" (*Collected Papers of Charles Sanders Peirce,* ed. Charles Hartshorne and Paul Weiss [Cambridge: Harvard University Press, 1931], vol. 1, par. 284). One finds this same theme in William James's *Essays in Radical Empiricism and a Pluralistic Universe* (New York: Longmans, Green & Co., 1974). I am indebted for the insights on Peirce to Richard J. Bernstein's essay, "Action, Conduct, and Self-Control," in his *Perspectives on Peirce* (New Haven: Yale University Press, 1965), 66-91.
3. One has only to examine the table of contents of van der Leeuw's *Religion in Essence and Manifestation,* or Mircea Eliade's *Patterns in Comparative Religion,* trans. Rosemary Sheed (New York: Sheed & Ward, 1958), to see how much space is devoted to such topics as sky and sky gods, sacred stones, and sacred water and fire.
4. See Rudolf Otto, *The Idea of the Holy,* trans. John W. Harvey, 2d ed. (Oxford: Oxford University Press, 1958); van der Leeuw, *Religion in Essence and Manifestation;* Joachim Wach, *The Comparative Study of Religion,* ed. J. M. Kitagawa (New York: Columbia University Press, 1958); Mircea Eliade, *Patterns;* idem, *The Sacred and the Profane: The Nature of Religion,* trans. Willard R. Trask (New York: Harcourt, Brace & World, 1959); and idem, *The Myth of the Eternal Return,* trans. Willard R. Trask (New York: Pantheon Books, 1954).
5. Joachim Wach, *Sociology of Religion* (Chicago: University of Chicago Press, 1944).
6. Marcel Griaule, *Dieu d'eau Entretiens avec Ogotemmeli* (Paris: Éditions du Chêne, 1948).
7. A. E. Jensen, *Das religiöse Weltbild einer frühen Kultur* (Stuttgart: August Schröder Verlag, 1948). The Hainuwele myth is translated by Joseph Campbell in his *The Masks of God: Primitive Mythology* (New York: Viking Press, 1959), 173-76.
8. Eliade has referred to this tendency negatively, and I must agree that this opposition is negative, but there is a positive meaning attached to this negativity. It is the desire for an autonomous human realm. This intention of the human consciousness should not be spoken of in purely negative terms. See Eliade, *Patterns in Comparative Religion,* 43, 52.
9. W. E. H. Stanner, *On Aboriginal Religion,* Oceania Monograph, no. 11 (Sydney: University of Sydney, n.d.), 39.

10. Godfrey Lienhardt, *Divinity and Experience: The Religion of the Dinka* (Oxford: Clarendon Press, 1961), 37. The myth does not tell us what the goal of this action is. We can only interpret this goal as it is embodied in concrete expressions of ritual and thought. The coincidence of the opposites dependence/independence and intimacy/autonomy is the perspective that now governs the religious orientation.
11. Lienhardt, *Divinity and Experience,* describes this communion in two chapters, one entitled "Divine Unity and Multiplicity; Free Divinities," the other entitled "Divine Unity and Multiplicity; Clan Divinities." The availability of divinity is present through the forms of individual and social experience, and social life and individual life symbolize concretely the opening of experience to divinity. The concrete symbols of experience are more than indicators; they possess, in the words of V. W. Turner, "an oretic as well as a cognitive function. They elicit emotion and express and mobilize desire" ("Ritual Symbolism, Morality and Social Structure Among the Ndembu," in *African Systems of Thought,* ed. M. Fortes and G. Dieterlen [London: Oxford Univ. Press, 1965], 87). Stanner gives us a similar description of this point among the Australians. His analysis is especially acute in describing the sacramental nature of the totemic principle. "The Murinbata," he says, "themselves make a kind of picture of the articulation of the segmental groups. They use sticks or stones in such a way that what emerges looks a little like a branching tree or a flung fishnet. But it is not a picture of sociality. That picture exists in the dramatization given by *Punj* in complex symbolisms of mime, song, dance, and rite. The ontological reality stated there is not reducible to points of force on a network. A 'theory' of that reality would have to be a rationalization of a reality which, if my account is correct, the Murinbata put to themselves as a joyous thing with maggots at the centre. It takes considerable temerity to try to improve on this imagery" (Stanner, *On Aboriginal Religion,* 37).
12. Lienhardt, *Divinity and Experience,* 58-64.
13. Stanner, *On Aboriginal Religion,* 83.
14. Turner, "Ritual Symbolism," 87.
15. Eliade, *Patterns in Comparative Religion,* 454.
16. Dominique Zahan, *La dialectique du verbe chez les Bambara* (Paris and The Hague: Mouton & Co., 1963).
17. Ibid., 11.
18. Ibid., 153.

# Chapter 3

## Archaism and Hermeneutics

### Introduction: From History to Phenomenology

The study of archaic and primitive religious phenomena has always constituted a great part of the work of the historian of religions. E. B. Tylor's *Primitive Culture* was published in 1870, and F. Max Müller, the first modern historian of religion, published his *Lectures on the Origin and Development Of Religion* in 1880. It is not surprising that a great deal of cross-fertilization went on between the young disciplines of comparative religion and anthropology. Both were interested in understanding the origins of human culture and its institutions, and to a great degree applied the same evolutionary theory to their data.

Because Tylor and Müller believed they were dealing with the earliest form of their data, the oldest forms of language and worship, and because both felt they possessed a universal norm for culture and language, it was easy for them to arrive at normative statements regarding the meaning of religion. This position resulted in Tylor's minimal definition of religion as a "belief in Spiritual Beings" and Müller's definition of mythology as a "disease of language." In both cases one is able to see that these men arrived at their definitions of the archaic and the primitive because they saw their phenomena under the guise of a law exterior to their data. They thought certain structural and regulative principles were operative in the evolution of nature and mind which could be applied as an interpretive scheme for culture and history.

The door to the history and cultures of non-Western peoples which they had slowly and timidly cracked burst wide open in the early part of the twentieth century. The disciplines of prehistory, archaeology, ethnology, Sinology, Indian studies, Near Eastern studies, and so on thrived, producing a mass of new data and methods.

As a consequence of this new development the theories of these two famous innovators were discredited. Tylor's definition of religion and Müller's

---

Originally published in *The History of Religions: Essays on the Problem of Understanding*, ed. Joseph Kitagawa, with the collaboration of Mircea Eliade and Charles H. Long (Chicago and London: University of Chicago Press, 1967), 67-87.

theory of the development of Indian religion were corrected by subsequent research. In both instances they were, in fact, dealing with cultural and religious materials of a comparatively late period. In each case it was the data of history which obscured the answer to the question of origins.

The reevaluation of these new religious materials from historical and ethnological study was accomplished by a complex relationship between the new methods of historical investigation and the employment of more systematic methods in the study of religion. The new tools of historical investigation, archaeology, and the resulting technique of historical-cultural stratification brought to the attention of scholars remnants of cultures much older than any now existing (though still not the earliest) and allowed researchers to sketch out the broad outlines of the relationship between various forms of culture and specific techniques and discoveries. A universal history of humankind now loomed as a possibility. The differences between cultural stages could now be related to the discovery of a new technique or the acquisition of a new artifact from another culture. From this point of view, culture could no longer be encompassed within the dry and neutral definition put forth by Tylor. Tylor had defined culture as "that complex whole which includes knowledge, belief, art, law, morals, custom, and any other capabilities and habits acquired by man as a member of society."[1] Culture from this new perspective was now seen as the expression of human creativity in history. It was through the medium of culture that expression was given to those forms of life which defined the human as a spiritual being. The difficulty of subsuming cultural creativity under the abstract laws of evolution left the problem of the correct norm for cultural life open and flexible.

One of the earliest forms of this systematization occurs in Chantepie de la Saussaye's phenomenology of religion. He proceeded by placing together similar forms of religious phenomena to see if they revealed a coherent and internal structure. Here in the work of Chantepie we are able to discern one of the problems of the phenomenology of religion: Does the same internal structure refer to an analogous structure of human consciousness?

This early phenomenology sought the meaning of the historical expression within the expression rather than in general abstract laws. The watershed of phenomenological studies in the field is represented by Rudolf Otto's *The Idea of the Holy*. Otto attacks the problem head on by describing the *a priori* religious category of human consciousness. Religious expressions and their peculiar modalities are manifestations of a *sui generis* religious consciousness.

Several objections may be raised to the position taken by Otto. First, Otto did not specify clearly the forms of the world through which the religious consciousness manifested itself. He was content to stress the modalities, the qualitative feelings of *mysterium fascinosum* and *mysterium tremendum*. This lack may be due to the fact that the model for his study was religious mysticism.

Second, his theory of the religious *a priori* operated as one of Kant's regulative ideas. The role of the historical subject undergoing or giving expression to experience in the world is therefore neglected. We, therefore, seem to be dealing with an explanatory *law* of religious experience and expression — a law not derivative from historical experience. The possibility of another subject's having or understanding such an experience and expression is mentioned only once and then in a polemical manner. Otto warns those who can never remember the last stomach ache to put the book aside, for they will never understand it.

Third, his phenomenology is an attempt to describe the fundamental nature of religious experience, and he discovers that this nature is nonrational. Although nonrational elements may appear in religious expression and experience, it is saying too much to equate religion with the nonrational. Despite these objections, Otto's work cleared the air and laid bare the problems with which the phenomenologists of religions must deal. It is evident from Otto's discussion of the religious *a priori* that he was trying to move beyond historicism. The religious consciousness did not come into being as simply an expression of historical experience; thus the expressions and manifestations of religion could not be understood by limiting them to the categories of history. Otto's work cut through all the evolutionary theories of religion and provided a structure of the consciousness which manifests itself in the same manner throughout the history of human culture.

But is this conquest of historicism a real victory? Otto's restatement and resolution of the problem on a level beyond historicism leaves us with many of the problems of historicism unresolved. The meaning of the varying historical manifestations of specific religions remains a problem.

Gerardus van der Leeuw takes up the problem from the side of religious expression and manifestation. His unique handling of a mass of religious data has made his *Religion in Essence and Manifestation* a classic in the history of religions field. But, in the last analysis, van der Leeuw refers all of the religious manifestations to one notion — power. He does not seem to have taken too seriously some aspects of his own phenomenological method. He states concerning the phenomenological method:

> Phenomenology, therefore, is not a method that has been reflectively elaborated, but is man's true vital activity, consisting in neither losing himself in things, nor in the ego, neither in hovering above objects like a god, nor in dealing with them like an animal, but in doing what is given to neither god nor animal, standing aside and understanding what appears into view.

It is clear from this statement that van der Leeuw wishes to avoid all of the scholarly "isms" prevalent in the human sciences — historicism, naturalism, idealism, and psychologism. This avoidance is prompted by his desire to approach the human presence from a nonreductionistic perspective. He believes that the phenomenological method can be a valuable asset for historical study because it enables the investigator to deal with the givenness of human expression. The avoidance of the "isms" indicates that he refuses to make any one of the disciplines implied by the "isms" into a world view which would immediately categorize the data, but he fails to tell us just how one must deal with the background of interpretation, for in the last analysis these disciplines define to a greater or lesser degree the situation of the interpreter in life.

Van der Leeuw is aware of this issue, but his work does not reveal how he deals with it. He makes remarks concerning "the interpolation of the phenomenon into our lives,"[3] and he defines the phenomenon as "an object related to a subject and a subject related to an object."

This note seems to be lost in the hermeneutic which van der Leeuw applies in his work. Indeed, he seems to be "hovering above objects like a god." There is a disengagement of the subject from the historical object in his work which causes the phenomenon to lose its existential character. This may be required at a certain stage in any hermeneutic, but a complete hermeneutic cannot avoid the interrelationship of the historical subject and object. We must remember that the phenomenological method, from its very beginnings with Edmund Husserl, attempted to transcend the problem raised by the historical existence of the subject through the eidetic translation which changes the historical subject into a transcendental ego — a moment of consciousness which permits the perception of the essence of the phenomenon.

It may be that van der Leeuw played down the role of the subject, for if the systematic study of religion is ever to become a true science, it must, as every other science, show that any cognition recognized by the interpreter as objectively valid must be recognized as being necessarily so for any other possible subject. This kind of objective rigor has allowed historians of religions to present with precision and clarity the structure and morphology of religious data. The problem presented by the interpolation of these data into our lives remains. It remains because phenomenologists of religion have not resolved the issue of phenomenology and history. If phenomenology is in truth "but man's vital activity," then the biases arising from its roots in Descartes and Husserl must be overcome before it can serve as a legitimate hermeneutic.

Husserl understood European (Western) culture as primarily and essentially an exfoliation of Greek forms. All of the modalities of experience are thus reduced too quickly and directly to a rational model. (Otto's designation of religion as a form of the nonrational is a protest against this tendency.) The fact that Husserl did not see the roots of the West in its Jewish-Christian religious heritage may account for his failure to deal adequately with the issues of rationality and historical contingency. It was only late in his life that he came to appreciate the problem of historical contingency.

Raffaele Pettazzoni, however, takes up the issues of phenomenological structure and historical contingency and poses a resolution.[5] Pettazzoni sees religious symbolism arising out of human existential anxiety in history. The symbolism is thus a representation of the human being's "existential situation."

> Existential anxiety is the common root in the structure of the Supreme Being, but this structure is historically expressed in different forms: the Lord of animals, the Mother Earth, the Heavenly Father. All these structures have profound relations with different cultural realities which have conditioned them and of which the various Supreme Beings are expressions.[6]

This statement explains at once too little and too much. While one must agree that particular symbols are discovered and predominate in particular cultural historical periods, is it enough to limit the meaning of the symbolism simply to a reflection of the world view of the period? And while existential anxiety may be a general characteristic of all human life, the modalities through which one expresses this anxiety take on different forms. What more than existential anxiety is expressed in religious symbolism? The question remains because of the wide variety of religious symbolism. Pettazzoni's resolution does not explain the persistence of the same symbolism in different cultural historical periods; nor does it suggest how it is possible to understand religious symbols of other times and places. In short, with Pettazzoni's marriage of phenomenology and history we regress to Dilthey's dilemma of world view.

All of the methods employed to understand the relationship of phenomenology to history have proven to be ineffectual for one primary reason.

*All have made a direct relationship between historical expressions and a law or ontology.* This procedure has minimized the specific nature and structure of the historical expressions (all religious symbols are expressions of power [van der Leeuw]; all religious expressions proceed from a religious *a priori* [Otto]; or all religious symbols express existential anxiety [Pettazzoni]).

This section began with a discussion of the problem of origins in the history of religions. Origins were first sought in objective history and later with the advent of phenomenology in the human consciousness. I have been critical of the first attempts, because they derived the meaning of their data from an exterior norm. I have leveled a criticism at the phenomenological method, because it has tended to lead to one-dimensional interpretations of the variety of religious expressions and, in addition, has failed to deal with the interrelationship of the subject and the world.

In the last analysis, both procedures are ineffectual, for their clarity has been obscured by history. In the case of Tylor and Müller, the historical shadows have come from the historical data, and in the case of the phenomenologists, the immersion of the subject in history while seeking to understand history dims the clarity of Otto's religious *a priori* and van der Leeuw's notion of power. The new historical methods and materials that served in part to disprove Tylor's and Müller's theories revealed layers of history extending far back beyond existing cultures, for history at a certain point turns into archaeology, and cultural anthropology at a certain point turns into physical anthropology. If we couple this knowledge with the one stable meaning from our phenomenological analysis — that there is an enduring structure to religious experience and expression — we must conclude that the search for origins, the archaic in objective history, must now be complemented by a search for the archaism of the subject. The archaeology of history and culture should be matched by an archaeology of the subject. This archaism is no longer a search for origins in objective history, for, as we have seen, this poses an impossible task. This "new archaism" arises in relationship to the universal structure and intentionality revealed in religious symbols. We now wish to understand the meaning of the archaic as a constitutive element in human understanding of self and world.

### The Archaeology of the Subject: From Phenomenology to Hermeneutics

There seems to be a rather natural affinity between phenomenology and the history of religions. It was, we must remember, in the first real phenomenology of religion, Otto's *The Idea of the Holy*, that the transfer of the problem of origins from objective history to the subjectivity of consciousness took place. I suspect that there is more than a simple clarification of method present here, for phenomenology, beginning with Husserl's *Cartesian Meditations*, was also concerned with first philosophy. With the obscuring of the problem of objective historical origins by history, it became clear that

> ...the significance of empirical history which seeks a causal explanation of events is ultimately based upon the "intentional history" which seeks to reveal the acausal genesis of meaning and the advent of truth constituted by men's existential assumption of pre-objective meaning structures in the contingency of their situation.[7]

Husserl's early attempts to move beyond the empirical to the acausal and thus to first philosophy involved the removal of the subject from history in the ultimate moment of understanding. This was possible, for the ego was conceived as a pure thinking subject. In his late work, *Phenomenology and the Crisis of European Culture*, he changes his views and admits that all experience begins with our corporeality. Prior to this, "reflection" had always meant a turning inward, not to the psychological activity of consciousness, but to the ideal act of consciousness which possessed an objective structure. In his late work he changes this conception and admits that there is an *Umwelt* or *Lebenswelt* — "a world in consciousness that has not been rendered 'thematic' which is simply taken for granted — it is the familiar world in which men perforce live."[8] Husserl goes on to admit that

> ...human spirituality is, it is true, based on the human physis, each individually human soul-life is founded on corporeality, and thus too each community on the bodies of the individual human beings who are its members.[9]

Here we see Husserl's admission that each thinking subject has a background and that this background must be taken into consideration if one is to develop a rigorous science of consciousness.

Husserl's pupil, Heidegger, has undertaken an analysis of the human being on this level in his *Being and Time*. Neither Husserl nor Heidegger intended to reduce humankind to a function of *Umwelt* or *Lebenswelt* with the introduction of this level of analysis. They intended, rather, to demonstrate the modalities of being in relationship to this dimension of the human consciousness. Heidegger subsumes the problem of hermeneutics under his general analysis of Being. Comprehension is no longer a mode of knowledge but a mode of being — the mode of that being who exists in comprehending Being. In Heidegger's analysis, historical knowledge is subordinated to ontological comprehension as an aspect of this type of understanding. For example, we have only to note Heidegger's attitude toward the use of ethnology in his discussion of the "Existential Analytic and the Interpretation of Primitive Being."

> But heretofore our information about primitives has been provided by ethnology. And ethnology operates with definite conceptions and interpretations of human *Dasein* in general, even in first "receiving" its material, and sifting it and working it up. Whether the everyday psychology or even the scientific psychology and sociology which the ethnologist brings with him can provide any scientific assurance that we can have proper access to the phenomena we are studying, and can interpret them and transmit them in the right way, has not been established.... Ethnology already presupposes as its clue an inadequate analytic *Dasein*.[10]

Although this may be true, one should not avoid the disciplines through which the problem of Being is stated. It is not, however, clear just how historical knowledge is in fact derivative from this ontological analysis. I prefer to see the problem stated in the opposite manner. Ontological analysis should arise from historical understanding. This would mean that before one could undertake an elucidation of an historical ontology, one would first have to understand the intentionality of both historical method and content. I propose to illustrate this procedure by taking my historical method and materials from the history of religions.

The discipline of the history of religions seeks to understand, from a description and analysis of all of humankind's religious expressions, the nature of religious experience and expression. Though one may begin by following a linear chronology of religious expression from prehistory to the present, this approach is not motivated by a search for origins as an objective history. Our first concern with this mass of data is, to quote Georges Dumezil, that "it is under the sign of logos and not *mana* that we place our research today."[11] The nature of our task as it relates to logos represents the attempt to order our materials so that they appear as a true structure of these phenomena — a structure that would appear true for any observer. Such an order may be seen in Mircea Eliade's *Patterns in Comparative Religion*. Eliade in his explication of the modalities of the sacred implies that every religion can be considered as a variation on the themes he has outlined.

His analysis describes the pre-objective, latent meaning structures of religious expression. For example, in speaking of sky symbolism, he is able to say:

> The transcendental quality of "height" or the supraterrestrial, the infinite, is revealed to man *all at once,* to his intellect, as to his soul as a whole. The symbolism is an *immediate notion* of the *whole consciousness,* of the man, that is, who realizes himself as man, who recognizes his place in the universe; *these primeval realizations are bound up so organically with his life that the same symbolism determines both the activity of his subconsciousness and the noblest expression of his spiritual life.*[12]

This type of structuring of the primary religious expressions does not arise from the metaphysical desire to construct the world. The intent of this structure is a more modest one. Through this structure a pattern, a "language" of the sacred, is revealed, a language that describes human immersion in life — in this case as a confrontation with the sacred. It is through this language that the human being deciphers the meaning of the sacred in history. This language or structure of the sacred is the medium through which historians insert themselves into the historical being of others. The use of every structure, whether biological, aesthetic, or religious, points to the endeavor to find a common form for the self and the "other" which is the object of interpretation. Structure is thus a mode of communication.

Every adequate hermeneutic is at heart an essay in self-understanding. It is the effort to understand the self through the mediation of the other. By self-understanding I do not mean the reduction of the other to the dogmatic categories of contemporaneity. Self-understanding through the mediation of the other involves the principle of reciprocal criticism. It is this reciprocal criticism of self and other which permits the interpolation of the phenomenon into our lives.

Paul Valéry once made an apt remark regarding this type of transaction. He said:

> There is no question in poetry of transmitting to one person something intelligible happening with another. It is a question of creating within the former a state…[which] communicates the intelligible something to him.[13]

This communication of the "intelligible something" (in our case religious structures) should lead to an opening of ourselves and permit us to order unexplored areas of our lives. Our return to the archaic and traditional religious forms does not express a desire merely to trace causal connections.

It is a return to the roots of human perception and reflection undertaken so that we might grasp anew and reexamine the fundamental bases of the human presence.

Such reorientation lies behind Heidegger's return to the pre-Socratics, Husserl's return to Descartes and the modern artist's return to primitive forms. Freud's exploration of the unconsciousness is a description of the archaeology of reason.

This archaism, or return to beginnings, is predicated on the priority of something already there, something given. This "something" may be the bodily perceptions, as it is for Alfred North Whitehead and Maurice Merleau-Ponty, or a primal vision of aesthetic form, as it is for the artist. In our case, this priority and otherness is the history of those primary religious intuitions — religious symbols and their intentionality.

The return to the archaic modality does not mean a recapitulation to objective archaic history, however. We do not wish to live the life of the noble savage. As I have said above, it is a hermeneutical procedure. It presupposes modernity. It was Paul Ricoeur who rightly described our historical period as the moment of forgetting and remembering.[14] According to him, the forgetting of hierophanies of the sacred is the counterpart to the task of nourishing humanity and satisfying human needs through the technical control of nature. But it is just at such a moment that we have a dim recognition which prompts us to restore the integrity of language. He continues:

> For we moderns are men of philology, of exegesis, of phenomenology of religion, of the psychoanalysis of language. The same age develops the possibility of emptying language and the possibility of filling it anew. It is therefore no yearning for a sunken Atlantis that urges us on, but the hope of a recreation of language.[15]

André Malraux reminds us that by a paradox of history it was left to the first agnostic culture that the world has known, "when it resuscitated all other cultures, *to recall to life their sacred works.*"[16]

These statements are examples of a critical phenomenology. They demonstrate the fundamental meaning of the epoche, the bracketing of experience in order to understand the givenness of the data to an observer. This epoche is not a "leap out of our skins." Through the epoche we try to find again through the phenomenon that link which establishes our existence with the world. By taking account of all the conditioning factors of our existence we are able to understand our life as a possibility among others. The epoche permits a meditation on our own existence — a meditation possible through the appearance of the "other."

## *Beginning and Reflection*

Authenticity and clarity seem to be the twin norms of contemporary meaning. We are persuaded to accept the death of God, secularism, or some form of existentialism as the price of our modernity. Through one of these orientations we are to achieve a realization of our authentic selfhood. Each one of these orientations defines elements in our contemporary situation, and from a positive point of view they express the desire for a new beginning. But as van der Leeuw put it in his provocative essay "Primordial Time and Final Time":

> The riddle of time is the riddle of the beginning. We know that there can be no true beginning. Something has always gone before. In the beginning lies the whole past. The beginning is the past.[17]

We must therefore subject all of these orientations to the same judgment we applied to Tylor and Müller. The clarity of the beginnings is obscured by history, by the layers of humanness which lie behind them. The negative character of the orientation is expressed by the explicit need to cut the self off from the thickness of experience and relations. There is a certain iconoclasm present in the movements which tends to define the self as a lonely ego. A kind of heroic clarity and authenticity is thereby achieved. But in the words of Whitehead, we must seek clarity and then distrust it; or equally, as in the way of Merleau-Ponty, we must always take the phenomenon back into the shadows.

These aphoristic statements are more than slogans. They point to the pretension of the ego which tries to define itself in isolation. All of the cultural forms through which our experience is mediated have a prehistory. Every ontology of the self should begin with a comprehension of some particular aspect and expression of being before arriving at an ontological statement. It is only through the manifestations of being in the fullness of time and space that we come to know who we are.[18]

The historical *cogito* is a *cogito* whose horizon and intentionality may be defined as memory — a mode of perception that anchors our life in prereflective experience. It is this horizon and its intentionality which has been overlooked by those who portray the subject as an ego isolated in contemporaneity.

Richard McCleary, in his introduction to Merleau-Ponty's *Signs,* has defined the hermeneutical function of Western culture as follows:

> Western thought and culture have a historically privileged position among men's creations. The West has invented an idea of truth which requires examination of all cultures in an attempt to incorporate them as aspects of a total truth, and a technology capable of one day sustaining a world culture. Consequently, it has the historical task of *re-examining all things (in terms of their source in the historical life world) in order to face up to the crisis of human culture by revealing its primordial unity and to achieve the new creations of effective cross cultural unity which are the only justification for its privileged position.*[19]

This program of reexamination and new creation cannot be carried out without the development of a historical memory. This historical memory must be commensurate with the forms of reality as these forms are delineated by modern disciplines. Such a memory must acknowledge its relationship with all historical forms, behaviors, gestures, objects, and ideas. The new definitions of the human being introduced over the last one hundred years add to the designation Homo sapiens supplementary or alternative descriptions of the human. Compare, for example, the following as descriptions: *Homo geographicus, Homo ludens, Homo laborans, Homo faber, Homo religiosus.*

It was obviously common knowledge prior to the last one hundred years that human beings lived in a landscape, played, made tools, worshipped, and so on. But what was not so obvious was the importance and status of these dimensions of life as a part of a total definition of the human being. These definitions refer to ordinary prereflective life. The human being as Homo sapiens is always rooted in some precise and specialized manner to the roots of knowledge. "La réflexion est pourtant toujours réflexion d'une réalité préréflechie."[20]

Historical memory is aided by a hermeneutic of the archaic in two ways. In the first instance, a hermeneutic of the archaic raises the problem of the constitution of the subject in the process of knowing. If it is the aim of historical knowledge to understand behavior and objects as well as ideas, the interpreting subject must be pushed back to a level of consciousness commensurate with the forms that the subject wishes to understand. This is the radical empirical level of meaning which is expressed in the forms of history. I understand, for example, Eliade's notion of religious symbolism as an expression of this primary prereflective experience.

The technical character of modern cultural life tends to dim this level of experience. We are able to be authentically and legitimately concerned with experience on this level as it is obscured in the "languages" of modernity — history, ethnology, linguistics, psychoanalysis, and so on. To prevent this level of experience from being subjected too quickly to the dogmatic categories of contemporaneity, we should try to understand it in culture and history where it is expressed as great cultural symbols. It is here that the history of religions plays an important part. In the premodern cultures, this symbolism has received a definitive expression.

This is not to say that primitive and archaic peoples expressed themselves only on the symbolic level, but it is to say that they are only consciously aware of the symbolic level of expression. It is clear from the work of anthropologists — for example, Godfrey Lienhardt, *The Religion of the Dinka* (London, 1960), and Claude Lévi-Strauss, *Structural Anthropology* (New York, 1963) — that a logical structure is present in primitive symbolism. That which is obscured in their expression is the rational. On the other hand, that which is obscured in the expression of modern cultures is the symbolic.[21]

We must now ask how these symbols revealed in the history of religions are to be interpolated meaningfully into the life of modernity. Paul Ricoeur is probably the only philosopher who has worked consistently with the meaning of religious symbolism as it is understood by historians of religions. Ricoeur accepts Eliade's understanding of religious symbolism; for him, the symbol presents to us the possibility of a new hermeneutical meditation. Ricoeur goes beyond Eliade's morphology of religious symbols to philosophical reflection. His formula "Le symbole donne à penser" ("Symbol invites thought") is the key to his philosophical reflection on symbols.[22] It is Ricoeur's contention that the symbolic level already contains everything. Like the Delphic oracle, it does not speak or dissimulate but signifies. The oracle must, however, be deciphered, and this is the task of rationality. Rationality for Ricoeur does not imply the reduction of the symbol to rational categories; rather, rationality is the tool that will unlock the enigma of the symbol.

Ricoeur illustrates this procedure when he deciphers the symbolism of evil, showing how Augustine, Kant, Spinoza, and Hegel have all delineated in their philosophies one or more of the elements in the symbolism. It is, however, only by reference to the primary level of symbolism that we are able to recognize the total intentionality of the problem of evil. The symbol is total and inexhaustible. A critique of the various theologies and philosophies of evil is possible when one subjects the more discursive form of thought to the basic intentionality of the symbol. By referring our rational categories back to their roots in the primary symbol, philosophical thought is renewed.

Eliade's procedure is more radical. Like Ricoeur, he too hopes that the philosophical tradition might be renewed through contact with situations and resolutions that have emerged from other cultures. But unlike Ricoeur, he is impatient with the model of Greek philosophical thought as the only possible way to do philosophy. Eliade believes that religious symbols present to us a spiritual universe. Although these symbols may invite thought, the thought that they invite must not be restricted to the categories of the West. It may be that the symbols by their very nature invite different and varying types of thought.

Instead of deciphering symbols along the lines of Western philosophical thought, Eliade moves from this morphology of symbols to the level of comparison, criticism, and dialogue. The most extensive example of this process is found in his best-known work, *The Myth of the Eternal Return* (New York, 1954), where he compares and contrasts the differences between the archaic and the modern notions of temporality. In his article "Mythologies of Memory and Forgetting"[23] he compares the modern notion of history with the older notion of anamnesis. He takes up this problem again in his essay "Religious Symbolism and Modern Man's Anxiety."[24] Here he plays with the equation, modern historical consciousness equals the moment of death.

> It is, in many religions, and even in the folklore of European peoples . . . at the moment of death [that] man remembers all his past life down to the minutest detail.... . Considered from this point of view, the passion for historiography in modern culture would be a sign portending imminent death.[25]

In nonmodern cultures, death is not an absolute end or nothingness but an initiation which prepares the human being for a new life. Eliade hopes that historical study may also be an initiation, a therapy that will prepare our culture for a new beginning. A new beginning is possible if we take seriously that which is revealed to us through historical study. In Eliade's case, this is the religious world — our confrontation with the sacred. I am never clear about the following point, since Eliade has not, as far as I know, made an explicit statement concerning it. It seems clear to me, however, from a reading of his works that he hopes to abolish the dogmatic categories which limit the meaning of human life to its historicity — through the study of history! He hopes to renew the West by seeing it within the context of a universal history, as its past and a world culture as its present and future.

From this perspective the hermeneutical nature of our study is an absolute necessity. Through such a hermeneutic, new levels of reality otherwise closed to us may be opened.

I have presented without critical comment two examples of the manner in which religious phenomena may be interpolated into our lives. Both examples presuppose the historical subject as a being possessing an "archaic" structure. Through religious symbolism we may find a new and authentic basis for reflection. Reflection proceeding from religious symbolism has the merit of correlating the interpreter on a search for the inner being of self and humanity with a level of historical expression commensurate with this intention. As the interpreter moves from symbolism to rationality, another movement will become necessary — a movement back into the shadows of one's ego and history — for the interpreter will discover that one's being is mirrored in the reality of life and history and simultaneously created in the moment of interpretation.

## Notes

1. E. B. Tylor, *Primitive Culture* (London: J. Murray, 1871), 1.
2. Gerardus van der Leeuw, *Religion in Essence and Manifestation* (New York: Harper & Row, Harper Torchbooks, 1963), 2:676.
3. Ibid., 674.
4. Ibid., 671.
5. See Raffaele Pettazzoni, "The Supreme Being: Phenomenological Structure and Historical Development," in *The History of Religions: Essays in Methodology*, ed. Mircea Eliade and Joseph M. Kitagawa (Chicago and London: University of Chicago Press, 1959).
6. Ibid., 66.
7. Richard C. McCleary in the preface to Maurice Merleau-Ponty, *Signs*, trans. Richard C. McCleary (Evanston, Ill.: Northwestern University Press, 1964), xxiv.
8. Quentin Lauer in the introduction to Edmund Husserl, *Phenomenology and the Crisis of Philosophy*, trans. Quentin Lauer (New York: Harper & Row, Harper Torchbooks, 1965), 67-68.
9. Husserl, *Phenomenology and the Crisis of Philosophy*, 152.
10. Martin Heidegger, *Being and Time*, trans. John Macquarrie and Edward Robinson (New York: Harper & Row, 1962), 76.
11. Georges Dumezil in the preface to Mircea Eliade, *Traité d'histoire des religions*, 2d ed. (Paris: Payot, 1964), 5. By *mana*, Dumezil has reference to the problem of the origin of religion which centered around this Polynesian term.
12. Mircea Eliade, *Patterns in Comparative Religion*, trans. Rosemary Sheed (New York: Sheed & Ward, 1958), 39 (italics mine).
13. Paul Valéry, *Collected Works of Paul Valéry*, Bollingen Series, no. 45 (New York: Bollingen Foundation, 1956), 6:157.
14. See Paul Ricoeur, "The Hermeneutics of Symbols and Philosophical Reflection," *International Philosophical Quarterly* 2, no. 2 (1962): 191-218.
15. Ibid., 192ff.
16. André Malraux, *The Metamorphosis of the Gods* (New York: Doubleday & Co., 1960), 1 (italics mine).
17. Gerardus van der Leeuw, "Primordial Time and Final Time," in *Man and Time*, ed. Joseph Campbell, vol. 3 of *Papers from Eranos Yearbooks* (Princeton: Princeton University Press, 1957), 325.
18. There is a strand in modern philosophical and theological analysis which treats this problem. Heidegger's *Being and Time* and Alfred North Whitehead's *Process and Reality* raise the problem in a formal manner. In Whitehead's *Science and the Modern World*, some content is given to the formal categories in his discussion of the English romantic poets. I prefer the works of Merleau-Ponty and Paul Ricoeur, for they seem to be acutely aware of the historical dimension of the problem, and for this reason their categories emerge in a different way. Both Ricoeur and Merleau-Ponty proceed from a critique of the Cartesian *cogito*.

Ricoeur's philosophical analysis reveals that the Cartesian *cogito* is a vain truth. It is the positing of an ego which cannot be mirrored in objects, works, or acts and therefore cannot be judged by criteria which we apply to the aforementioned forms. It is in reality a void *(une place vide)* which is filled with a false *cogito*. The presumption of the isolated thinking subject always leads to a bad conscience (see Paul Ricoeur, "Existence et herméneutique," in *Interpretation der Welt, Festschrift für Romano Guardini,* ed. H. Kuhn, H. Kahlefeld, and Karl Forster [Wurzburg: Echter Verlag, 1965], 32-51. Merleau-Ponty sees three possible meanings to the *cogito*: (1) There is the *cogito* as the psychic fact that "I think." This is an instantaneous constatation and is possible only under the condition that experience has no duration. I, therefore, adhere immediately to what I think and cannot doubt it. This is a skeptical understanding which cannot account for the idea of truth. (2) In the second way the "I think" of the *cogito* is combined with the objects which this thought intends. Both the "I think" and the things thought have in this context an ideal existence. (3) Finally, there is the third meaning, "the only solid one...I grasp myself, not as a constituting subject which is transparent to itself and which constitutes the totality of every possible object of thought and experience, but as a particular thought, as a thought engaged with *certain* objects, as a *thought in act,* and it is in this sense that I am certain of myself." See Maurice Merleau-Ponty, *The Primacy of Perception,* ed. James M. Edie (Evanston, M.: Northwestern University Press, 1964), 21-24 (italics mine).

19. McCleary, in Merleau-Ponty, *Signs,* xxxv (italics mine).
20. G. Gusdorf, *Traité de metaphysique* (Paris: A. Colin, 1956), 62.
21. For a discussion of religious symbolism, see Eric Dardel's analysis of the use of symbolism in the ethnographic work of Maurice Leenhardt, in "The Mythic," *Diogenes,* no. 7 (1954), and Mircea Eliade, "Methodological Remarks on the Study of Religious Symbolism," in *The History of Religions,* ed. Eliade and Kitagawa, 86-7.
22. Ricoeur, "The Hermeneutics of Symbols and Philosophical Reflection," *International Philosophical Quarterly* 2, no. 2 (1962): 191-218.
23. Mircea Eliade, "Mythologies of Memory and Forgetting," *History of Religions* 2, no. 2 (Winter 1963): 329-44.
24. Mircea Eliade, *Myths, Dreams and Mysteries: The Encounter Between Contemporary Faiths and Archaic Realities,* trans. Philip Mairet (London: Harvill Press, 1960), chap. ix.
25. Ibid., 234.

# Chapter 4

## Silence and Signification

### Reflection on Religion and Modernity

"The eternal silence of these infinite spaces terrifies me." This statement comes at the end of the section of Pascal's *Pensées* entitled "From a Knowledge of Man to a Knowledge of God." It is the culmination of a somber meditation on the fragility and finite nature of the human being when compared to the infinity of the world and nature. It is somewhat strange to find such a poignant statement in the midst of that most creative and optimistic period in Western cultural history which we refer to as the Enlightenment. And this strangeness is increased when we are reminded that Pascal is not a scholastic theologian of the Protestant or Roman variety protesting the reduction of the world to a new rationalism or mathematization; he is a more complex person than this. He is, in fact, very much a part of his age; he knows its language, being one of the greatest mathematicians of his time, and is, for all intents and purposes, a product — a distinguished product of his age. The complexity of his character is revealed when we learn that he is not only a great mathematician and scientist but also an ardent advocate of Jansenism, that ethical-moralistic orientation in Catholicism which reminds us most of a kind of puritanical Protestantism.

Before we jump to conclusions, however, and place Pascal in the category of so many of those contemporary scientists whose understanding of religious and humanistic matters is still at the Sunday school level or worse, and whose knowledge in these areas is not at all commensurate with their sophistication in areas of scientific knowledge, we must take note of the fact that since the publication of the *Pensées* and his work on conic circles, these works have become basic documents for a proper understanding of the respective histories of theology and science. In other words, in confronting Pascal we are dealing not with a schizophrenic personality but with one of those rare human souls

---

Originally published in *Myths and Symbols: Studies in Honor of Mircea Eliade*, ed. Joseph A Kitagawa and Charles H. Long (Chicago and London: Univ. of Chicago Press, 1969), 141-50.

who struggles simultaneously with the fundamental problems of human creativity and human nature.

Pascal expresses in this statement and throughout the *Pensées* the fundamental crisis of his historical period. The precision with which he delineated the problem of theodicy for his time is attested to by the fact that Voltaire turned again and again to a refutation of his arguments, for Voltaire knew that in Pascal he was confronting a thinker who struggled with the problem of God and human with the same diligence, intelligence, and wholeness that he devoted to his scientific investigations. The importance of the problem is attested to again by the other systematic genius of the Enlightenment, Immanuel Kant, who was the only thinker of this period to address this problem with equal acuteness.

But Pascal is more than simply an expression of his age. He is, to be sure, especially in his *Pensées*, writing a kind of existential treatise, a treatise and meditation on the state of the human heart in his time, and it is just because he is a man so engaged with the fundamental problems of *his time* that he expresses meanings that are valid for the human problematic of the entire modern period. His orientation in the *Pensées* bears resemblances to a pattern and logic of human thought that is present in all religious orientations, a pattern of thought that has become crucial for our contemporary period. In the face of the creativity that has come into being through the new understanding of nature, God as a structure of intimacy has disappeared and a new world latent with creative possibilities and terrifying dread appears. Let us listen to Pascal's words, for they express the freshness of this problem; they give us a chance to see how this issue was stated *at the beginnings*.

> For who will not marvel to find our body, which a moment ago was not visible in the universe, which was itself imperceptible in the bosom of the whole, is at present a colossus, a world, or rather, a whole when compared with the world which lies beyond our ken?... Anyone who regards himself in this way will be terrified at himself, and seeing himself sustained in the body that nature has given him, between two abysses of the infinite and the void, will tremble at the sight of these wonders, and I think that, as curiosity changes to wonder, he will be more disposed to contemplate them in silence than to presume to question them.[1]

In this passage Pascal traces a pattern of experiences that is a response to this new form of scientific nature. There is first the experience of the marvelously new, the sheer fabulous character of it; then there is awe and fear, a trembling at the sight of these wonders; and finally, Pascal says, "as curiosity changes to wonder, he will be more disposed to contemplate them in silence than to presume to question them." I shall return to this pattern later, but first I shall say something about this pattern as it expresses itself in the history of religions.

We know from the studies of such historians of religions as Wilhelm Schmidt, Raffaele Pettazzoni, and Mircea Eliade that one of the central problems in recent study of the history of religions is the problem of the High God. It was Mircea Eliade who observed that the problem of the High God among primitives became a central issue for historians of religions in the same generation that Nietzsche proclaimed the "death of God." And, Eliade continues in his observation, one of the most important elements in the structure of the High God symbol is the tendency of the High God, who is always the creator-deity, to become a *deus otiosus* after the world has been created. He describes this tendency explicitly in his *Patterns in Comparative Religion*.

> What is clear is that the supreme sky god everywhere gives a place to other religious forms. The morphology of this substitution may vary; but its meaning in each case is partly the same: it is the movement away from the transcendence and passivity of sky beings towards more dynamic, active, and easily accessible forms. One might say that we are observing a "progressive descent of the sacred into the concrete"; man's life and his immediate surroundings come more and more to have the value of sacred things.... Every substitution marks a victory for the dynamic, dramatic forms so rich in mythological meaning over the Supreme Being of the sky who is exalted, but passive and remote.... The supreme divinities of the sky are constantly pushed to the periphery of religious life where they are almost ignored; other sacred forces, nearer to man, fill the leading role.[2]

And then there is this final statement which I should like to use from Eliade's work:

> This slipping of the omnipotence, transcendence, and impassiveness into the dynamism, intensity, and drama of the new atmospheric fertilizing vegetation figures, is not without significance. It makes clear that one of the main factors in the lowering of people's conception of God...is the more all-embracing importance of vital values and of "Life" in the outlook of economic man.[3]

Eliade's description of the history and structure of the High God may be summarized as follows: (1) he is a being who created the world; (2) his symbolism is related to the sky and thus he always represents transcendence, power, and wisdom; (3) after the creation of the world, the High God becomes *deus otiosus*, removed from the world he has created; (4) in his place are substituted the dramatic deities of fertility and creativity; (5) the High God is not completely forgotten, but he is no longer a part of the human life of the world; he has no cult, and worship is not addressed to him; (6) he is called upon or remembered in moments of strife or catastrophe when the basic structure of the world is threatened and when no help can be gained from the deities of fertility and creativity.

This pattern of elements and experiences in the structure of the High God bears a similarity to the structure of experience of the marvelously new. Subsequently there is the experience of awe and trembling fear before the wonder of the world, and finally, for Pascal there is the movement to silence. Although there is a similarity, not a one-to-one relationship between the two structures, the similarity is so marked that it might give us some insight into the religious experience of modernity; it might show us how, within the context of modernity, some basic patterns of human religiousness may be discerned.

Pascal, unlike the enthusiasts of the Enlightenment, possesses the insight of double vision. He is able to see the infinite world of possibility which the new science makes possible, but he discerns at the same time that God has departed from this world and he is terrified by the infinite spaces, the void. In his meditations on God and the biblical tradition he keeps alive the memory of a God who has disappeared, but even here there is the remembrance of a kind of skeletal structure of the Divine Creator. While his insights are penetrating and precise, the structure of the Supreme Being in the very moment of his most ardent advocacy is still detached and abstract. It is the Supreme Being as a giver of laws and the guarantor of the moral life; there is little of the joy of intimacy and relatedness in the *Pensées*.

Nevertheless, it is at this point that Pascal has almost predicted the course of modern Western cultural life since the Enlightenment. Can any of us deny that Western culture moved from the enthusiastic euphoria of the marvelously new world of the new science to a contemplation of this wonder with trembling fear and awe, and finally, as I shall argue, to a spirit of contemplation with silence? We have only to remember the enthusiasm of Voltaire, Auguste Comte, and the leaders of the French and American revolutions to understand this response to the marvelously new world and its possibilities. But already, before the great wars, Goethe and several others knew that this world contained evil and terrifying implications. The wars, the instability of these centuries, the enormity of Buchenwald and Auschwitz, of Hiroshima and Nagasaki, seem to be summed up in the statement made by

Robert Oppenheimer when he saw the first atomic explosion: "Thou hast become Death, destroyer of worlds."

### Creativity and Silence

The results of the new world and the new creativity have not been unambiguously good. From a religious point of view one might say that human beings have lost their religiousness — that God is dead and that the human no longer has any model or guide for conducting life. This way out is too easy, for such a position reduces the religious imagination to ethics and fails to understand that religion is the continual quest for the meaning of human existence. In addition, this easy position overlooks two major facts, one of which is a product of the modern period itself; the other is of more ancient vintage. The modern fact is that humankind must be understood as one species, and any assessment of the meaning of humankind in any ultimate sense cannot be limited to the meanings of one culture or one historical period. The ancient fact is its correlate: the religious being knows that humanity participates in a reality which is more than historical and cultural — religiously, the human being is an ontological being.

While the Western world became the dominant cultural area of the world during the modern period, its meanings and understanding must be seen against the cultures and histories of the world. This means that the language of Western cultural creativity is not the complete language of humankind during this period. I have used the term "language" metaphorically here, for this metaphor enables me to relate aspects of the modern world which are too often overlooked. The new language of reason modeled on the mathematical symbols of Newton expressed a universal intention. As over against the language of transcendence of the Abrahamic tradition, with its exclusivistic pretensions, it was a language that included all humankind.

It would have been difficult for the enthusiasts of the Enlightenment to foresee that the technicalism resulting from the new science would become the vehicle of extreme nationalism, divisiveness, colonialism, conquest, and so on. This is not, however, the whole story of this creativity; one must also take account of those peoples who had to undergo the "creativity" of the Western world — those peoples and cultures who became during this period the "pawns" of Western cultural creativity. They were present not as voices speaking but as the silence which is necessary to all speech. They existed as the pauses between words-those pauses which are necessary if speech is to be possible — and in their silence they spoke. As opposed to the existential and historical presumptions of human beings making their world, those who lived as the *materia prima* (raw material, I think, is the economic way of expressing this) kept the ontological dimension open through their silence. This silence was as necessary as it was forced. It is not strange that in the nineteenth century, when the Western world admitted the death of its God, at just that moment it sought God not in its own traditions and cultures but in the cultures of primitive and archaic peoples. It was from this silence that the Western world tried to evoke once again a sign of intimacy and relatedness to ontological meaning.

There is another place where this "voice of silence" may be heard. It is internal to Western culture itself. I am speaking of the exhaustive pursuit of all forms of human expression in the Western world. With the removal of the traditional restraints, the West began an exhaustive pursuit of the infinitely large and the infinitely minute and subtle structures of life and the world. This conquest of a new world led to both beneficial and monstrous results. Every aspect of geographical, social, sexual, artistic, psychological, and intellectual life has been almost exhaustively explored. Modern abstract art as well as *musique concrète,* the era of colonialism and human and economic exploitation, the creation and the destruction of the novel as a literary genre — all of these meanings and events are products of this period. Its monstrosities are Buchenwald, Hiroshima, Nagasaki, the evils of racism in America, and the political enslavement of peoples in every nation on the planet. In the very pursuit of authentic selfhood, the Western world has come face to face with silence, with the exhaustion of the forms of the world. What more is to be said after Buchenwald or after a flight to the moon or after one has said that God is dead?

Modern western cultures in the midst of their tremendous creativity and noisiness find themselves confronting an awesome silence — a silence that cannot be banished by the clamor of activity. It is the wonder and monstrosity of our deeds which has evoked this mood of silence. The great language of creativity which we used to subdue and exploit the world has been placed in jeopardy; its mighty words are overwhelmed by the silence of the pauses between the words. This language has been prostituted by the very techniques that brought it into being; after having been used and misused for so long by so many, this language has come to be distrusted by the cultures of the West.

This silence which has come about in the modern period may well be a sign of a kind of cultural catastrophe, for when a culture is unable to trust its own language and the names that it has assigned to things, it is indeed in trouble. As in the myths of the creation of the High God, in a period of catastrophe, the human community is unable to gain help from the lesser gods of cultural creativity, and must turn again to the creator of the beginning. This is a characteristic religious orientation. It is the *"Be still* and *know* that I am God"; it is the Hindu *muni* whose silence is a testimony to God's holiness; it is the silence of Meister Eckhart, who, after ascending to the godhead, found an unspeakable void; and again, it is the Delphic oracle of Socrates which does not speak but signifies.

## *The Irony of Silence*

It is difficult to get at the meaning of silence, for, though a kind of power is signified through its quality, the power of silence is so unlike the power of words that we have no words to express it. Or, to put it another way, the power of silence can only be expressed through the words — words which are able to move beyond and break through their own creative intent to the intentionality of silence. Silence is thus radically ironic. It brings us up short in the same manner as the prime minister who, upon being asked for advice from his king, told the king that the best advice he could give was that he should not accept advice from anyone.

The fact that silence presupposes words is what gives it this ironic twist. Without words there can be no silence, yet the sheer absence of words is not silence. Silence forces us to realize that our words, the units of our naming and recognition in the world, presuppose a reality which is prior to our naming and doing. This attentiveness reminds us, in the words of Maurice Merleau-Ponty, that

> …we must consider speech before it is spoken, the background of silence which does not cease to surround it, and without which it would say nothing.[4]

Something of this same irony is present in Ludwig Wittgenstein's *Tractatus*. It is doubly ironic that a philosophical work which brought about the major orientation in philosophy to linguistic analysis speaks also of the limits and impotence of language. In a philosophical work devoted to language, we find one of the clearest expressions of silence. One of the most profound statements in the *Tractatus*, and indeed in all recent philosophy, is Wittgenstein's aphorism, "What can be shown cannot be said."[5] Max Black, author of one of the commentaries on the *Tractatus*, explains Wittgenstein's aphorism in this manner:

> Showing, however we understand it, has to be conceived as quite unlike assertions by means of configurations of objects standing as proxies for objects.... It is we the users of language who "say things," make assertions by means of arbitrary co-ordinations we have assigned to words; but whatever shows itself, independently of any arbitrary conventions we may have adopted — *what is shown is not something we express.*[6]

In other words, what shows itself is prior to speech and language and the basis for speech and language; furthermore, because it shows itself, it cannot be said — it is silent. But it is not only in the notion of showing that Wittgenstein places limits on language, for he places all value outside the world of language. Finally, at the end of the *Tractatus* he makes the following surprising statements:

> 6.522. There are indeed things that cannot be put into words. *They make themselves manifest.* They are what is mystical.
> 6.54. My propositions serve as elucidations in the following way: anyone who understands me eventually recognizes them as non-sensical, when he has used them as steps to climb beyond them. (He must, so to speak, throw away the ladder after he has climbed up it. He must transcend the propositions, and he will see the world aright.)
> What we cannot speak about we must pass over in silence.

The strangely ironical use of language as a testimony to silence may very well be a sign that the possibility of moving from Pascal's trembling and terrifying awesomeness to a contemplation in silence is at least a possibility, and if a possibility, the basis for a new ontology.

What is distinctly new in this position is that we are given a philosophical orientation that sees all language as enveloped in silence. In other words, the interrelation of language and silence gives us a new understanding of the totality of the language and range of experience of the human being. The value of the new position is that it is possible to include within it that which goes by the name of rationality and that which is historical.

The old distinction between existence *in intellectu* and existence *in re* which lies behind the discussion of Anselm's ontological argument could be radically transformed. Could not existence *in intellectu* be transformed into the silence of Being, a mode of being that does not make itself known through the demonstration of a language that stands for objects but through that kind of showing in silence which is necessary for speech and all the objects to which speech refers. Existence *in re* could, from this point of view, refer to the denotative nature of language and its propositions. As I have tried to show in my previous remarks, silence does not mean absence; rather, it refers to the manner in which a reality has its existence. The silence of the non-Western world during the period of colonialism did not mean that these cultures did not exist; it only pointed to the mode of their existence and — we have learned in our study of the history of religions — indicated that the expression of their existence through symbols and myths was at the same time the expression of an ontological position. It means that silence is a fundamentally ontological position, a position which though involved in language and speech exposes us to a new kind of reality and existence.

If any of these hints are correct, it means that being than which nothing greater can be conceived is not simply a concept of the intellect but, in fact, refers to the signification of silence, the world of symbols, values and meanings which throughout human history has been deciphered from the silence which shows itself, which manifests itself, and which forms the basis of our worlds of making sense. It means that any new ontology must take account of the historical expressions of all cultures — those prehistoric, archaic, colonial, Western, and Eastern cultures whose silence expresses a fundamental ontology of both objectivity and intimacy. It is a silence which may no longer terrify us, and it is a silence which in its showing might give us an understanding of the human mode of being which moves us beyond conquest, enslavement, and exploitation. In acquiring this understanding, we may recover the patience and the sensibility which lie at the heart of a religious attitude: "Be still and know that I am God."

## Notes

1. Blaise Pascal, *Pensées,* trans. Martin Turnell (New York: Harper & Row, 1962), 216.
2. Mircea Eliade, *Patterns in Comparative Religion,* trans. Rosemary Sheed (New York: Sheed & Ward, 1958), 43-52.
3. Ibid., 127.
4. Maurice Merleau-Ponty, *Signs,* trans. Richard C. McCleary (Evanston, Ill.: Northwestern University Press, 1964), 46.
5. Ludwig Wittgenstein, *Tractatus Logico-Philosophicus,* trans. D. F. Pears and B. F. McGuiness (London and New York, 1963), 51.
6. Max Black, A *Comparison to Wittgenstein's Tractatus* (Ithaca, NY: Cornell University Press, 1964), 190.
7. Wittgenstein, *Tractatus,* 151.

*Part Two*

*Religion and Cultural Contact*

*Part Two*

*Religion and Cultural Contact*

All of the essays in this section are devoted to a form of demasking. This is accomplished through an examination of certain metaphors used in describing modes of thought and thinking and a correlation of these metaphors with a meaning at another level of human existence. Thus in the essay "Human Centers," the notion of the center as the initiating and controlling moment of thought is correlated with the form of the ceremonial center and later the urban form as the authoritative structure in social life. The power of the center as mode of thought and the power of the metropolitan centers of modern Western culture are specified.

This specification leads to several forms of signification from the center. One of the most powerful cultural languages of signification centers around the discourses set forth from the distinction between the "primitive" and the "civilized," the subject of the second essay. What appears as a description and an innocent distinction becomes the vehicle for a cultural language to invoke powerful valences of authority and subordination into what then reappears in the modes and languages as "natural perceptions."

The essay "Conquest and Cultural Contact in the New World" defines the cultural contact situation itself as a religious locus. From the point of view of those cultures and religions which had to undergo conquest, this meaning has always been noted and affirmed, but the reverse relationship has hardly ever been admitted, at least from the point of view of modern Western culture. The study of the situation of contact from the point of view of the victors has always been injected with the methodological discourse of objectivity at this juncture. The distantiation of objectivity, while making possible a "scientific" language, also creates a gap that prevents the examination of the reciprocity of meaning and thus the loss of a cultural language that is expressive of the true situation of contact.

In the following essay "Cargo Cults as Cultural Historical Phenomena," I interpret the cargo cult as a religious phenomenon that describes the situation of cultural contact from the point of view of those who had to undergo conquest. I emphasize the new language of the cult and the desire on the part of the cult leader to create a new form of humanity. The situation of cultural contact places the cultures in question under severe tension; the hegemonic and authoritative orders of both cultures are threatened, and in the case of the conquered culture these orders are, more often than not, destroyed.

I then hint, or, if you will, make a hyperbolic leap or analogy from the cargo cult to the professional association of teachers and scholars of religion in the United States, the American Academy of Religion; this essay is the substance of my presidential address in 1973. The Academy at that time and presently cannot be defined in terms of common methodological or disciplinary structures. To use a term used by M. M. Bakhtin in describing the novel, the Academy is an expression of polyglossia. The Academy proper came into being in 1963, growing out of its parent group, The National Association of Biblical Instructors. The change of name was accompanied by a change of structure, a greatly expanded membership, and the inclusion of a wider variety of scholars, subject matters, and disciplines devoted to the study of religion. These changes have as their societal backdrop all of the political and social upheavals of the 1960s that continued into the early 1970s.

The declining clarity of focus on the Bible as defining the study of religion, the growth of several departments of religious studies in state universities, the receding of the normativity of the mainline Protestant traditions, the inauguration of black studies, women's studies, and ethnic awareness, all have had an effect on the meaning and understanding of the nature and meaning of religion in the United States. In making this analogy, I felt that in the study of religion we were experiencing the impingement of "America upon the Americans," and thus that the amorphousness of the American Academy of Religion had some analogues to the cargo cult.

# Chapter 5

## Human Centers:
## An Essay on Method in the History of Religions

One of the dominant ways in which scholars of Western cultures tried during the modern period to formulate a science of the human was to turn to an examination of foreign and exotic cultures (the primitives) and discuss and analyze these cultures in terms of their religions. Furthermore, they tended in their work to emphasize the irrational nature of religion in these cultures. The unexamined assumption contained in these investigations was that primitive cultures represented an early stage of human development, an irrational stage gradually being supplanted by the rationality of modern thought and life. What they failed to grasp was that their ideals of rationality and objectivity, rather than being the self-evident properties of critical method, reflected an ideological bias which prevented them from seeing and understanding the phenomena they were studying. By means of a critical analysis of problems of method in the history of religions I want to show how our rational Western intellectual tradition, rooted in a cited tradition, has blinded us to an adequate appreciation of the diversity of the human. A critical consideration of these problems has, I believe, broad implications for a new sense of the human in all humanistic studies and in the human sciences.

### *Rational Methods and Irrational Data*

Joachim Wach never tired of telling his students that the history of religions as an academic discipline had its origins in the Enlightenment. "Die moderne Religionswissenschaft is ein Kind der Aufklärung."[1] It surprised me that Wach should make so much of the Enlightenment genesis of the discipline, for he was a student of Rudolf Otto and as Wach's students we cut our teeth on *Das Heilige*. Otto's approach to the study of religion was, if anything, more an heir of Romanticism than of the rationalism championed by Enlightenment thinkers. One might consider Romanticism a dimension or even the left-wing of the Enlightenment. But in this more precise context

---

Originally published in *Soundings* 61, no. 3 (Fall 1978): 400-414.

one wonders, given the choice, why Wach as a historian of religion would emphasize a cultural definition of the discipline that implied texts such as the Kantian *Critiques* and Hume's *Dialogues* rather than the works of Herder, Schleiermacher, and Schelling.

It took me some time to realize the wisdom of Wach's statement. The import of the statement is carried in the two words, *moderne Religionswissen-schaft*. *Religionswissenschaft*, or the science of religion — referred to in America as the history of religions — emphasized systematic study and inquiry. The adjective *moderne* carried everything implied by Enlightenment critical inquiry, hence our study of Hume and Kant. While the Enlightenment presented us with a variety of philosophical and intellectual orientations, the common notion underlying these positions was the attempt at an empirical, analytical, and systematic treatment of religion. Religion appeared as a valid area of human concern, an area that could be subjected to the methods valid for the study of any human phenomenon, and thus the possibility for the scientific study of religion was opened — a study that was not to be determined by the biases of theology.

Unlike the other human sciences that also had their origins in the Enlightenment, however, the history of religions has never gained the prestige that accompanies a clearly articulated academic discipline. Anthropology, history, and later, sociology, are now well established as disciplines of the Academy. The history of religions and religious studies in general have only lately been accepted in the Academy. Even where this acceptance has taken place, the area defined by religion frequently remains in the position of a stepchild.

Several reasons may be given for this situation, especially within the American context. I refer here to the constitutional issue of the separation of church and state and the dominance of theological studies over religious studies. I think, however, that the fundamental issue lies elsewhere; it constitutes an unresolved and often unrecognized methodological tension within religious studies.

The Enlightenment orientation in the history of religions represents the continuation of a classical Western epistemological stance. Its methodologies, while critical of former positions, tended to relocate the epistemological center of inquiry as new data were confronted, yet it remained wedded to the notion of a centered consciousness as the locus of inquiry. Its systematic inquiry presupposed the locus of an ordered and centered intelligence in human consciousness. The problem of reductionism in all the human sciences stems from this issue; it is most acute in the area of religious studies.

Let us illustrate an early version of this problem. Alongside Enlightenment epistemology we must recognize the influence of Romanticism. Romanticism in any of its several variants was a radical empiricism — a passionate empiricism. For the history of religions it meant the engulfment of rational categories by the contingent historical situations; it was a return to experience as the source of phenomena. No historian of religions can fail to see the line that runs from Giambattista Vico to Rudolf Otto. The movement is from rational categories and concepts of religion to religious experience itself, and it is not surprising that Otto introduces the notion of the "nonrational" as the modality of religious experience.

Otto's usage is predicated on his knowledge of religious forms; his *The Idea of the Holy* is the first religious phenomenology. He attempts to make sense of the primary data of religion. David Hume had reminded the Deists that the primary data of religion were, more often than not, grotesque, strange, and weird. Hume sought to undercut the overly rational and moralistic conceptions of religious life as a negative rejoinder to the Deists. Otto represents the constructive side of this same problem. We may pose Otto's problem in this manner: "What do the Kantian *Critiques* have to do with *mana, taboo, wakanda,* divination, and bloody sacrifices?" If these terms are descriptions of *what is the case* in the religious life, they carry the baggage of human existence. Such religious data do not permit us to view religion as what it ought to be, either in terms of the historical past or in terms of the future. To be sure, some scholars did attempt an interpretation through recourse to a form of evolutionism or progressivism. Phenomena such as those noted by Hume and Otto were relegated to an earlier stage of human life — to the primitives and to the irrational stages of culture, which stages, if they were not overcome in principle by the classical Greeks, were finally thought to be overcome by the Enlightenment. Both Hume and Otto reject this position, but for different reasons. Hume's discussion of the causal nexus is devastating for any theory of evolution. And Otto will not allow for any evolutionary stages in the religious consciousness. The structure of the religious consciousness is the same for the first human as it is for the last. The tension posed for *Religionswissenschaft* is apparent when the attempt is made to give order to religious experience and expression. If actual religious expressions cannot be reduced to the conceptual framework of Enlightenment rationalism, then what form of order is appropriate?

In addition to this intellectual problem, an ideological issue may also be discerned. Since rationality and conceptuality are considered the *sine qua non* of any intellectual endeavor, they have a privileged status in the Western intellectual tradition. Since the Enlightenment, the nonrational tends to be expressed with reference to non-Western cultures and traditions. This was not the case with Otto, for he drew on data from the Western and non-Western cultural traditions. Even so, the essential problematic nature of *Religionswissen-schaft* was posed for him by religious data from other cultures.

## Rationalism and the Centering Power of the City

It is in the work of Mircea Eliade that we begin to see some helpful resources for resolving this impasse within *Religionswissenschaft*. He has done the most creative work in the discipline of the history of religions over the last twenty years. His new interpretive framework, his precise monographs on *Yoga* and *Shamanism,* and his insistence that the history of religions constitutes an autonomous humanistic discipline have gained for Eliade a preeminence accorded probably to no other scholar since F. Max Müller.

While Eliade's study of myths, his notion of archetypes, and his assessment of the religious value of history are fairly well known, one of his notions, though often repeated, has not received the prominence it deserves in his interpretive schema. I refer to his notion of the center as a religious reality. He devotes a major section of *The Myth of the Eternal Return* to a description of the center. An entire chapter is given over to it in *Images and Symbols,* and it is a running theme in *Patterns in Comparative Religion*. A summary description of the center must suffice.

> This elementary notion of the place's becoming, by means of a hierophany, a permanent "centre" of the sacred, governs and explains a whole collection of systems often complex and detailed. But however diverse and variously elaborated these sacred spaces may be, they all present one trait in common: there is always a clearly marked space which makes it possible (though under very varied forms) to communicate with the sacred.
>
> This symbolism of the centre…is as much involved in the building of towns as of houses: every consecrated place where hierophanies and theophanies can occur, and where there exists the possibility of breaking through from the level of earth to the level of heaven.[3]

For Eliade the center defines the locus of reality. Accessibility to the center through the construction of domes, temples, and other architectural forms is given as evidence of the pervasive notion of centered existence as denoting the religiously real. Again, the prestige of the beginnings in Eliade's thought is predicated on his conception of the center as symbolizing the beginnings, representing the novelty of creation to a human community. In traditions emerging after the rise of cities, a return to the beginnings through cyclical rituals is at the same time a return to the center. The center for Eliade is the locus of revelation par excellence.

Around the center, other dimensions of life are organized; the center gives coherence to the common life, and through the center the common life participates in reality. The center holds together in symbolic forms human, natural, and supernatural realities. It is through the center that life receives meaning and value; the center is the source of human value.

Working from Eliade's notion of the religious center, three recent works dealing with the history of citied traditions have given empirical historical verification to the religious meaning of the center: Lewis Mumford's *The City in History*,[4] Robert McCormick Adams's *The Evolution of Urban Society*,[5] and Paul Wheatley's *The Pivot of the Four Quarters*.[6] Especially in the last two works we are presented with detailed archaeological and historical analyses of the beginnings of citied traditions in the ancient Near East, Mesoamerica, China, India, and Africa. Wheatley, in his well-researched study, shows that citied traditions are based upon a metaphysical notion of effective space. Citied traditions begin as ceremonial centers which later develop into embryonic cities. It is not that ceremonial centers always develop into cities; it is simply that before there can be a city there must first be a ceremonial center. The ceremonial city is the symbol of the metaphysical notion of effective space. The discernment of the sacred in the ceremonial center is a recognition of a surplus of power (Eliade's kratophany), and from this place power may be allocated. The power and prestige of the ceremonial center are transferred to the city, and thus the early, and for that matter all, citied traditions express centrifugal and centripetal dynamic forces; they tend to bring power into their centers and redistribute the power from the center. One might say that there tends to be an imperialistic principle inherent in even the earliest citied traditions.

This pattern may be observed in the economic, political, and military structures of citied traditions. It is equally documented in rituals and ceremonies. Social relationships are of a hierarchical nature in these traditions. The sedentary, agricultural, allocative, centripetal-centrifugal character of citied traditions stands in marked contrast to the nomadic egalitarian traditions of the hunters and gatherers of pre-citied cultures.

It was in the context of a nonegalitarian citied tradition that the critique of myth in the classical Western tradition by Aristotle and Plato expressed a new meaning of the center as human reality. This critique, which generated the pervasive and persistent understanding of rationality, of the concept and the category, formed the epistemological structure of Western philosophical thought. It represented the meaning of rationality and logic, the possibility of a *common* mode of knowledge in all human knowing. This common mode, expressed through the form of an epistemological center, was correlative to an ordering of consciousness. It is highly significant that this order of the knowing faculty was formulated within the context of hierarchical citied traditions. It is presupposed in the mystery of the "other" to be known, which is at the heart of every problem of knowledge; yet it is equally presupposed that the issue of knowledge itself was part and parcel of a class structure and a privileged position, not only in regard to rationality but also and simultaneously in regard to sociological context. The criticism of myth in the classical Western tradition is at the same time the criticism of and the beginning of the deterioration of the city as center of a ceremonial order — an order that is homologous with cosmic and biological structures of nature. This development is the beginning of the institutionalization of a notion of the irrational.

I do not mean to remind us here of the sociology of knowledge or of a form of historicism that would limit every meaning to an explicit and *sui generis* sociological and historical context. I refer to this context of knowledge because it is related directly to the meaning, process, and character of knowledge in the human sciences today. At least within the history of religions a great deal of the methodological impetus has emerged from the study of peoples or data that did not possess the forms of order which we refer to as rationality. Or we might say that those who articulated data, if the data displayed rationality, were themselves unaware and unreflective concerning the rationality they expressed (or so the investigators would have us believe).

In Max Müller, the father of history of religions, we see one of the earliest statements of this dichotomy. Myth for Müller is a disease of language — a disease, that is, if one attempts to make sense of its content. For Müller and the other early German Sanskritists, it is clear that the Sanskrit language represents one of the highest forms of order. One might say that they considered Sanskrit almost a perfect language. The paradox for Müller and many of his followers had to do with the ability of the human mind to fashion such a logical form (language in general and Sanskrit in particular), and simultaneously to use this logical form to give expression to illogicalities on the order of myths.

We are again reminded of the hermeneutical structure of this epistemological modality. The center of the epistemology was in the Western world; the data or the *other* that was to be interpreted came from those removed in time and/or in space. The problem of knowledge thus constituted a structure of distance and relationships. Objectivity as a scientific procedure allied itself with the neutrality of distancing in time and space. The issue of relationship was a bit more difficult to negotiate. At what level of the knowing subject did one find a correspondence between what was known and the epistemological center? Cultural evolution might be invoked at this point. The *others* represent the childhood or adolescence of the human race, a stage familiar to us but long past, since the cultures of the epistemological center are forms of adulthood in this evolutionary metaphorical sense. When some form of the cultural evolutionary structure was not invoked, one had recourse to general theories of pathology, fantasy, emotionalism, hysteria, and insanity.

In the Western philosophical tradition, the metaphysical notion of effective space is translated into the notion of the centeredness of human consciousness. The episteme refers to this centering as a mode of human consciousness.[7] In the form of *eidos, arche, ousia*, God, or Consciousness, the episteme refers us to the constancy of a centered principle from which human thought may have validity. As such, it is the *basis* for thought, truth, and verification.

But the epistemic principle constitutes at once a presence and an absence. The paradoxical nature of the epistemic principle consists in the fact that the principle itself can never be known; it constitutes a presence that allows one to generate data, along the periphery, so to speak, but the actuality of the epistemic principle cannot be known itself. The epistemic principle, the center of *Homo sapiens*, cannot be known in itself; it is always transported out of itself into its surrogate, to the data of the periphery.

Just as citied traditions through their centeredness brought a new power into the world — a metaphysical and social power that is identified with civilization — this same principle presided over the emergence of the centered nature of Homo sapiens; it gave rise to that form of intellectual curiosity which leads to knowledge as scientific inquiry. It is not strange, therefore, that there is almost a one-to-one relationship between citied traditions and the epistemic principle in the cultures of the West. The Enlightenment origins of the history of religions are part of this continuity.

Something new and rather strange happened in this young "science of religion." The data that appeared for systematic study tended to resist all efforts of order. As early as 1870, Émile Bournouf stated in his *La science de religions:*

> This present century will not come to an end without having seen the establishment of a unified science whose elements are still dispersed, a science which the preceding centuries did not have, which is not even yet defined, and which, perhaps for the first time, will be named science of religion.

Such a science had not been established as a unified discipline when, as late as 1965, Mircea Eliade had reason to deplore the timidity and lack of daring in the work of historians of religions.

> A creative hermeneutics does not seem to guide the work of historians of religions because, perhaps, of the inhibition provoked by the triumph of "scientism" in certain humanistic disciplines. In the measure that social science and a certain anthropology have endeavored to become more "scientific," the historians of religions have become more prudent, indeed, more timid.

In my opinion, this timidity and failure of historians of religions to articulate a "new science" or a total hermeneutics is related to methodological tensions. These tensions arise because the data with which the religious historian deals tend to undercut any systematic methodology. An epistemic principle which has allowed the data to appear only on the periphery raises basic questions regarding the epistemic principle itself.

We have only to remember again the classic formulation of this problem in the work of Rudolf Otto, who was forced to speak of the nonrational as both methodological principle and as description of his data. We might equally recall the formulations of Lucien Lévy-Bruhl, who had recourse to notions such as the "law of participation" and "pre-logical mentality" in his explanation of primitive and archaic religion. And we must remember that the Melanesian notion of *mana* was not only a discovery about the nature of Melanesian religion but the source of a methodological principle for many historians of religions.

In the light of these discoveries we might well ask whether the data of the historians of religions have not taken over the privileged place of the center by displacing the rational epistemic principle and relegating it to the periphery. This move might appear to be an easy resolution of our dilemma, but it would not change the structural problem of method; the center would still hold in citied traditions and in their sciences. By challenging this epistemic center, the history of religions would simply become an even more isolated discipline.

Methodological problems of the same character as the center/periphery dichotomy have been raised in other disciplines. In recent anthropological discussions it has taken the form of the nature/culture distinction. Claude Lévi-Strauss resolves this issue in his analysis of the incest prohibition.[10] He finds that the incest taboo provides an empirical case in which the nature/culture dichotomy is undercut. The incest taboo is common to all cultures and unique to each. This discovery leads him to a reevaluation of human societies. For Lévi-Strauss, every marriage is a divine mystery. In marriage the human species, in fulfilling a law of nature, creates the specific human form of culture. The institution of marriage is not the only cultural form created; it is, however, the symbolic institution from which all other rules and categories of culture emerge. The prohibition against incest, in Lévi-Strauss's mind, is not so much a category of morals as it is a category of logic. It is necessary for human culture. A similar movement of analyzing the structure of the irrational can be seen in Freud. The realm of sexuality and the pulsations of desire form the basis for ordering relationships in human society.

The admission of these archaic and irrational forms of humanness into the authenticity of meaning and value can no longer be seen simply as additive dimensions of an older rationalism and humanism; but neither is it advisable to re-create the excesses of Romanticism and allow these archaic forms to move into the center. These modalities of human consciousness, discovered and interpreted by modern forms of thought, are part and parcel of that larger world of human experience which, through the categories and concepts of an older rationalism and humanism, were interpreted in a derogatory way as archaic and irrational. Viewed as archaic and irrational, their structure and significance were not adequately appreciated. It is precisely this point which is at stake in the argument between Jean-Paul Sartre and Claude Lévi-Strauss. When Sartre championed post-World War II decolonization and upheld the dignity of the former primitive and colonized peoples as being *now human* because they were taking their rightful place in world history, Lévi-Strauss's rejoinder was that they were already human and had always been human. The issue at stake is: What is the meaning of the human now that the West must realize that those who were formerly considered lesser or second-class human beings have in fact always been fully human?

From a hermeneutical point of view the issue is at once important and torturous. It is important because human sciences such as psychology, sociology, economics, and the history of religions must trace their origins back to the confrontation with an irrationality. Yet the very possibility of discovering the significant structure of this irrationality is rooted in the centered rational consciousness of the *l'homme bon sens*. One cannot simply dismiss this epistemic structure. A discourse and methodology must be found that are capable of putting things in their right places and assigning the correct values to them. Centered rational notions of epistemology must be seen as heuristic devices and not as somehow ontological givens. Or to put it another way, all dimensions of human consciousness are ontological and all human groups and persons are ontologically real. There are no privileged positions. In Whiteheadian terminology, all actual entities are real.

I see a similar movement in the work of Mircea Eliade. In his description of religious symbols he finds his own empirical case of resolution by discerning significant structure in what previously had been interpreted as irrational. Eliade lists six aspects of religious symbols.[11] I shall emphasize two of them in this discussion.

> The symbol is thus able to reveal a perspective in which heterogenous realities are susceptible of articulation into a whole, or even integration into a "system.[12] Perhaps the most important function of religious symbolism ... *is its capacity for expressing paradoxical situations.*[13]

Through his interpretation of religious symbolism Eliade pushes us back to the actual historical situations in which these symbols articulated meanings of the world. He is equally aware of the historical situation which has allowed us to confront these meanings. In both instances we are nearer to Otto's and Wach's emphasis on religious experience. This decentering of methodology in the history of religions is part and parcel of a more general movement in contemporary philosophy. Especially among philosophers who have been attracted by the linguists, the movement of thought is not from logic and grammar but from rhetoric; it is from speech-acts, rather than the other way around. With the absence of a center, everything becomes discourse, or, to put it in religious terms, with the absence of a normative center, religious expressions and manifestations are able to reveal their own specific modalities.

This decentering process represents one of the major methodological shifts in the late modern world. Already in Wilhelm Dilthey the focal interest is shifting away from *pure* reason to historical reason, and, as we just observed in Freud, from the rational moral consciousness to the structures of unconsciousness and of libidinal powers and drives. In the historical schools the shift from Leopold von Ranke to Johann Gottfried von Herder is typified today in the Annales school by Lucien Febvre, Marc Bloch, and Fernand Braudel.

## Rationalism as Western Ideology and New Openings to the Meaning of the Human

It is significant to note that though these shifts have been part of the intellectual scene for some time, it is in the area of religion that they have found a locus for discussion and extensive discourse. When I say "in religion," I am first of all speaking of the new discipline of the history of religions, which itself emerges from the shifts in modern scholarly understanding; in another sense I shall be speaking of a broader context where the issue of a new humanism and an ultimate definition of the human is at stake.

In Max Müller's life and work, the basic issues of what Paul Ricoeur refers to as a "conflict of interpretations" are set forth. We see these issues posed in his avowal of the Aryan myth and in his claims concerning the prestige of Sanskrit in general and of the Indo-European languages in particular; in his attempt to understand myth through an analysis of the history and evolution of language; in his editing of non-Western "sacred books"; in his discussion of the problem of human origins from the point of view of the general history of languages and the specific history of Indo-European languages; and, finally, in his overall attempt to keep the methodological problems raised by these studies within the context of a Neo-Kantian frame of reference.

All of these inquiries take place within a context of ideology. Or stated more precisely, these inquiries constitute aspects of an ideology out of which new paradigms for the study and understanding of religion emerge. On the cultural-historical level, one does not have too much trouble placing Müller within the German ideology. Seen from another point of view, Stanley Hyman in his book *The Tangled Bank* reveals how a new religious mythology can be discerned in the literary styles of the modern giants (in Vico's sense of that word): Darwin, Frazer, Freud, and Marx. And along similar lines John Cuddihy has suggested that Freud, Marx, and Lévi-Strauss each express in the undercurrents of their work a critique of the norms of modern Western gentile culture as an adequate definition of the new humanity.

The definition of ideology implied in the above discussion is that of Louis Dumont who says:

> It is probably expected at this stage that I should distinguish more or less substantially between ideology, on the one hand, and science, or rationality, or truth, or philosophy, on the other. To make such a distinction is the last thing I would do.

He continues:

> We do not take as ideology what is left out when everything true, rational or scientific has been preempted. We take everything that is socially thought, believed, acted upon, on the assumption that it is a living whole, the interrelatedness and interdependence of whose parts would be blocked out by the a priori introduction of our current dichotomies. The ideology is not a residue; it is the unity of all — a unity that does not exclude contradiction or conflict.[14]

In my opinion, the locus of ideological issues has fallen within religious studies because religion is the only area within the humanities and/or the human sciences that could hold together authentically all of the varied orientations; also, it can best provide space for discussing what is *common* to all human beings in the late modern period. Let me illustrate this point again. Note that Dumont's definition of ideology bears a structural resemblance to Eliade's definition of the religious symbol. And observe that the first phenomenology of religion, Rudolf Otto's *The Idea of the Holy*, speaks of the numinous and nonrational in terms that are neither pathological nor evolutionary. Furthermore, and to revert to the father of the discipline again, Max Müller, we see an interest in written "sacred texts," while the nonwritten languages of human nature were being discussed in religious terms beginning with E. B. Tylor through R. H. Codrington, James Frazer, Émile Durkheim, and others. And finally the arena of religion held open the possibility for the interpretation of the human in the ultimate sense as *Homo symbolicus*.

Another part of the late modern ideology has to do with the subjugation of vast areas of the globe through the technological, economic, and military power of the West. I do not mean to imply that the human sciences were simply and merely the ideological counterpart to this subjugation. I should, however, make the case that these sciences come into being presupposing this situation. A great deal of the practical and theoretical meaning of the "others" is related to this colonial situation. Whereas the history of the West is replete with historical events and heroes, the cultures of the world of "others" is filled with static, eternally present social structures, and *mythological* events. The West is rational, the "others" nonrational; the West logical, the "others" illogical or prelogical; the West civilized, the "others" primitive.

Whether we are in the philosophical meaning of hermeneutics observing a mirror effect in this binary dichotomy or whether we are simply dealing with a practical description of differences is beside the point, for these dichotomies and binaries are most important for the assessment of the programs and hermeneutics of modernity. The reviewer of the English[15] translation of Braudel's *The Mediterranean and the Mediterranean World in the Age of Philip II* noted that Braudel's method and his historiography represented a decentering of Europe in terms of wider global considerations and a decentering of the volitional human event as the key to human history; we see again here the thrust of the meaning of this new discourse regarding the human. And it is equally significant that this kind of history with its emphasis on the long event, and seeing the past in varying rhythms, continuities, convergences, and discontinuities, is able to give prominence to the authenticity of those nonhistorical, nonliterate, nonpowerful — in the modern sense of those terms — meanings of the human. This is a religious meaning, for it pushes beyond all the specific modern modes and paradigms, whether of language, logic, or writing, to the fullness and poverty of being which is designated by the term "sacred."

Can there be a science of religion with specific data, methods, and discourse? Yes, there can be such a science, but it must be a *new* science in the sense of a Vico or a Bacon. This new science must be part and parcel of a new humanism and as such it must be a hermeneutical science, a science capable of seeing law and rule in the most contingent and voluntary acts, a science which never gives up the definite and fragile moments of the human image. Such a science is possible, I say, if it is capable of devising methods and procedures consistent with those moments of being and imagination which the human is graced to repeat and embody.

## Notes

1. This same position is upheld by Gustav Mensching in *Vergleichende Religionswissenschaft* (Heidelberg, 1937) and Ernst Cassirer, *The Philosophy of the Enlightenment* (Princeton: Princeton University Press, 1951).
2. Mircea Eliade, *Patterns in Comparative Religion*, trans. Rosemary Sheed (New York: Sheed & Ward, 1958), 368.
3. Ibid., 373.
4. Lewis Mumford, *The City in History: Its Origins, Its Transformations, and Its Prospects* (New York: Harcourt, Brace and World, 1961).
5. Robert McCormick Adams, *The Evolution of Urban Society: Early Mesopotamia and Prehistoric Mexico* (Chicago: Aldine Publishing Co., 1966).
6. Paul Wheatley, *The Pivot of the Four Quarters: A Preliminary Enquiry Into the Origins and Character of the Ancient Chinese City* (Chicago: Aldine-Atherton, 1971).
7. I am greatly influenced here by Jacques Derrida's philosophical analysis. See his *De la grammatologie* (Paris, 1967); *L'écriture et la différence* (Paris, 1967); and "Structure, Sign, and Play," in his *The Structuralist Controversy*, ed. Richard A. Macksey and Eugenio Donato (Baltimore: Johns Hopkins Press, 1970).
8. Eugène Bournouf, *La science des religions*, 3d ed. (Paris, 1870).
9. Mircea Eliade, "Crisis and Renewal in History of Religions," *History of Religions* 5, no. 1 (Summer 1965): 7.
10. Claude Lévi-Strauss, *The Elementary Structures of Kinship*, rev. ed. (Boston: Beacon Press, 1969), chap. 1.
11. Mircea Eliade, "Methodological Remarks on the Study of Religious Symbolism," in *The History of Religions: Essays in Methodology*, ed. Mircea Eliade and Joseph M. Kitagawa (Chicago and London: University of Chicago Press, 1959), 86-107.
12. Ibid., 99-100.
13. Ibid., 101.
14. Louis Dumont, *From Mandeville to Marx: The Genesis and Triumph of Economic Ideology* (Chicago and London: University of Chicago Press, 1977), 17, 22.
15. Richard Mowery Andrews, review of *The Mediterranean and the Mediterranean World in the Age of Philip II*, by Fernand Braudel, *New York Times Book Review*, sec. 7, May 18, 1975.

# Chapter 6

## Primitive/Civilized: The Locus of a Problem

In 1967, Professor Charles J. Adams published an article, "The History of Religions and the Study of Islam."[1] In his essay Adams expressed a singular problem regarding methodology in the discipline of the history of religions. While the discipline purports to study, investigate, and render a systematic and comprehensive understanding of all religious phenomena, the source of most of its important theories is derivative from an interpretation of primitive and prehistoric religious cultures. This trend may be seen in the works of Nathan Söderblom, Gerardus van der Leeuw, and Mircea Eliade. Even when nonprimitive historical-cultural forms of religion — for example, Hebrew, Christian, Islam — are dealt with, they are confronted on the levels of their "primitive" aspects to conform to the methodological orientation of the historian of religions. One does not have to agree with every detail of this criticism to acknowledge that the study of primitive religions has loomed large in the history of the history of religions. This may be explained historically by showing how the origins of the discipline took place in the milieu of E. B. Tylor's researches into primitive cultures, of Charles Darwin's evolutionary theories, and of the popularity of James Frazer's *Golden Bough*. The central cultural issues were expressed in terms of "origins," of the search for the first and simplest forms, and of explanatory systems that traced the evolutionary course of human development over historical time.

This milieu accounts for certain initiatory emphases in method, but it does not explain the continuing and inordinate concern for the data of primitive religions and methods growing from their interpretations. Let us explore this problem by relating the concern for primitive religion to the more general orientation of primitivism.

Arthur O. Lovejoy and George Boas in their classical work define two generic forms of primitivism.[2] One form, chronological primitivism, is concerned with the question of the temporal distribution of good or value in the history of humankind, whether this has occurred in the past, is in the present, or will be in the future. Cultural primitivism, the second form, expresses the discontent of the civilized with civilization or with some conspicuous or characteristic feature of it. It is the expression of a nostalgia for a simpler and less sophisticated form of life than that obtaining in the present situation.

In both forms, chronological or cultural primitivism, one notes a generic ingredient of civilization. Lovejoy and Boas are not careful to define what they mean by civilization; for them, it is a relative term which might extend from the cultures of prehistory to the present. What is important for them is the critical element in the orientation of primitivism, for it expresses the inquietude of human consciousness itself. We might also note that the documents of their text are from West Asian, Indian, and Greco-Roman cultures.

The concern for primitive religion in our time might well be the expression of either or both kinds of primitivism in late modern Western culture. I think, however, that something much more fundamental is at stake in this concern. The texts of Lovejoy and Boas cover literary, philosophical, and imaginary genres; the worlds embodied in primitivism exist as modes of thought and imaginative speculation.

The milieu that forms the context for Tylor, Darwin, and Frazer is of a different kind.[3] It is different in at least two senses. First of all, the term "civilization" has a definite and self-conscious meaning for the intellectuals of this period. Second, the meaning of this term cannot be understood apart from the geographies and cultures of the New World that are both "other" and empirical.

It is clear that the New World itself — the new worlds of the western hemisphere and later the South Pacific — made an extraordinary impact on the European consciousness. Nothing before or since has equaled this discovery. This should not imply, however, that the modality and structure of the "empirical other" is unknown in Western culture prior to this time. Initial perceptual forms for the New World were more often than not based upon a prior history.

## *Empirical Others*

I use the phrase "empirical others" to define a cultural phenomenon in which the extraordinariness and uniqueness of a person or culture is first recognized negatively. However, because the recognition of the person or culture is necessary for interpreters of cultural identity, various stratagems of description and/or diagnosis are employed to represent the other in the relationship.

One example of this kind of meaning can be gained from Ilza Veith's history of the disease hysteria.[4] In her research she traces the history of the disease from ancient Egypt to the work of Freud.

Hysteria throughout this history is classified as a woman's disease; its name is derived from the Greek *hystera*, which means uterus. The symptom of this disease is a marked emotional tension expressing itself in fainting spells or violent pathological behavior. Throughout the history of this disease, various diagnoses are made, many defining the uterus as an animal that tends to wander through the body out of its place. A standard remedy prescribed for this disease throughout its history is heightened heterosexual activity. In other cases, vapors or watery solutions were to be inserted into the vagina. It is especially interesting to note that in the Kahun Papyrus of the Egyptian Middle Kingdom, aromatic agents were to be incorporated in the shape of the ibis. The aroma from this wax upon entering the womb is supposed to pacify the womb. The ibis, a bird, is the symbol of Thoth. Thoth is a male deity personified by the moon and related to the sun. He is also the inventor of writing and the scribe of all the other gods.

Veith notes that "this specific instance of the ibis used for vulvar insufflation inevitably gives rise to further speculations that bear on modern psychological theories. The employment of the image of a powerful male deity to lure a wandering female organ is highly suggestive of the nature of the underlying ideas concerning hysteria even if it is nowhere spelled out in detail."[5]

Another instance of "empirical other" in the modality of an internal European "otherness" may be seen in the mythological structure of the wild man.[6] Elements of this mythological structure may be traced from Enkidu in the Gilgamesh epic to the Tarzan of the cinema, but the exemplary form of this figure is found in its medieval European manifestation. This figure is neither human nor beast; falling somewhere in between these species, it expresses in a grotesque way some of the proclivities of both. It is usually pictured as a hairy creature that walks on two legs, possesses a tail, and is often endowed with boar's tusks growing from the corners of his mouth.

The wild man is a child of nature, his natural habitat is the forest. His great strength is matched by his appetite for carnal connections with human female and the flesh of human beings. Nothing about the wild man prepares him for participation in civil society. When confronted with human beings, he may take to flight or, conversely, offer steadfast resistance to the death. This mythological figure is found on the folkloric, literary, theatrical, and artistic levels of medieval society.

Richard Bernheimer's history of the mythology of the wild man is matched by Michel Foucault's history of madness.[7] Foucault sees a connection between the disappearance of leprosy at the end of the Middle Ages and the confinement of persons considered to be mad.

Prior to the confinement of mad persons, they were able to lead a wandering existence. As a matter of fact, the *Narrenschiff* of mythological lore became literally a "ship of fools," a ship on which mad persons, driven from various cities, were forced to embark. While all mad persons were not placed on ships of this kind, the symbolic meaning of the navigation of mad persons expressed a peculiar valuation.

> But water adds to this dark mass its own values; it carries off, but it does more, it purifies. Navigation delivers now to the uncertainty of fate; on water, each man's voyage is at once a rigorous division and an absolute Passage. In one sense, it simply develops, across a half-real, half-imaginary geography, a mad-man's liminal position on the horizon of medieval concern.

But the watery wanderings of the mad did not continue; in the course of time since, mad persons have been confined, first of all in the abandoned leprosariums, then in places built especially for them. The locus of this confinement is sometimes on the periphery of the city and sometimes in the center of the city.

This brief discussion of certain extraordinary behaviors and beliefs within Europe was undertaken to form a basis for the symbolic and mythological languages used to describe and interpret the new worlds discovered by the Europeans since the fifteenth century. First of all, attention is given to biology and anatomy, but what is the normal anatomical and biological structure of the "other" appears to the authoritative interpreter as the mode of the extraordinary, or the pathological and the irrational. Second, there is the issue of loci. In the case of hysteria, we are confronted with a wandering animal within the body of the female, an animal that will not stay in its place and must be induced to do so by clinical procedures or actions that have the salutary side effect of providing pleasure for men.

Wild men are separated from human society. The natural place for these ambiguous creatures is the forest, removed from human habitation. Wild men are tempted to leave the wilds out of an inordinate and destructive desire for human flesh, expressed carnally or cannibalistically. Their biological structure is ambiguous, partaking of the human and the beast, uncontrolled by human reason; their great natural and bestial strength poses a threat to human society.

In the case of madness, if we follow Foucault, until the middle of the sixteenth century mad persons were wanderers, their lack of fixity of mind paralleled by their abandonment in space.[9] Their first confinement was in a kind of quasi prison — a ship of fools that confined them in a pilgrimage over the waters. Later confinements were within old leprosariums, where they inherited many of the valuations of the former lepers simply by being in those places. Subsequently, confinement in places built for the mad expresses the ambivalence of the society regarding the locus of unreason. Is the place of confinement to be, as in the case of Bedlam, located within the city? And again, what are the functions of unreason? Is it a mysterious malady that should be isolated or is it a spectacle to be observed for the sake of amusement or sober reflection?

It is not at all strange that notions such as these formed the archetypes for the descriptions and taxonomies that Europeans used to make sense of the new worlds. It is normal to describe the new by reference to the old that is already known. However, a new factor of necessity must be observed in regard to the New World. This factor has to do with those movements — political, economic, and religious — which took place within Western Europe from the late fifteenth century to the end of the eighteenth century. In a word, this is symbolized by the notion of civilization. While civilization is used most often as a term to describe the ideas, technology, religion, manners, morals, and so on, of citied traditions throughout the world since the Near Eastern urban development, the precise word "civilization" does not appear in Western languages until the late eighteenth century, first in France in the writings of Marquis de Mirabeau and fifteen years later in England in 1772 in Boswell's *Life of Johnson*.[10] The incident of the appearance of the word in the English language is instructive regarding the new range of meanings implied by the term.

> On Monday March 23, [1772] found [Dr. Johnson] busy preparing a fourth edition of his folio Dictionary.... He would not admit *civilization*, but only *civility*. With great deference to him I thought *civilization*, from to *civilize*, better in the sense opposed to barbarity than civility, as it is better to have a distinct word for each sense, than one word for two senses, which civility is, in his way of using it.[11]

Émile Benveniste surmises from this statement of Boswell's that the term "civilization" was already in use in England and not a neologism of his own invention. It may, therefore, be the case that the term has an earlier appearance in England than the year 1772.

In any case, one is able to find a proliferation of usages within a short time after this date, and one is led to presuppose that it was part of the *lingua franca* of the intellectual class. Adam Smith, in his *An Inquiry Into the Nature and Causes of Wealth of Nations*, makes use of the term in almost a casual manner.[12] As a matter of fact, Benveniste was able to find the term used as common parlance among Scottish intellectuals in John Millar's *Observations Concerning the Distinction of Ranks in Society*, published in 1771.[13] It is safe to say that by the middle of the eighteenth century the word had become a necessary descriptive term for certain cultural processes at work in France and England. Norbert Elias has described these processes as "civilizing processes" that find expression in what he terms sociogenetic and psychogenetic processes. These processes refer to the gradual changes taking place in Western Europe over a two- or three-century period — changes on the psychic and social levels that produced the culture we refer to as modern Western civilization.

> This concept [civilization] expresses the self-consciousness of the West. One could even say: the national consciousness. It sums up everything in which Western society of the last two or three centuries believes itself superior to earlier societies or 'more primitive' contemporary ones. By this term Western society seeks to describe what constitutes its special character and what it is proud of: the level of *its* technology, the nature of *its* manners, the development of *its* scientific knowledge or view of the world and much more.[14]

Outside of internal developments in Western Europe, this formation of culture is caused by or correlative with the discovery of the New World by the West. The self-conscious realization of the Western European rise to the level of civilization must be seen simultaneously in its relationship to the discovery of a new world which must necessarily be perceived as inhabited by savages and primitives who constitute the lowest rung on the ladder of cultural reality.

The sociogenesis and psychogenesis of this formation are equally formed by the explorers, adventurers, merchants, and literary artists whose field of opportunity and expression was the brave New World of savages and primitives beyond the Atlantic sea.

### *Hermeneutical Excursus*

> It would be easy, too easy, at this point to interpret the formation of modern Western culture in political and ideological terms, pointing out the relationship between universal education and literacy as aspects of mercantile imperialism and a tool of the rising bourgeoisie, the primitives and primitivism in general serving only as a camouflage and justification for conquest.
> 
> Resistance to this temptation should not imply that these kinds of factors are not at work and even though inordinate attention to these features might render a too simplistic interpretation, this is not why such a temptation must

be resisted. The resistance is, rather, based on the hermeneutical nature of this enterprise. What is at stake and what has appeared is the symbol, civilization — a symbol that includes the meaning and definition of primitive. This symbol, at least as far as our interpretation has gone, is an expression of the will to power, and at this juncture the problem of truth and error must be subordinated. One must employ at this juncture what Paul Ricoeur has called the hermeneutics of suspicion.[15]

The issue is whether the symbol civilization is simply the context for a necessary lie (the appearance of crude and debased cultures and the demonstration of the superior power of the Europeans) or a new sacred power in the world (the bringing of all cultures into communication with one another and the beginnings of the possibility for a new meaning of human freedom in the world). Both interpretations are equally as true as they are false. Both inhere within the epistemological valence of civilization. Both are products of false consciousness as much as each makes a claim for truth. The very notion of civilization is now suspended within the web of a hermeneutic of suspicion.

And this is as true for those who form its heritage as it is for those who see themselves as its victims. The champions of civilization still speak in continuity with the rhetoric of imperialists and mercantile classes, and its victims clamor for recognition and authenticity of their histories and heritages in the name of civilization, protesting against the unfairnesses of civilization for reducing them to the semantics of tribes and primitives within the very taxonomies of the civilization, which is in point of fact their *bête noir*.[16] Both come to know themselves and define their presence within the rhetoric of "civilization."

The hermeneutics of suspicion reveals the authenticity residing within the ambiguities of the existential. It may be seen as part and parcel of our history after the Second World War, the vogue of anticolonialism, the rise of the Third World, and so on. In this sense, it emphasizes a capacity for iconoclasm, destruction, and nihilism. But all of this in the name of true human authenticity and being. It is, however, impossible to make sense of the being of the human in strictly existential language. The being of the human requires a recognition of depth, whether that depth is defined as history, givenness, creation, or in terms of the vague shadows that accompany the clarity of identity. And so this critical iconoclastic element within a hermeneutics of suspicion already anticipates a hermeneutic of recollection and memory.

## Utopias and Hermeneutics

The term "civilization" — a term that embodies the notion of the primitive — became a part of Western languages in the eighteenth century. Elias has shown that this term is the synthesis of a number of processes that can be understood empirically in Western culture since its medieval period. But if civilization represents a clarity and an identity regarding cultural formation, it throws shadows on histories, imaginations, and meanings that are obscured by the very clarity of the symbol of civilization.

The West as a symbol is historically and logically prior to civilization as a symbol. The West as symbol has had many and varied moments of authenticity, but from the point of view of civilization, the West evokes a dialectical and synthetic orientation to the meaning of "human world." The semantic range engenders a history that is both ideological (suspicious) and normative (a curiosity regarding the nature of being human).

> Two relations, separate but indivisible, are always apparent in the European consciousness. One is the realm of political life in its broadest sense, in the atmosphere of — if I may describe it so — concrete relations with concrete non-European countries, peoples and worlds.... The other relationship has reigned in the minds of men. Its domain is that of the imagination, of all sorts of images of non-Western peoples and worlds which have flourished in our cultures — images derived not from observation, experience, and perceptible realities, but from a psychological urge. That urge creates its own realities that are totally different from the political realities of the first category. But they are in no way subordinate in either strength or clarity since they have always possessed that absolute reality value so characteristic of the rule of myth.[17]

Henri Baudet's statement regarding the formative elements in Western culture goes far in explaining its penchant for the dialectical and the binary and the exemplary form of the symbol as the coherence of paradoxical elements.

Many of these structures were alive in the history of the Renaissance and medieval period prior to the rise of that extension of Western cultural formation which we denote by the term "civilization." It is represented not by symbols and images of an empirical other, but by symbolic imaginative others. It opens us to the symbol of the noble savages of antiquity, of paradisial myths, of imaginary geographies and other worlds.

It is against such a background that the cartographers and explorers of the fifteenth century prepared for their explorations of new worlds.[18] Since the time of the Crusades, the myth of the kingdom of Prester John, who ruled a Christian kingdom in Ethiopia, reigned in the minds of Europeans. This kingdom had a vague basis in biblical and classical literature, and the existence of such a kingdom raised hopes for aid against the assault of the Muslims. In addition to this, according to biblical sources, the kingdom of Ethiopia should lie close to the geographical location of the paradisiacal Garden of Eden. The image of Ethiopia led to concrete expression in the search for its geographical and cartographic reality.

In concert with this image, the legend of the Magi underwent new inte rpretations.[19] To the symbol of time represented by them originally is added the geographical symbol of space. The Magi appear already in a sixth-century Armenian gospel as King Melchior of Persia, King Casper of India-Ethiopia, and King Balthazar of Ethiopia. Another version of this spatial morphology has them recapitulating sons of Noah: Ham with Africa, Shem with the East, and Japheth with Greece, the West.

These myths of recollection and reminiscence are the basis for the geographical and cartographic images regarding the nature of the world during the Renaissance. This geographical and cartographic interest indicates how the imaginary was used as a clue and tool for the understanding of the concrete world; it actually became the basis for voyages into the *terra incognita*. It is this historical and imaginary background which forms the latent structures of thought for the discovery of America and the extension of the power of modern civilization.

Through an ingenious form of logical and philosophical reasoning, Edmundo O'Gorman has sought to dispel the notion that Christopher Columbus *discovered America*.[20] The reasons for this critique are not ideological; the aim is not to put forward a previous discovery by the Norse or the Phoenicians, nor to make the obvious claim that the aborigines of this continent came from somewhere at sometime before the appearance of Europeans.

O'Gorman's critique presupposes the European understanding of America — and his point of departure is the adventures of the Admiral of the Ocean Sea — as an extension of the meaning of the West. His critique is logical and historical, but because it is so, both the history and the logic must be seen in terms of that structure wherein cartographies lead to historical consequences.

Succinctly put, Columbus did not discover *America*, for in terms of the imaginary cartographic and geographical knowledge of his time, the meaning and existence of a space that could be America did not exist. Is it possible to discover that which does not exist? Added to this logic are the facts of Columbus's biography; to his dying day and after four voyages across the

Atlantic, he believed that he had discovered what did in fact exist, either the shores of Cathay or a watery route to the Indian seas.

O'Gorman does not rest his case on the history of this period, nor on the biography of Columbus. As a historian, his method must verify his historical judgment. Two rather long quotes from O'Gorman will reveal that philosophical logic undergirding his historiography.

> This conclusion led me to understand that the basic concept for the historian is that of "invention," because the concept of creation which assumes that something is produced *ex nihilo* can have meaning only within the sphere of religious faith. Thus I came to suspect that the clue to the problem of the historical appearance of America lay in considering the event a result of an inspired invention of Western thought not as the result of a purely physical discovery, brought about, furthermore, by accident.[21]

> We ask whether or not the idea that the American continent was "discovered" was acceptable as a satisfactory way of explaining its appearance on the historical scene of Western culture. We may now answer that it is not satisfactory, because this interpretation does not account adequately for the facts that it interprets; it reduces itself to an absurdity when it reaches the limits of its logical possibilities. The reason for this absurdity is the substantialistic concept of America as a thing in itself. We must conclude that it is necessary to discard both this obsolete notion and the interpretation that depends on it.... If one ceases to conceive of America as a ready-made thing that had always been there and that one day miraculously revealed its hidden unknown, and unforeseeable being to an awe-struck world, then the event which is thus interpreted [the finding by Columbus of unknown oceanic lands] takes on an entirely different meaning, and so, of course does the long series of events that followed. All of these happenings which are now known as the exploration, the conquest, and the colonization of America, the establishment of colonial systems in all their diversity and complexity; the gradual formation of nationalities; the movement toward political independence and the economic autonomy; in a word, the sum total of all American history, both Latin and Anglo-American, will assume a new and surprising significance.... Historical events will no longer appear as something external and accidental that in no way alters the supposed essence of an America ready-made since the time of Creation, but as something internal which constitutes its ever-changing mobile, and perishable being, as is the being of all that partakes of life; and its history will no longer be that which has happened to America, but that which it has been, is, and is in the act of being.[22]

It is O'Gorman's argument that Amerigo Vespucci really discovered America, for in his voyage of 1501-02 along the coast of what is called South America, Vespucci discerned that he had found a "New World." His interpretation was based on an *a posteriori* foundation. Vespucci's voyage became the empirical determinant that opened up the possibility of explaining the new-found lands in a way different from and contradictory to the accepted picture of the world.[23] Vespucci says in his description of this New World that he is going to write about things unknown by either ancient or modern authors.

It is through this process, according to O'Gorman, that the *being* of America, the New World, unfolds. The imaginary cartography of the Renaissance that led Europeans to undertake their initial voyages is broken by the sheer facticity of the existence of the new land mass and the impossibility of fitting it into the older symbolic structure without doing violence to the structure or the empiricity of the new lands. But if the geographical images were broken, the historical elements of this image remained intact. The inhabitants of the new world would bear the name "Indians," a carryover from the imaginary geography of Columbus. Their historical meaning would fluctuate between those of Western antiquity, biblical and classical, as archetypes, on the one hand, and would be deciphered in the terms of a norm of nature on the other. The norm of nature often combined in one image that of the older "empirical others" of Europe and a passive paradisiacal understanding of nature.

From this process several images of the primitive emerge. The aboriginal inhabitants of North America appear as noble savages, as metaphors of the wilderness and as wild men. These images come to fruition through a combined fertilization of theological-philosophical, economic-political, artistic-literary, and scientific concerns on the part of the Europeans.[24]

The semantic range, from a virgin land in North America inhabited alternatively by noble or ignoble savages to models based on the extension of the archetypes of the crusades in Mesoamerica and South America, indicates the speculative arena in which these images took shape. In the South Pacific, that other vital source of primitivism in the modern period, the varying meanings of the norm of nature as a deciphering tool were dependent on two European traditions of artistic depiction, both traditions represented simultaneously on Captain Cook's voyage of 1768. On this voyage were two kinds of painters. One type had been trained by the British navy and were revered by the Royal Society for their accuracy and scientific attention to detail. The second type represented the tradition of neoclassicism. For them, nature was to be depicted not with imperfections clinging to it but in ideal perfected forms. Both traditions of painting and the literary traditions of high and popular culture stemming from them in England contributed to the ambiguous image of the natives of the South Pacific.[25]

These images, in spite of their variations, constitute a coherency to the extent that they all refer to the "other world" of the primitives, for coherency was based on a singular contrast with the mode of civilization. The voyages from Vespucci to the end of the nineteenth century had almost dispelled the earlier imaginary cartography and providential history of the late fifteenth and sixteenth centuries; the actual and empirical outlines of all the lands of the world were known. The inhabitants of these lands became the loci of a new *terra incognita*. They were not imagined in the symbols of a totally imaginary archetype, reminiscent of, let us say, that of Prester John; more often than not, they immediately became confined within the structures of the prison of medieval Europe's "empirical others," and European contact with them created a new modality of primitivism in the West that was experienced as a fatal impact by the natives of these new worlds.[26] The utopian quest of the Renaissance had been altered. The aesthetic satisfaction and scientific knowledge to be gained from exploration had already been blunted in the motivations of the first voyages by the search for riches; thus political considerations were already present, but vestiges of the aesthetic and scientific meaning of perfection in knowledge of the world continued as one of the reasons for undertaking a voyage of exploration. However, given the inner dynamics of Western civilization during this period, the Utopias were more often than not defined in more concrete economic terms. It is the Hakluyts, the Purchases, the Hawkesworths of the rising mercantile class who promise the Utopias in the new world, and their manipulation of the primitives or the ideology of primitivism is related directly to their existential concerns.[27] The utopia of the new world from this point of view must necessarily create its fatal impact in the creation of the primitive.

## *Demythologizing and Reorientation*

The concern for primitivism may well be as Lovejoy and Boas indicated, a concern of civilization throughout the history of this cultural form. However, that concern for primitivism which has expressed itself in the imaginary and empirical knowledge of extra-European peoples from the fifteenth century to the present represents a unique form for several reasons. In the first sense, the peoples and culture who were the data for this form of primitivism were not *simply* imaginary structures of reality either in terms of their cultural reality or their geographical loci.

Second, this present meaning of primitivism contained an imaginary dimension, but it possessed more than an imaginary meaning for the civilization that had defined it in those terms. The civilization of Western Europe during this period could not have defined itself apart from the empirical existence of the primitive cultures and their exploitation. The range of significations for the meaning of primitivism during this period is much wider and bears a greater depth of meaning. Third, the background and context for this understanding are within the framework of the democratization of western Europe and the universalizing of Western civilization.

There is obviously not a relationship of identity between the academic community and ordinary citizens, but they share common semantic orientations especially as cultural meanings affect the economic and popular levels of culture. To the extent that learned societies expressed a meaning of truth that was not simply class oriented — a truth arrived at through scientific investigations — such truths about the primitives were communicated quite easily to persons on the popular levels of culture.[28] For this reason, the ideology of primitivism constitutes a pervasive influence in modern Western cultures, on the learned as well as the popular level. The problem surrounding the usage of the term "primitive" as a proper designation for certain cultures, histories, and religions must therefore be seen as a crisis of the term "civilization."

Other terms have been forthcoming to replace the term "primitive" — noncivilized, nonliterate, cold cultures, and so on. These changes will not suffice, for the cultural language of civilization that brought forth the structure of the primitive has not changed.

The problem defines a hermeneutical situation. Since the beginning of the modern period in the West the primitives have been understood as religious and empirical "others," empirical from the point of view of those disciplines and sciences which take these peoples and their cultures as the data of their inquiry — for example, anthropology, ethnology, and history of religions. These "others" are religious in two senses. In the first sense, the primitives form one of the most important bases of data for a non-theological understanding of religion in the post-Enlightenment West. In the second sense, the "primitives" define a vague "other"; their significance lies not in their own worth and value but in the significance this other offers to civilization when contrasted with it. The primitives operate as a negative structure of concreteness that allows civilization to define itself as a structure superior to this ill-defined and inferior "other."

The disciplines of hermeneutics are responses to this crisis of civilization. The importance of hermeneutics for our time can be seen in the movement from hermeneutics as the interpretation of biblical texts to a general hermeneutics — a field in which the problem of understanding covers the range of the disciplines of the human sciences. These disciplines, whether economics, depth psychology, or the history of religions, are related to certain existential problems of our civilization. A favorite pattern can be discerned in their methodological procedures. Once an issue has been raised as problematical or pathological within our culture — for example, the problem of production and class structure in economics; the problem of the sexual in depth psychology; the loss or absence of the religious sensibility in modern culture — primitivism or the primitives appear as a methodological tool or stratagem that enables one to analyze the problem or pathology in a culture and history where it appears nonpathological or problematical and fully expressive. This other situation for modern Western civilization has become the world of the ethnological primitives.

We began with the citation of a suspicion about the relationship of the history of religions to the study of primitive religions. A discourse concerning primitives, primitivism, and civilization then followed. Another suspicion is encountered, this time a suspicion surrounding the necessary relationship obtaining between primitives, primitivism and civilization. By implication, this second suspicion is at the same time a suspicion regarding civilization and religion.

Our discussion of the designation of those "others" referred to as "primitives" occurred in the attempt to demythologize the symbolic myth of civilization. We must now ask whether we are able to discern a structure of symbols and meanings that will establish a new integrity for the status of primitive religions, on the one hand, and demonstrate the proper place for this study within the history of religions on the other.

The religions of the "primitives" are too often seen as static, externally existing in the present, and as such they constitute the basis for a minimum definition of religion. Some elements of all religions appear under this guise, for to the extent that religions manifest the status of the human in relationship to the transcendent, myths and symbols express this atemporal dimension. Too often this dimension of primitive religions is taken to define the total meaning of the religion, so that the temporal dimension is entirely lost or neglected. In the case of the New World, we must take account of these religions as they are described in their pre-European integrity, as well as their existence during and after the European contact and subsequent conquest.

The movement of Europeans to the West was undertaken in many cases under the aegis of utopian and eschatological symbols. America is the result of a European diaspora. But there have been eschatological dimensions in the pre-European traditions of aborigines in several parts of the world. An understanding of this form of sacrality in non-European traditions would throw light on the nature of this religious symbol.

But more important than this is the possibility of studying the living traditions of the contact between Europeans and aborigines in the various situations in which this happened. It is the myths of conquest, or the myths of virgin lands, that have obscured the traditions and languages of this religious meaning. We have, to be sure, several studies of cargo cult movements in various parts of the world; these studies are important and we shall return to them in the last essay in this section, but we are speaking here more of the kinds of studies represented by Nathan Wachtel's study of the religious tradition for the conquest itself in the history of Mesoamerica and South America.[29] Jacques Lafaye's work on the Mexican tradition is a more elaborate description, but the possibility of this kind of study is not unique to the history of Mexico.[30] Eva Hunt's work is also situated in Mexico, but like Wachtel's, its fundamental data are those of the folkloric tradition, as in Gary Gossen's study of the Chamulas.[31]

For North America, Francis Jennings's study reveals a rich mine of data available for the study of the Puritans and the aborigines.[32] I am pointing to a simple fact: scientific studies and reports on the primitives are usually made after some two hundred years of cultural contact with Europeans. This fact must be understood as part of the religious meaning of these traditions. If primordial structures are revealed in these religions, such symbols might simultaneously refer to a mythical past and a history of cultural contact.

One aspect of this religion of contact is the phenomenon of cargo cults. They provide a unique and alternate meaning of human freedom in the modern world. Their traditions demythologized through contact with the modern world, the cargo cult prophets undertake a new quest for a world of sacred meaning. This quest is not a return to the precontact situation, nor a mere acquiescence to the conquerors. The ingredients of the past and the present are reconceived as sacred forms, and from this sacrality new human beings are to be created. A revalorization of matter, time, money, and human exchanges is adumbrated in these movements, for they represent one of the most powerful attempts of modern human beings to live an authentic sacred life.[33]

The problematical character of Western modernity created the language of the primitives and primitivism through their own explorations, exploitations, and disciplinary orientations. Recourse to the "primitives" cannot bring about new insight. The world and language that emerged from the imaginary geographies of the Renaissance through the conquest of the Americas and the later conquest of the South Pacific can no longer be returned to as a lively hermeneutical option.

The marks that provided the basis for internal distinction and contrast between the primitive and civilization are no longer valid. This is as true of nudity (the sexuality of savages) as it is for language (writing) and for rationality. From Lucien Lévy-Bruhl's recantation to Claude Lévi-Strauss's enunciation of the logic of the concrete, from E. B. Tylor's theory of animism to Mircea Eliade's notion of a primitive ontology, the distinctions are blurred. The ultimate contrast based upon writing has evoked the most brilliant critical analyses from the pen of Jacques Derrida.[34]

No one denies that there were and are peoples and cultures in the world who possess different technologies, customs, manners, and so forth; the general designation of these forms of human reality as primitive is less than a description and more than a definition. The withering away of the distinction represents a critique of civilization itself. A new and different "other" is present for our understanding.

We can only come to terms with this reality through the tools and data we have at hand. A first step would be to reexamine the modes by which this primitive other came to be in the beginnings of our civilization and its disciplinary orientations. This would include a careful analysis of the problem of internal others as well as the others of exoticism. But the most important task would be epistemological. This combines the issues of knowing and naming. If the symbol of civilization is demythologized, if this symbol no longer possesses an ontological prestige among the other symbols of human culture, in what manner do the others appear?

What is now the proper *topos* for the modalities of rationality, the sacred, civilization? There may well be a prerational that is the correlate of the rational consciousness; a primordial that undergirds the existential; a primitive that is a modality of the civilized, and, as Derrida has argued, there may be a writing before writing. But if any of these assertions are admitted for investigation, they should be so as expressions of universal human conditions and should not be imputed to or limited to one time or place.

If the West demythologized and demystified the religious traditions of aboriginal cultures throughout the modern period, a proper study of these traditions might enable us to demythologize in turn our own discipline, and thereby extend our understanding of religion.

## Notes

1. Charles J. Adams, "The History of Religions and the Study of Islam," in *The History of Religions: Essays on the Problem of Understanding*, ed. Joseph Kitagawa, with the collaboration of Mircea Eliade and Charles H. Long (Chicago and London: University of Chicago Press, 1967), 177-93.
2. Arthur 0. Lovejoy and George Boas, *A Documentary History of Primitivism and Related Ideas* (Baltimore: Johns Hopkins Press, 1935), 1-22.
3. Stanley Diamond argues that the power and influence of figures such as Darwin, Marx, Frazer, and Freud are due in substantial part to their ability as *imaginative* writers; see Stanley Hyman, *The Tangled Bank* (New York: Atheneum Publishers, 1962).
4. Ilza Veith, *Hysteria: The History of a Disease* (Chicago and London: University of Chicago Press, Phoenix Books, 1970).
5. Ibid., 6.
6. I am dependent on Richard Bernheimer's *Wild Men in the Middle Ages* (New York: Octagon Books, 1970). See also Edward J. Dudley and Maximillian E. Novak, eds., *The Wild Man Within: An Image in Western Thought from the Renaissance to Romanticism* (Pittsburgh: University of Pittsburgh Press, 1973), especially Hayden White, "The Forms of Wildness: Archaeology of an Idea," 3-38; Stanley L. Robe, "Wild Men and Spain's Brave New World," 39-54; and Geoffrey Symcox, "The Wild Man's Return: Enclosed Visions of Rousseau's *Discourses*," 223-48.
7. Michel Foucault, *Madness and Civilization: A History of Insanity in the Age of Reason* (New York: Random House, Vintage Books, 1973).
8. Ibid., 11.
9. Ibid., chap. 7.
10. See Émile Benveniste, *Problems in General Linguistics*, trans. Mary Elizabeth Meek (Miami: University of Miami Press, 1971), chap. 28, "Civilization: A Contribution to the History of the Word," 289-96.
11. Ibid., 293.
12. It is interesting to observe the influence of the Scottish moral philosophers' contribution to the discussion on civilization. Most prominent are Adam Smith and John Millar. Ronald Meek, *Social Science and the Ignoble Savage* (Cambridge: Cambridge University Press, 1976), credits this school with the stadial theory of cultural evolution.
13. Norbert Elias, *The Civilizing Process: The Development of Manners* (New York: Urizen Books, 1977).
14. Ibid., 3-4.
15. See Paul Ricoeur, *Freud and Philosophy* (New Haven: Yale University Press, 1970), 26, 32-36. I am employing "hermeneutics of suspicion" here because the meaning of primitive religion is couched within the Western ideological understanding of "primitivism." And given the history of modern Western civilization, the authenticity of the actual cultures and peoples called primitives has been conflated with "primitivism."
16. For a polemic on the discipline of anthropology and the "primitives," see Dell Hymes, ed., *Reinventing Anthropology* (New York: Random House, Vintage Books, 1974), especially William S. Willis Jr.'s essay, "Skeletons in the Anthropological Closet," 121-52. For insight into the practical and disciplinary nature of this

dilemma, see Wole Soyinka, *Myth, Literature and the African World* (Cambridge: Cambridge University Press, 1978), especially the preface.
17. Henri Baudet, *Paradise on Earth: Some Thoughts on European Images of Non-European Man*, trans. Elizabeth Wentholt (New Haven: Yale University Press, 1965), 6.
18. See John Parker, ed., *Merchants and Scholars* (Minneapolis: University of Minnesota Press, 1965). For an understanding of the aesthetic appeal of Renaissance cartography, see Joan Gadol, *Leon Battista Alberti: Universal Man of the Early Renaissance* (Chicago and London: University of Chicago Press, 1969).
19. For a thorough discussion of the transformation of the "three wise men," see J. Duchesne-Guillemin, "Die drei Weisen aus dem Morgenlande und die Anbetung der Zeit," *Antaios* 8, no. 5 (September 1965): 234-52.
20. Edmundo O'Gorman, *The Invention of America* (Bloomington: Indiana University Press, 1961).
21. Ibid., 4.
22. Ibid., 117.
23. Ibid.
24. See Robert F. Berkhofer, Jr., *The White Man's Indian* (New York: Alfred A. Knopf, 1978); Benjamin Keen, *The Aztec Image* (New Brunswick, NJ.: Rutgers University Press, 1971); Philip D. Curtin, *The Image of Africa* (Madison: University of Wisconsin Press, 1964).
25. Bernard Smith, *European Vision and the South Pacific* (Oxford: Clarendon Press, 1960).
26. The phrase is from Alan Moorehead, *The Fatal Impact: An Account of the Invasion of the South Pacific 1767-1840* (New York: Harper & Row, 1966); see also, for North America, Francis Jennings, *The Invasion of America: Indians, Colonialism, and the Cant of Conquest* (Chapel Hill: University of North Carolina Press, 1975).
27. Samuel Purchas, *Hakluytus Posthumus or Purchas his Pilgrimes...* , 4 vols. (1625); J. Hawkesworth, *An Account of the Voyages Undertaken by the Order of His Present Majesty for Making Discoveries in the Southern Hemisphere*, 3 vols. (London, 1773). Both were writers whose depictions of the New World were designed to attract investment and settlement. Hakluyt was Purchas's business partner.
28. The image of the New World found profuse expression on the learned and popular levels of European society, in philosophical discussion, in theater, and in literary creations. See Antonelli Gerbi, *The Dispute About America*, and Gilbert Chinard, *L'Amérique et le rêve exotique dans la littérature francaise au XVII et au XVIII siècle* (Paris: E. Droz, 1934).
29. Nathan Wachtel, "The Vision of the Vanquished," in *Social Historians in Contemporary France: Essays from Annales*, ed. Marc Ferro (New York: Harper & Row, 1972), 230-60.
30. Jacques Lafaye, *Quetzalcóatl and Guadalupe: The Formation of Mexican National Consciousness*, trans. Benjamin Keen (Chicago: University of Chicago Press, 1976).
31. Eva Hunt, *The Transformation of the Hummingbird* (Ithaca, N.Y.: Cornell University Press, 1977); Gary H. Gossen, *Chamulas in the World of the Sun: Time and Space in a Maya Oral Tradition* (Cambridge: Harvard University Press, 1974).
32. Jennings, *The Invasion of America*.
33. Kenelm Burridge, *New Heaven, New Earth: A Study of Millenarian Activities* (New York: Schocken Books, 1969).
34. Jacques Derrida, *Of Grammatology*, trans. Gayatri Spivak (Baltimore: Johns Hopkins University Press, 1976). See especially pt. II.

# Chapter 7

## Conquest and Cultural Contact in the New World

The theoretical and methodological bases for our discussion may be seen in two formulations of the meaning of religious experience. First, religious experience is a primordial experiencing of that which is considered ultimate in existence. Since the brilliant formulation of Rudolf Otto of religious experience as *mysterium tremendum et fascinosum* or Joachim Wach's notion of religious experience as the experience of ultimate reality, students of religion have understood religion — or, more precisely, the holy, the sacred — as the basic element in the constitution of human consciousness and human community.[1]

Second, implied in this notion of religious experience is that of human orientation — the meaning that human communities give to the particular stances they have assumed in their several worlds. Orientation refers to the actual situation of the particular stance and the reflections and imaginations attendant to it.[2]

As a biological species, human beings are equipped with the capacity for internally motivated movement. This self-evident observation looms large in any discussion of human cultures prior to the beginnings of the cited traditions. The cultures of Paleolithic and Early Neolithic were transhumance cultures. Human beings in these cultures came to a knowledge of themselves and their world by passing through and over the space of the earth.

The erect stance characteristic of human equilibrium must be seen against the background of the ever-present spaces of the earth, sky, topographies, and flora and fauna over which the human passes. But this externality is simultaneously an internality. Human consciousness emerges as the right configurations and approximations of the actual and potential meaning of this stance. The world as a cosmos, a home, and receptacle for the human mode of being, is based upon this perception of space and the human transversal through it. The sacred as orientation and as those forms perceived from this orientation is defined in this movement. As a species we have maintained this mode of being for most of our existence on this planet, and though it is not given the status and prestige in cited traditions that it retains in hunting and gathering societies, it remains a residual value even within the cited traditions of modernity.

The citied traditions, beginning during the Upper Neolithic in the Fertile Crescent, represent a new human venture. While previous human cultures moved across the land and through space, these newer cultures introduced the meaning of the human as a sedentary being — as situated in a specific space — a center defining the human condition. This centeredness as location and orientation was not absolutely new; it was known and practiced in the cultures of transhumance, but in these later cultures the centers changed quickly; they were flexible, changing with the movement of the community, and thus they never retained the absoluteness of power as eternal and inflexible.

Early prehistorians such as V. Gordon Childe, and some contemporary Marxists, contend that the beginning of these earliest citied traditions is the result of new economic and material conditions. More detailed research by Robert McCormick Adams, Thorkild Jacobsen, Paul Wheatley, Mircea Eliade, and S. J. Tambiah presents an alternative and more plausible view of this beginning.[3] Let us summarize.

A particular space manifests itself in some extraordinary manner — this manifestation is sacred. The sacred is kratophanic; it is saturated with power. Instead of becoming a limited and specific flexible center, this center becomes the organizing principle for all habitable space. As such, this particular space is venerated by the community as a ceremonial center. As ceremonial center, it is the model for all habitable space and the basis for the effective use of space as human habitation. All early cities are built on the site of a ceremonial center or are defined on the model of a ceremonial center. Power radiates out from the center in a centrifugal manner and returns to the center centripetally. The center is at the same time the locus for an axis between the earth and the sky. As a matter of fact, the center may be seen as a model of the astrocosmic powers that establishes its legitimacy, authenticity, and coherence.

This is the model for the citied traditions of the ancient Near East, Asia, Africa, and Mesoamerica. It represents at once the sacred valorization and the domestication of space as an effective human habitat. The economic, commercial, political, military, and technological expressions of the citied traditions are modes of domestication of this space rather than its cause. Patterns of citied traditions of this kind persisted in all traditions of the ancient world; the new modern city either is built upon the residual structures of this pattern or is the extrapolation of one of the functions of its domestication, whether economic, technological, or military.

The kind of cultural contact that will be discussed in this essay is an aspect of this kind of sacred ideology of the conquest and domestication of space and spaces. For the greater part of history, cultural contact has come about as a result of the centrifugal/centripetal power of the citied traditions — the tendency to expand the power of the center over ever wider spatial areas, thereby bringing these spaces under the reign of the center and its ideology, assuring them a place in the legitimate and authentic structure of that reality designated and symbolized as this center.

This is the broader contextual structure for my remarks. I shall in the main explore the religious situation defined, on the one hand, by those who reside in the center and, on the other, by those who form the peripheries of this center in that long series of cultural contacts in the world since the European discovery of the New World in 1492 C.E.

## *First Impressions: Inner and Outer Pilgrimages*

The voyages of exploration commencing with Christopher Columbus are understood as continuing the older religious traditions of the religious pilgrimage.[4] The pilgrimage is that peregrinative ritual which retains the older meaning of the human as a being who moves across space. But the pilgrimage is a product of the citied tradition. The ceremonial center, or a replica of it, is always presupposed in a pilgrimage ritual. After accomplishing the goal of the pilgrimage, the pilgrim must return to the original source of stability, the city of departure. The pilgrimage in one form or another is present in all periods of the Western Christian tradition. This tradition of pilgrimage expresses a tension between two religious attitudes contained within the structure of the pilgrimage — stability and curiosity. In the early centuries of the Christian church, many believers, following the imitation of Christ as the homeless one, took up a life of peripatetic existence, residing in deserts, wandering with no predetermined itinerary or goal. They were condemned by the orthodox because of their instability. The normative pilgrimage for the orthodox was represented by the Jerusalem pilgrimage. Leaving home offered the pilgrim the chance to realize the spiritual value of forsaking the familiar world for an alien environment; but the act of pilgrimage also presumed a return home where each Christian must live and work — this return symbolized the restoration of stability and order.

Curiosity, wandering in space or wandering in mind, was held to be a sin by the Christian community well into the Middle Ages. In spite of its valuation as sinful temptation, pilgrims allowed themselves to be enticed and distracted by wondrous sights along the way, intensifying the tension between stability and curiosity in the act of pilgrimage.

Columbus understood his voyages as pilgrimages. He gave minute details of the algae on the waves as indications of shallow water and the proximity of land, the constellations in the sky as signs of positions, scars on the Indians as signs of bellicose relations with neighboring tribes, gold rings as signs of gold mines. What he noticed in the world he traveled through were landmarks, and these marks were placed within the context of an inner piety and faith recorded in his spiritual diaries, combining the inner and the outer pilgrimages in a manner reminiscent of stations of the cross.

The tension exemplified in the diaries of the great admiral soon broke down and the pilgrimage as a voyage of discovery — an exercise of curiosity — became the rule.[5] From the time of the voyages of Columbus through the nineteenth century, European hegemony was established through economic, technological, military, and, to a certain extent, religious means throughout the world. This was, in the words of Immanuel Wallerstein, the beginnings of the modern world system. This cultural contact had a tragic effect upon all non-European cultures, but that is a history we need not discuss at this juncture. These voyages of discovery, especially the discovery of the New World (referred to by the Spanish as the Other World), had an impact of equal intensity upon Europe, especially in the sixteenth and seventeenth centuries. There were the obviously economic, military, and political meanings of these discoveries, but the intellectual impact was even more intense and far-ranging, and this impact is all too often not taken into account.

> Its discovery [the New World] had important intellectual consequences, in that it brought Europeans into contact with new lands and peoples and in so doing challenged a number of traditional European assumptions about geography, theology, history, and the nature of man.

Let me place this intellectual impact within the structure of the pilgrimage — the inner pilgrimage of curiosity occasioned by the discovery of worlds that appeared new and strange to the European. I shall have in mind those processes which have gone into the "making of the European mind," under the impact of these discoveries. It is the first impressions of this New World which open up a new inner space alongside the reorientations characterized by the terms Reformation and Renaissance. It is here that religion as orientation in time and space, externally and internally, forms a locus. The New World was intellectually and economically a matter of ultimate concern. This new locus of religiosity expressed a dynamic; like the pilgrim, it expressed mobility, and this movement formed the questions which occurred before the formal questions of a scientific and cultural inquiry were asked regarding the New World and the new peoples confronted in the cultural contact.

Stephen Greenblatt in his *Renaissance Self-Fashioning* has given us a brilliant study of the power of the New World on the literary imagination of six sixteenth-century English figures. They are Thomas More, William Tyndale, Thomas Wyatt, Edmund Spenser, Christopher Marlowe, and William Shakespeare. All of these men produced classics of English literature. But they were not simply writers, they were men of affairs, often holding high civil, military, and religious responsibilities. Their literary productions help to define the new space of religious and cultural consciousness in much the same manner as the works of John Locke, Thomas Hobbes, or Montaigne did in the area of political and moral philosophy.

In their personal lives and in their writings, they represent in dramatic form the ways in which the New World brought about a new orientation of European consciousness. In their "self-fashioning" we observe the impact of the Other World upon those "who stayed at home to travel." Greenblatt offers the following general characteristics for all of them:

> All of these talented middle-class men moved out of a narrowly circumscribed social sphere into a realm that brought them in close contact with the powerful and the great. All were in a position as well…to know with some intimacy those with no power, status, or education at all…. The six writers here then are all displaced in significant ways from a stable inherited social world, and they all manifest in powerful and influential form aspects of Renaissance self-fashioning.[7]

In addition, Greenblatt has noted ten meanings common to all of them. Five of these will suffice at this point:

1. None of the figures inherits a title, an ancient family tradition, or hierarchial status that might have rooted personal identity in the identity of a clan or class.
2. Self-fashioning is achieved in relation to something perceived as alien, strange, or hostile. The threatening Other — heretic, savage, witch, adulteress, traitor, antichrist — must be discovered or invented in order to be attacked and destroyed.
3. The alien is perceived by the authority as that which is either unformed or chaotic (the absence of order). Since accounts of the former tend inevitably to organize and thematize it, the chaotic constantly slides into the demonic, and consequently the alien is always constructed as a distorted image of authority.

4. Self-fashioning is always, though not exclusively, in language.
5. The power generated to attack the alien in the name of authority is produced in excess and threatens that which it sets out to defend. Hence self-fashioning always involves some experience of threat, some effacement or undermining, some loss of self. Self-fashioning occurs at the point of encounter between an authority and an alien, that which is produced in this encounter partakes of both the authority and the alien that is marked for attack, and hence any achieved identity always contains within itself the sign of its own subversion or loss."

Two examples from the enormous corpus of these literary giants will be discussed here. The first example is the destruction of the Bower of Bliss in book 2, canto 12 of Spenser's *The Faerie Queene*.[9] After a perilous voyage Guyon, the Knight of Temperance, arrives with his companion, the old man Palmer, at the realm of the beautiful and dangerous witch, Acrasia. After quelling the threats of her guards, they enter the witch's exquisite bower. There, aided by Palmer's counsel, Guyon resists a series of sensual temptations. Guyon then systematically destroys the Bower and leads the tightly bound Acrasia away.

Greenblatt suggests that the structure of *The Faerie Queene* is derivative from the descriptions, voyages, and pilgrimages of explorers of the New World. Even Spenser refers to the Bower of Bliss as Eden itself in a manner in which Columbus had already stated in 1498: "I am completely persuaded in my own mind that the Terrestrial Paradise is in the place that I described." Similarly, Sir Walter Raleigh in his description of the Orinoco had suggested the same Edenic vision: "On both sides of the river, we passed the most beautiful country that mine eyes had ever beheld." And Peter Matyr in his collection of exploration accounts had recorded: "Surely, I marvel not at the gold and precious stones, but wonder with astonishment with what industry and laborious art the curious workmanship."

But this seductive beauty of the New World like that of the Bower of Bliss is dangerous. The danger is not present in things that are described as repugnant to the perceiver; the danger lies precisely in the fulsomely attractive and wonderful beauty of the New World and the Bower. The Edenic quality of the New World is the backdrop and screen onto which the Europeans projected their fantasies of evil in the New World. The Indians are often portrayed as beasts without intelligence; they are absolutely indiscriminate in their sexual relations, they are cannibalistic — eating their children and relatives. They lack discipline and often make wretched slaves, and if left to their own devices, they wander up and down and return to their old ways. It is indeed ironic that the Indians are accused of wandering by a class of people and a culture that has institutionalized, spiritualized, and commercialized the pilgrimage of curiosity. Even as acute an observer as Alexis de Tocqueville is under the sway of the Bower of Bliss notion as late as the early part of the nineteenth century. de Tocqueville in *Democracy in America* repeats the story in this fashion:

> When the Europeans landed on the shores of the West Indies, and later of South America, they thought themselves transported to the fabled lands of the poets. The sea sparkled with the fires of the tropics; for the first time the extraordinary transparency of the water disclosed the ocean's depths to the navigators. Here and there little scented islands float like baskets of flowers on the calm sea. Everything seen in these enchanted islands seems devised to meet man's needs or serve his pleasures. Most of the trees were loaded with edible fruits, while those which were least useful to man delighted him by the brilliance of their varied colors. In the groves of fragrant lemon trees, wild figs, round-leafed myrtles, acacias, and oleanders, all interlaced with flowering lianas, a multitude of birds unknown to Europe displayed their azure and purple feathers and mingled the concert of their song with the harmony of a world teeming with vivid life.
> 
> *Death lay concealed beneath this brilliant cloak, but it was not noticed then, and moreover, there prevailed in the air of these climates some enervating influence which made men think only of the present, careless of the future.*[10]

The Bower of Bliss in *The Faerie Queene* is destroyed not because it represented sensuality and sexuality, for there is a legitimate place in the drama for these meanings in the Temple of Venus. The Bower of Bliss is destroyed because it is immoderate, excessive, and extraordinary, and within the structure of the drama it does not enhance the fashioning and crafting of a gentleman.

In contrast, the heroes and characters of Christopher Marlowe's dramas are given to excess and immoderation.[11] They are also homeless, but not in imitation of the homelessness of Christ; their homelessness is the sign, not of humility and love, but of lostness. Indeed, Greenblatt points to the dramatic problem of representing this sense of the ever-moving, being nowhereness — this grim utopia — on a stage. In *Tamburlaine the Great* Marlowe attempts to efface all differences and to insist upon the essential meaninglessness of theatrical space. Space has lost qualitative meaning. It is the space of the new cartography, the map that is simply the abstract grid upon which one locates where one is and where one wants to go. This mapping expresses conquest, and it is the organ of wants never finished and of an infinite homelessness.

Precisely because Marlowe's plays are deployed in this manner, his characters do violence as a means of marking boundaries, effecting transformations, signaling closures. The mark of one's being is the ability to carry out a decisive and aggressive event upon this abstract grid of the world. His characters give one the sense that they are attempting to use up, to consume fully all experience — their appetites are insatiable. Marlowe wrote in the period in which Europeans embarked on the extraordinary career of consumption and conquest; one intellectual model after another of the conquest was seized, squeezed dry, and discarded along with the exhaustion of the world's resources. The temporal processes created in this mode were understood in quantitative terms — time and space could be exhausted. We use and kill time, and this is the sense dramatically set forth in Marlowe.

What I have attempted through the above summary of Greenblatt is to portray the making of the modern "myth" of the European, and European exploration of the new cultures and other worlds of the non-Europeans since 1492. I am using the term "myth" in the sense taught by Mircea Eliade — it is a true story. Likewise I include those elements of the myth which are anonymous and autonomous. It may be objected that the anonymity and autonomy of the myth have been lost or at least compromised, since it is portrayed and fashioned by specific persons. My rejoinder is that the persons are doing exactly that — giving dramatic meaning to forces, desires, and impulses that are realities for their age — and that in various ways the explorers and their explorations are the raw materials for the myths at the same time that they are making use of the myth as the interpretive screen for their observations. The objective and empirical referent of the myth is the New World — first in the Americas, later in the South Seas. But the New World is at the same time an Other World. Greenblatt notes the element of Otherness in the myth of self-fashioning when he points out that all of the dramatists had to achieve an identity in relation to a threatening Other — an other that had to be invented or discovered in order to be attached and destroyed. Furthermore, this Other is perceived as unformed and chaotic, the parody of order.

It is interesting to note in this connection that Edmundo O'Gorman, arguing on strictly historical and logical grounds, has put forth the notion that America was an invention and not a discovery of the Europeans. In like manner, historian J. H. Parry commented that "Columbus did not discover a new world; he established contact between two worlds, both very old."[12] The myth of the New World obscured the reality of the contact. The "true story" of the contact has yet to be told. For some time we have known the facts of this contact. We know, for example, that Europeans in North America were absolutely dependent on Indian culture for several generations after their arrival. We know that North America was not a "virgin land." What is more important, the early European settlers knew it! In the middle colonies of North America, Virginia and the Carolinas, the contact between the two cultures took on the normal ambiguities attendant to such human contacts. The English settlers of the early generations saw their role in America as tutelary. The Indians were not simply their brethren, they were their "younger brethren." Karen Kupperman makes much of this distinction when she analyzes the meaning of this rhetoric among the English.

> Younger brethren, like women, were dependent in English society of this period. After the death of the father, younger brothers in gentry families owed obedience to the inheriting older brother similar to the obedience they had shown their father. If younger brothers did not show proper respect and obedience to the oldest brother he could effectively cut them off from marriage and career opportunities.... The superior knew what was best for the dependent.[13]

While such notions may have made sense to the English and may have had the ring of theological soundness about them, they obviously made no sense at all to the Indians and were violently resisted when they became the cornerstone of English colonial policy.

In the day-to-day working out of the relationship with the inhabitants of these new lands, the Europeans came to a more realistic assessment of the relationship. Each colony learned in its own way that the Indian would not submit to vassalage. The Indians were not willing to forsake their cultures for "civilization." Nor was English technology an attraction; in many instances, Indian technology and know-how rivaled or were superior to the technology and know-how of the English. The Indians were willing, however, to share, and in several instances, for longer or shorter periods, this sharing took place, but the cultural language for this notion of sharing with the Indian never came into being. The Indian was, in all the reigning cultural languages, ultimately taken as a race apart and different from the European. Once the differences between two groups come to be seen as important and continuing, it is a short step to seeing the different life of the Indian as less valuable than the European way of life and attributing the differences to qualities inherent in each group. When African slaves were imported to North America in the seventeenth century the idea of categorizing purely on the basis of race applied to African and Indian alike.

This was not simply a transfer of negative categorizations; the notion of race became the theater of the entire European myth of conquest, while the color of the Indian assured his admission to the theater on the basis of race. The myth of the Indian and the African as inferior human beings, lazy, savage, heathen, wild, noble and ignoble — the crass and vulgar side of the dramatic myths of the Elizabethans — took on popular expression only after the real issue of domination had been decided, at a time when the native peoples of the Americas could no longer hamper European exploration and exploitation.

By this time the language of pilgrimage had imperceptibly changed into the notion of progress; the meaning of novelty and otherness into the calculus of color. The economic and military conquest was accomplished, but another conquest more subtle and with even longer-lasting effects had taken place. This was the linguistic conquest. Obviously there was an imposition of empirical European languages in areas conquered by them, but on the deeper level I am referring to the creation of that form of language which is the myth and the metaphysical. In the encounter with the New and Other worlds, a new form of self-world structure is articulated and the new people and their worlds are located within it. This is a metaphysical world which imposes through archetypes its meanings upon the empirical and physical realities encountered. It has the power of the myth in that it becomes the normal manner in which realities are observed and understood.

Samuel Daniel in his poem of 1599, the *Musophile,* renders this meaning poetically and directly:

> And who in times knows wither we may vent
> The treasures of our tongue, to what strange shores
> This gaine of our best glorie shall be sent,
> T'inrich unknowing Nations with our stores?
> What worlds in th' yet unformed Occident
> May come refined with th' accents that are ours.

The New World for Daniel is a vast rich field for the plantation of the English language. Language in the poem is both empirical and mythological. From an empirical point of view, the Indian languages were taken to be gibberish, guttural utterances. Since the Indian often went nude, it was presupposed that this nakedness corresponded to a blank mind and a cultural void. In order for the myth of the wild man and the savage to stick, it had to be buttressed with a linguistic interpretation. The nudity inferred a blankness of mind and culture, thus making the native transparent to every meaning, definition, and myth of the colonizer and conqueror. The colonizers in this sense were essentially dramatists who imposed the "shape" of their own culture embodied in speech on the New World and made that world recognizable and habitable by them. The colonist and the dramatist in their mutual raids upon what they assumed to be the inarticulate penetrated new areas of their own experience; their language expanded the boundaries of their cultures and made the new territories over in their image.

But the Indians and all other non-Europeans possess and possessed specific and definitive empirical and imaginative languages. Each of these languages reflected and substantiated the specific character of the culture out of which it sprang. Specific empirical languages are not transparent; they are opaque. Europeans in the sixteenth and seventeenth centuries had as much difficulty accepting this notion as we do today. When opacity (the specific meaning and value of another culture and/or language) is denied, the meaning of that culture as a human value is denied. By not dealing with this opacity, one is able to divorce oneself from the messy, confusing welter of detail that characterizes a particular society at a particular time and to move to the cool realm of abstract principles symbolized by the metaphorical transparency of knowledge.[14]

## *Visions of the Vanquished*

> Originating in the neighborhood of Vailala, whence it spread rapidly through the coastal and certain inland villages, this movement involved on the one hand, a set of preposterous beliefs among its victims — in particular the expectation of an early visit from their deceased relatives — and, on the other hand, collective nervous symptoms of a sometime grotesque and idiotic nature. Hence the name Vailala madness seems apt enough and at least conveys more meaning than any of the various alternatives.[15]

This is the beginning of that classic study of F. E. Williams which launched the anthropological interest in that phenomenon called "cargo cults." The report, published in 1923, is certainly not the beginning of the phenomenon referred to by the name of the Vailala Madness. This kind of dramatic religious behavior is at least as old as the encounter between Hernando Cortez and Montezuma in 1519.[16]

There is a history of the contact of those who were already at home when the conquerors came. There was, indeed, a *new* world and an *other* world for them also. The great disadvantage of those who came into contact with the Europeans after 1492 was the simple fact that these natives of extra-European lands knew who they were. They had an identity and were secure within it.

It was beyond their imaginations to encounter a mode of the human with such insecurities, with such enormous appetites, and whose identity had to be made in a combative and destructive posing of themselves against others and the OTHER. Their dramas, dreams, and visions tell another story — a story in dramatic form which is the only language we have of the true meaning of the cultural contact. In many respects these dramas are analogous to those of the Renaissance Elizabethans, but they differ in one very important respect, and this difference makes all the difference. They are dramas in the opaque mode.

This opacity of vision forces the vanquished to come to terms in a concrete manner with what has happened to them. They had to take account first of the conquerors and their initial wrong perceptions of them and their intentions. They had to make sense of the trauma of the decentering and destruction of their cultures. They had to come to terms with the fact that their cultures would never be the same. In addition to these factors, they were forced to sort out carefully the specific meanings and qualities of the conquerors' culture that had qualitative meaning for them. Attendant to these general elements of reorientation, there were the specificities of the meaning of writing as a mode of communication, the use of money as a token of exchange, and the professed understanding of the god and religion of the conquerors as definitions of the conqueror's world. In the case of the vanquished, the alien and the other are empirical concrete facts. The threatening Other does not have to be invented or discovered so that it may be attacked and destroyed; for them, the threatening Other is not a structure of mind but a fact of history.

The imaginary and visionary emerge in their dramas as forms that allow them to reconceive of the concreteness of their existence. Their myths and dreams outline a religious drama of the conquest. Myth-dreams are a series of themes, propositions, and problems that are to be found in myths, in dreams, in the half-lights of conversations, and in the emotional responses to a variety of actions. The appropriate term "myth-dream" was coined by Kenelm Burridge and he discusses it in this manner:

> All people participate in particular myth-dreams: they are not only to be found amongst pre-literate peoples. Myth-dreams are not intellectually articulate, for they exist in an area of emotionalized mental activity which is not private to any particular individual but which is shared by many. A community daydream as it were. But among literate peoples a portion of it may be intellectualized and set down in writing.[17]

Among peoples without written language the articulation of the myth-dream is through the charismatic leaders, who bear the articulation in their bodies, in their speech and actions. A cult drama develops which enables a larger community to participate in its elaboration and to become a part of its meaning.

In Mesoamerica and South America these dramas of the myth-dream, which began during the conquest, are still carried on in areas that were the domains of the Aztec, Mayan, and Inca empires.[18] A scenario of these dramas is as follows:

1. Dreams foretell the advent of the Spanish.
2. Preliminary meetings between Spanish and Indians are always conducted on the lower administrative levels.
3. The dramatic highlight is the meeting of the Indian and Spanish leaders.
4. The death of the Indian leader is followed by lamentations and the king of Spain appears like some *deus ex machina* to punish Pizarro, or Cortez.

These myth-dreams and patterns of dramas form a structural logic articulated by a particular form of praxis and produce an imaginary restructuring of the native societies; they express at the same time the fierce determination of the Indians to revive traditions. But these meanings take place in a situation that is post-conquest, made up of institutions, customs, practices, meanings, and patterns that both resist and sustain human activity. Freedom is not exercised arbitrarily. The natives both submit to the legacy of the past and the conquest and adapt it to their aspirations for the future. In some instances, views of the colonial world through native eyes legitimize the return to an earlier primordial state; but this return to the past at the same time foreshadows a new order, since, in a quasi-messianic hope, there is the expectation of the justice of the Spanish king that will presage one final cataclysm which will set the topsy-turvy world to rights.

In other parts of South America the adaptation itself is the critique of the meaning of the world of the conquerors. These myth-dreams, these magical beliefs, are revelatory and fascinating not because they are ill-conceived instruments of utility but because they are poetic echoes of the cadences that guide the innermost course of the world. Magic takes language, symbols, and intelligibility to their outermost limits, to explore life and thereby to change its destiny.

Michael Taussig has explored the meaning of the symbolism of the devil in the acculturative process of Indian and African slaves in Bolivia and Columbia.[19] The Indians, Africans, and their descendants view the new meaning of capitalistic production and the use of money as the basis of exchange as a sign of the devil. This devil is the religious symbol of evil taught to them by the Christians, but they have applied its meaning in their own manner. To them this new socioeconomic system is neither natural nor good. Instead, it is both unnatural and evil. The meaning that they give to the devil is very much like the definition given to this demonic form of sacrality by the early Christian fathers — he who resists the cosmic process. The market economy interposes itself between persons, mediating direct awareness of social relations by the abstract laws of relationships between commodities. They are filled with incredulity when the Europeans speak of the procreative powers of money. They ask quite seriously, "How and when does money copulate such that it is able to bear offspring?" They give value to gold because, in their cosmology, gold is a form of the maturation of substances in the earth, but it is to be used to bestow honor and prestige within the human community. The fact that it is used for exchange violates its essential meaning. In like manner, the growing of sugar cane makes sense, but they are unable to understand why the cane that is grown is bundled up and sent away to some place called the market. Why is it not used, and used up, by those who grow it?

Though they know that there is an authentic power in what appears to them as the magical power of the Europeans to transmute nature and natural relationships, for them it is the power of the devil. While they have been taught the power of a great and beneficent deity revealed in Jesus Christ, their own experience of the Europeans allows for this alternative theological formation. The world of the Europeans is ruled by their god, the devil, and it is not beyond the natives to venerate this demonic devil-god when they are engaged in activities that bring them into contact with the world of the Europeans.

These myth-dreams, behaviors, and orientations of the vanquished should not be seen in continuity with chiliastic movements in the Western world, for these presuppose the specific nature of modernity — the modern world system. Modernity itself is a form of critique. These movements, from this point of view, must be viewed as a critique of the critique. It is the modern Western world that created the categories of civilization, self-fashioning, the individual as an agent of production, the races, the primitives, and so on. These terms are part and parcel of the universalizing and critical structures of the modern Western consciousness. In many respects, the cultures that have given rise to visions of the vanquished, religions of the oppressed, were created for the second time by the critical categories and languages of the West. This is the source of what W. E. B. DuBois has called the double consciousness as one of their characteristic modalities. The oppressed long for or imagine the meaning of their existence as human beings prior to the definitions imputed to them in this second creation through the hegemony of Western languages. The first word about them in this second creation is abstract and categorizing. No intimacy of language is present in the definitions of the second creation. It is only in some such manner that we are able to understand the seemingly strange rituals, myths, and orientations of their religious experience and expression. Whether it is the American Indian Ghost Dance of the 1890s, the Vailala Madness, the Rastafarians, or even aspects of the black power movement in the United States, all of these movements have come face to face with radical contingency. Their myths, to paraphrase words of Claude Lévi-Strauss, "evoke a suppressed past and apply it, like a grid, upon the present in the hope of discovering a sense of those two aspects of that reality with which man is confronted — the historical and the structural — and to bring about coincidence of these two modes."[20] This critique takes place behind the veil, in the language of DuBois,[21] or in the twilight zones of half-light and quasi-physical infection inhabited by the semirealities of the modern Western world - this is the arena as described by Octavio Paz.[22] Or again, in the languages of the Annales school, in a kind of intrahistory.[23] In each case, the locus for this religious drama and language is opaque.

Expressions of the meaning of the cultural contacts that have taken place since 1492 are still with us, not as residual structures of an older history but as expressions of new forms of the human face. They will increasingly move from the local levels and take their place as some of the most serious efforts made to define a new world and a new self. Pablo Neruda, the Nobel Laureate Chilean poet and a descendant of one of those cultures, expresses his vision of the vanquished:

> As far as we are concerned, we writers within the tremendously far-flung American region, we listen unceasingly to the call to fill this mighty void with being of flesh and blood. We are conscious of our duties as fulfillers - at the same time we are faced with the unavoidable task of critical communication in a world which is empty but which is no less full of injustices, punishments, and sufferings because it is empty - and we feel also the responsibility for reawakening the old dreams which sleep in statues of stone in the ruined ancient monuments, in the wide-stretching silence in planetary plains, in dense primeval forests, in rivers which roar like thunder. We must fill with words the most distant places in a dumb continent and we are intoxicated by this task of making fables and giving names. This is perhaps what is decisive in my own humble case, and, if so, my abundance or my rhetoric would not be anything other than the simplest of events in the daily life of an American.[24]

## Notes

1. See Rudolf Otto, *The Idea of the Holy,* trans. John W. Harvey, 2d ed. (Oxford: Oxford Univ. Press, 1958), and Joachim Wach, *Types of Religious Experience* (Chicago and London: University of Chicago Press, 1951).
2. See Mircea Eliade, *The Myth of the Eternal Return,* trans. Willard R. Trask (New York: Pantheon Books, 1954), and idem, *Patterns in Comparative Religion,* trans. Rosemary Sheed (New York: Sheed & Ward, 1958).
3. For V. Gordon Childe, see his *Man Makes Himself in History* (New York: New American Library, 1951). Later researches are as follows: Robert McCormick Adams, *The Evolution of Urban Society: Early Mesopotamia and Prehistoric Mexico* (Chicago: Aldine Publishing Co., 1966); Paul Wheatley, "City as Symbol," Inaugural lecture delivered at University College, London, Nov. 20, 1967, and *The Pivot of the Four Quarters* (Chicago: Aldine-Atherton, 1971); Eliade, *The Myth of the Eternal Return;* S. J. Tambiah, "The Galactic Polity: The Structure of Traditional Kingdoms in Southeast Asia," *New York Academy of Sciences* 293 (1974).
4. See Samuel Eliot Morison, *Admiral of the Ocean Sea* (Cambridge: Harvard Univ. Press, 1942).
5. For the literature on pilgrimage, consult Donald R. Howard, *Writers and Pilgrims: Medieval Pilgrimage Narratives and Their Posterity* (Berkeley and Los Angeles: Univ. of California Press, 1980); Christian K. Zacher, *Curiosity and Pilgrimage: The Literature of Discovery in Fourteenth-Century England* (Baltimore and London: Johns Hopkins University Press, 1976); Anthony Yu, "Two Literary Examples of Religious Pilgrimage: The Commedia and the Journey to the West," *History of Religions* 22, no. 3 (February 1983): 202-30.
M. H. Abrams, *Natural Supernaturalism: Tradition and Revolution in Romantic Literature* (New York: W. W. Norton & Co., 1971), is a brilliant discussion of the pilgrimage of consciousness. The relationships between voyages of discovery and languages of discovery and description are dealt with in Daniel Defert, "The Collection of the World: Accounts of Voyages from the Sixteenth to the Eighteenth Centuries, "*Dialectical Anthropology* 7 (1982): 11-20.
6. J. H. Elliott, *The Old World and the New, 1492-1650* (Cambridge: Cambridge University Press, 1970), 6-7.
7. Stephen Greenblatt, *Rennaissance Self-Fashioning: From More to Shakespeare* (Chicago and London: University of Chicago Press, 1980). I shall be summarizing *in passim* the ideas set forth by Greenblatt.
8. Greenblatt, *Renaissance Self-Fashioning,* 7-9.
9. See Greenblatt, *Renaissance Self-Fashioning,* chap. 4.
10. Alexis de Tocqueville, *Democracy in America,* ed. J. P. Mayer and Max Lerner, new trans. by George Lawrence (New York and London: Harper & Row, 1966), 19-20.
11. See Greenblatt, *Renaissance Self-Fashioning,* chap. 5.

12. See Edmundo O'Gorman, *The Invention of America* (Bloomington: Indiana University Press, 1961), and John H. Parry, *The Spanish Seaborne Empire*, History of Human Society Series (New York: Alfred A. Knopf, 1966), 65.
13. Karen 0. Kupperman, *Settling with the Indians: The Meeting of English and Indian Cultures in America, 1580-1640* (Totowa, NJ.: Rowman & Littlefield, 1980), 170.
14. I am again indebted to Stephen Greenblatt for the quotation and for his influence on these observations; see his "Learning to Curse: Aspects of Linguistic Colonialism in the Sixteenth Century," in *First Images of America* (Berkeley and Los Angeles: University of California Press, 1976), vol. 2, 561-80. See also my working out of the meaning of opacity in "Archaism and Hermeneutics," in *The History of Religions: Essays in Interpretation* (Chicago and London: University of Chicago Press, 1966), and chap. 3 in this volume; "The Oppressive Elements in Religion and the Religions of the Oppressed," *Harvard Theological Review* 69, nos. 1/2 January-April, 1976): 397-412, and chap. 10 in this volume; and "Freedom, Otherness, and Religion and Theologies Opaque," in Chicago *Theological Seminary Register* 73, no. 1 (Winter 1983): 13-24, and chap. 12 in this volume.
15. F. E. Williams, *The Vailala Madness and Other Essays* (St. Lucia, Queensland: The University of Queensland Press, 1976), 331.
16. See Davíd Carrasco, *Quetzalcoatl and the Irony of Empire* (Chicago: University of Chicago Press, 1983): see esp. chap. 4
17. Kenelm Burridge, *Mambu, A Melanesian Millennium* (London: Methuen & Co., 1960), 148.
18. This interpretation is based on Nathan Wachtel, *The Vision of the Vanquished. The Spanish Conquest of Peru Through Indian Eyes, 1530-1570,* trans. Ben Reynolds and Siân Reynolds (Hassocks, Sussex, England: Harvester Press, 1977), passim.
19. See Michael Taussig, *The Devil and Commodity Fetishism in South America* (Chapel Hill: University of North Carolina Press, 1980), esp. pt. 1, chap. 2; pt. 11, chap. 5; and pt. III, chaps 11-14.
20. Claude Lévi-Strauss, *Scope of Anthropology* (London: Jonathan Cape, 1967), 7.
21. W. E. B. Dubois's famous statement describing the double consciousness is contained in his *The Souls of Black Folk* (Basic Afro-American Reprint Library, Johnson reprint; originally published in Chicago: A. C. McClurg, 1903).
22. Octavio Paz, "The New Analogy," *Third Herbert Read Lecture,* 25.
23. For a discussion of the Annales school, see Traian Stoianovich, *French Historical Method: The "Annales" Paradigm* (Ithaca, N.Y.: Cornell Univ. Press, 1976), and Patrick H. Hutton, "The History of Mentalities: The New Map of Cultural History," *History and Theory* 20:237-59.
24. Pablo Neruda, *Toward the Splendid City,* Nobel Lecture (New York: Farrar, Straus & Giroux, 1974).

# Chapter 8

## Cargo Cults as Cultural Historical Phenomena

Since the publication of *The Vailala Madness and the Destruction of Native Ceremonies in the Gulf District*[1] by F. E. Williams in 1923, the literature on cargo cults has steadily increased. Reports of similar phenomena have come from several parts of the world, and these reports have in turn forced scholars to take a new look at religious movements in the history of Western culture.

Theories, interpretations, and methodologies have kept pace with the citing of new phenomena of this type. Beginning with F. E. Williams's own theory of the cause of this religious phenomenon, that is, the destruction of native ceremonies and the attempt to substitute Western cultural forms in place of the indigenous culture, through Ralph Linton's refinement of this theory into one of cultural deprivation,[2] to the latest and most sophisticated theories of Peter Worsley and Kenelm Burridge,[3] the problem of cargo cults has presented such an issue to students of religion that I. C. Jarvie[4] has taken the *issue of cargo cults* as the *basis* for speaking of a "revolution in anthropology." If we are to take Jarvie seriously, the phenomenon of cargo cults looms as an issue comparable only to the older issue of totemism, as requiring not only explanation but also a reevaluation of a much wider range of anthropological theory and method. If the issue is as crucial as Jarvie has defined it for students of religion (and I am persuaded that he is correct in his assessment), it is then clear that around this issue center some of the fundamental problems of religious-cultural dynamics.[5]

But before going into this area, I will give some description of cargo cults, beginning with Williams's description of the Vailala Madness.

> Originating in the neighborhood of Vailala, hence it spread rapidly through the coastal and certain of the inland villages. This movement involved, on the one hand a set of preposterous beliefs among its victims — in particular the expectation of an early visit from deceased relatives — and on the other hand, collective nervous symptoms of sometimes grotesque and idiotic nature. Hence the name Vailala Madness seems apt enough and at least conveys more meaning than any of the various alternatives.[6]

---

This article was first presented as the 1973 Presidential Address at the American Academy of Religion annual meeting in Chicago, November 1973. Published in *The Journal of the American Academy of Religion* 42, no. 3 (September 1974): 403-14.

He continues:

> Perhaps one of the most fundamental ideas was that the ancestors, or more usually the deceased relatives, of the people were shortly to return to visit them. They were expected in a large steamer which was to be loaded with cases of gifts — tobacco, calico, knives, axes, food stuffs and the like.
>
> A feature of interest and importance is that in some places the returning ancestors or relatives were expected to be white and indeed some white men were actually claimed by the natives to be their deceased relatives.

For a more complete description I quote Burridge:

> Cargo movements, often described as millenarian, messianic, or nativistic movements, and also Cargo cults, are serious enterprises of the genre of popular revolutionary activities. Mystical, combining political-economic problems with expressions of racial tension, Cargo cults compare most directly with the Ghost-dance cults of North America, and the prophetist movements among African peoples. Typically, participants in a Cargo cult engage in a number of strange and exotic rites and ceremonies the purpose of which is apparently, to gain possession of European manufactured goods such as axes, knives, aspirins, china plates, razor blades, colored beads, guns, bolts of cloth, hydrogen peroxide, rice, finned food, and other goods to be found in a general department store. These goods are known as "cargo" or in the Pidgin English rendering Kago.[9]

In passing, I shall give a definition of millenarianism taken from an analysis of Western cultural materials:

> Millenarian sects or movements always picture salvation as
> a) collective, in the sense that it is to be enjoyed by the faithful as collectivity,
> b) terrestrial, in the sense that it is to be realized on this earth and not in some other-worldly heaven;
> c) imminent, in the sense that it is to come both soon and suddenly;
> d) total, in the sense that it is utterly to transform life on earth, so that the new dispensation will be no mere improvement on the present but perfection itself;
> e) miraculous, in the sense that it is to be accomplished by, or with the help of, supernatural agencies.[10]

## Religion and Power

The phenomenon referred to as the cargo cult constitutes a specific type of religious experience. It is specific in its manifestations and beliefs — possession, dreams, ecstasy, and so on — specific in its precise definition of salvation and cargo, and it is again specific because it occurs at a point of cultural contact, such contact defining a disequilibrium between the cultures involved.

In attempting to get at the cultural-religious dynamics of the cargo cult, I shall begin with a definition of religion as a kind of power, for at the heart of these kinds of movements the nature of power is central. Gerardus van der Leeuw, who has done a most thorough interpretation of religion as power, makes this statement:

> But when we say that God is the Object of religious experience, we must realize that "God" is frequently an extremely indefinite concept which does not completely coincide with what we ourselves usually understand by it. Religious experience, in other terms, is concerned with a "Somewhat." But this assertion often means no more than that this "Somewhat" is merely a vague "something"; and in order that man may be able to make more significant statements about this "Somewhat," it must force itself upon him, must oppose itself to him as being Something *Other.* Thus the first offer-motion we can make about the Object of Religion is that it is a *highly exceptional* and *extremely impressive* "Other."[11]

If we are to make use of van der Leeuw's approach, we must ask ourselves the following questions: What is the "vague Somewhat" that is confronted in order to create the cargo cultists? and, How does this "Somewhat" force itself upon the indigenous population as "Something Other"?

From the point of view of the indigenous culture, the vague somewhat is the scientific, industrialized Western culture with its religious ideology. The impact of this culture on the several cultural areas of the world since the fifteenth century has brought about the type of cultural disequilibrium appropriate to mercantile capitalism with all of its attendant vices and virtues. To be sure, we are speaking of domination and imperialism, but these terms are too abstract to describe the experiential poles of this confrontation.

While cultural deprivation took place and, to use the words of Williams, there was in fact "the destruction of native ceremonies," more than simply cultural deprivation and its attendant attempt to substitute Western cultural and religious categories is involved. If we take the implications of this statement seriously, namely, that the Westerners did not confront a *tabula rasa* and that economic, political, and military domination did not succeed in the total destruction of native cultures, we must then deal with the confluence of the two respective forms of cultural creativity.

The expectation of the return of deity, often a *deus otiosus*, or of the ancestor, or of a culture hero is already a religious possibility in many cultures prior to the coming of the Europeans. Indeed, this notion of the return of some divine being as the bearer of salvation is found in the so-called higher religions of Buddhism, Judaism, Christianity, and Zoroastrianism.

The coming of the Europeans has only intensified this original notion of return and renewal. Within the non-European primitive cultures, this return and renewal was localized within the tribal unit and was interpreted in cosmic rather than historical terms. It was one of the cycles of the eternal return, a mode of renewing the cosmos and time. Though mystery, awe, and even anarchy or Émile Durkheim's "cultural effervescence" accompanied the return and renewal, the mode and the time of coming of the divine beings were normalized and ritualized.

The Western impact on the primitive cultures of the world should be seen from the point of view of this mode of apprehension. These strange-looking beings who came in large ships from nowhere, bearing strange tools and artifacts and beliefs, were subsumed under the structure of this mythical apprehension. They were welcomed as the return of sacred beings who would bring about a new cosmic renewal. They were seen as the renewing power already latent in the natives' cultural myth.

New and powerful though they were, they were not new and powerful through the categories by which they (the Westerners) understood their power. They were subsumed under an indigenous structure of apprehension. In most cases, the initial meeting of these cultures was friendly; the indigenous cultures were often receptive to the Westerners and to their teaching of their culture and religion, for the Westerners not only possessed the power to dominate but were at the same time a fulfillment of the general notion of power already present in the indigenous cultures.

If, however, this continuity were the end of the process, we should be hard put to understand cargo cults — indeed, would they exist? The initial stage is simultaneously and subsequently the beginning of the opposition, for even at this stage the artifacts and beliefs of the Westerners have begun their eroding processes. A money economy and a work ethic take the place of trade and barter. The intimacy of relationships embodied in the cultural tradition is undercut by the necessity of productivity. The indigenous cultures have become part of the periphery of the great mercantile Western centers, and through this process they have lost their own centers.

The beliefs of the Westerners insofar as they speak of the sacred seem hypocritical, for not only do they not fulfill the structure of expectations related to cosmic renewal but they also fail in the minds of the indigenous peoples to live up to the new strange beliefs that they teach. Reverend R. Hanselmann quotes the following from a New Guinea Christian:

> How is it we cannot obtain the origin of wealth? You hide this secret from us. What is ours is only rubbish, you keep the truth for yourselves. We know that all that is the white man's work is forbidden to us. We would like to progress, but the white man wants to keep us in our state of Kanakas. The Mission, it is true, has given us the word of God, but it does not help us black men. The white men hide the secret of the Cargo.[12]

A state of resistance and oppugnancy sets in, and the initial responsiveness to the Westerners moves into a more complex and ambiguous situation. But just as the initial stage of contact does not constitute a continuity, so the oppugnancy and resistance should not be spoken of as a discontinuity. I remind you that we are speaking of religious experience and not a contractual obligation. The opposition of the indigenous culture to Westernization enables us to speak of the dialectic of sacred power — it at once attracts and repels; it is both *mana* and *taboo*. But more important, we are able to see the truth of van der Leeuw's statement that the vague Somewhat of Power "must force itself upon him, must oppose itself to him as Something Other."

It is at this point that the individual and collective experience of the cargo cultists can be understood. On the one hand, the members of the indigenous cultures must positively undergo their domination on the historical level, but on the other hand they actively participate in and think through the meaning of this historical domination in mythical modes. In other words, members of the cult undertake the mythicization of history, but this time it is not simply the reduction of the new culture to the old mythic categories; the mythic possibility remains, but the old myth has been ruptured by the new power. The cultists now undertake the creation of a new cultural myth that will enable them to make sense of the mythic past and the historical present in mythic terms.

It is well for us at this point to remember a statement by Lévi-Strauss concerning mythical history:

> Mythical history thus presents the paradox of being both disjoined from and conjoined with the present. It is disjoined from it because the original ancestors

were of a nature different from contemporary men: they were creators and these are imitators. It is conjoined with it because nothing has been going on since the appearance of the ancestors except events whose recurrence periodically effaces their particularity. It remains to be shown how the savage mind succeeds in overcoming this two-fold contradiction.... Thanks to ritual, the disjoined past of myth is expressed on the one hand through biological and seasonal periodicity and, on the other, through the conjoined past, which unites from generation to generation the living and the dead.[13]

Ritual is a form of religious behavior and it is precisely the madness, the possessions of the cultists individually and collectively, that is the expression of the continuity of structure and the novelty of the new mythic perception. From an analysis of states of possession we are able to distinguish a passive and an active appropriation of reality. Godfrey Lienhardt has pointed out that the Dinka image their reactions to experience in physical and social reality by separating the active subject from the passive object in experience;[14] the same is true of possession cults, for they have, or I should say, find it necessary to create, a possibility of creating a form of experience they desire and a possibility of freeing themselves symbolically from what they must passively endure. In responding to the experience of Western domination, the cults create on a symbolic level so that their own creativity will possess a value freed from Westerners' categories.

On this sacred level they can manipulate the symbols, even become them and act them out when possessed, and thus understand and dominate them, although they may consider themselves controlled by them. Possessed individuals consider themselves directed by omnipotent external forces, but these forces are directly related to the apprehension of reality.

Possession thus becomes an essential part of the ritual of the cultists. The rupture of the old myth, the appearance of a new power, and the creation of a new myth require the recollection of the structure of mythic power and the construction of a new myth from the elements of the present situation. The collective religious experience is the madness of Vailala.

On the personal level, the problematical experience is centered in the cult leader or prophet; Burridge has written one of the most profound and moving monographs of such a leader. Mambu, the title of this monograph, is also the name of a native of New Guinea who in the late 1930s led what has come to be known as a cargo cult.

Mambu is clearly a charismatic leader; by virtue of his charisma he is an exceptional man, but in Burridge's interpretation his charisma is directly related to his ability to give adequate interpretation to the myth-dream of Kanakas.

Mambu himself had experienced the acentric and marginal situation of the Kanakas in their contact with European culture. He was a converted Roman Catholic who assisted at the Mass.

Following are two versions of Mambu's life, the first from the Reverend Father Georg Höltker, the second the Kanakas:

> One Sunday towards the end of 1937, about a year after he had returned from a spell of contract labour in Rabaul, New Britain, Mambu came to the mission church at Bogia. He was much earlier than usual. He entered the church, removed the dust covers from the altar and tables near by, and proceeded to lay out the prayer books for Mass. Some minutes later the missionary sister, whose duty it was so to prepare the church, came in. She saw with some surprise, that Mambu had done her work for her. She was puzzled, but she made no fuss. Mambu, meanwhile, remained quietly in the church until Mass commenced. Then he went out.
>
> After Mass the missionary priest, who had heard of the morning's doings from the sister, sent for Mambu, and tried to get him to talk about what he had done, and why he had done it. But Mambu would say nothing.
>
> Then the Angelus bell sounded.
>
> Normally, a Catholic will stand with bowed head, repeating the Angelus prayer. Mambu fell straight to his knees and prayed with passionate fervour.
>
> As the prayer ended Mambu rose, took his leave of the priest, and departed.
>
> A few days afterwards there was another strange event in the mission. One of the missionary sisters woke up during the night, startled to find a Kanakas bending over her in the darkness. Very frightened as he started to clutch at her hands, she was about to call for help when the intruder, whatever his intention had been, slipped off into the night.
>
> The intruder was never positively identified. Those most closely concerned, the resident missionaries, could not but associate the third occurrence with the previous two, and, since there was no one else to suspect, they thought the man might have been Mambu. At a minimum reckoning, even if the incident was no more than a sister's imaginative impulse, it is clear that Mambu had attracted no little notice.
>
> Almost immediately after the nocturnal visitation Mambu started his activities in Apingam, his native village. But his own people would have none of him. There was a little trouble, and Mambu left Apingam for the settlement of Tangu. There, speaking in Pidgin, he seems to have found a few followers. The resident missionary was away at the time, and Mambu succeeded in collecting a sum of money — the "head tax" — which he said should be given to him and not to the administration.
>
> When the missionary returned to Tangu he got wind of what Mambu was doing and took immediate action. He recovered the money which Mambu had extracted from Tangu, returned it to the donors, and ordered Mambu to leave

Tangu forthwith. It was as a result of his expulsion from Tangu, says Father Höltker, that Mambu developed an implacable hatred for the mission.

From Tangu, Mambu went to the Banara hinterland, beyond Pariakenam. Here he found a welcome from the villagers, and here, comparatively isolated from both mission and administration, Mambu settled to his task.

According to Höltker the gist of Mambu's teaching was as follows:

At the present time, Mambu said, Kanakas were being exploited by white men. But a new order, a new way of life was at hand which was dependent on no longer submitting to white men whether they were missionaries, administrative officers, planters, or traders. The ancestors had the welfare of their offspring very much at heart. Even now some were in the interior of the volcano of the Manam island, manufacturing all kinds of goods for their descendants.

Other ancestors, adopting the guise and appearance of white men, were hard at work in the lands where white men lived. Indeed, said Mambu, the ancestors had already dispatched much cargo to Kanakas. Cloth for laplaps, axes, khaki shorts, bush-knives, torches, red pigment, and ready-made houses had been on their way for some time. But white men, who had been entrusted with the transport, were removing the labels and substituting their own. In this way, Mambu said, Kanakas were being robbed of their inheritance. Therefore, Kanakas were entitled to get back the cargo from white men by the use of force. The time was coming, however, when all such thievery and exploitation would cease. The ancestors would come with cargo for all. A huge harbour would be created in front of his [Mambu's] house in Suaru, and there the ships of the ancestors — laden with cargo — would make fast. When this time came, all work in the gardens should cease. Pigs, gardens — everything — should be destroyed. Otherwise, the ancestors — who were going to bring plenty for all — would be angry and withhold the cargo.

In the meanwhile, said Mambu, until a sign was vouchsafed them, certain things should be done. The administration had no right to demand a tax: instead, the tax should be handed to Mambu himself. If the administration asked for it the people should say that they had already given it to Mambu, "The Black King." Nor should the Kanakas clean up the roads or do any carrying; the administration should do it for themselves. Since, also, the missionaries had made common cause with the administration to exploit the Kanakas, natives should not attend the mission schools, nor go to their churches or stations. Those who disobeyed this injunction would not have a share in the glories of the new age. They would be completely outcast. Any Kanakas who happened to be in a mission church or school when the ancestors came would be burnt up and consumed in a holocaust.

Mambu used to pray by the graves of the deceased, and he demanded payment for doing so. He introduced a form of baptism which, he said, would give full dispensation in the rights of the new days to come. Men and women in couples — two men and two women, but not a man and a woman — would stand before Mambu, cast off their breech-clouts or grass skirts, and have their genitals sprinkled with water. Mambu said too, that it was not fitting that Kanakas should wear native apparel. Instead, they should wear European clothes, throw away their breech-clouts and grass skirts and bury them. By doing these things the ancestors would be pleased. And seeing the cast-off breech-clouts and grass skirts, they would say, "Ha! Our children are truly doing well."[15]

The Tangu account of Mambu follows:

Mambu, say Tangu today, was a Kanaka of the Bogia region who had been working in Rabaul. When he finished his contract he stowed away in a steamer bound for Australia. He was, however, discovered and hauled before the captain of the ship. The captain was very angry with Mambu for stowing away.

He was about to have Mambu thrown overboard lest by going to Australia he should chance upon the secret of the white man when Mambu's former employer, his "master," who was on the same ship, intervened and saved him. The same man, an Australian, saw Mambu safely to an Australian port.

Arrived in Australia, Mambu was clothed and fed. His master showed him the sights, gave him rice, spare clothing, beads, knives, canned goods, razor blades — heaps of good things. All this cargo was packed into cases and sent to the quayside for loading. The master's sister wrote a letter, stuck it into Mambu's hair, and told him to go down to the quay where he would find all his cargo marked with such-and-such a sign. Mambu was to board a certain ship together with his cargo and return to New Guinea. If there was any trouble, or if anyone questioned him, Mambu was to produce the letter.

Mambu boarded his ship. He survived several attempts by the captain to have him thrown overboard, but eventually he reached Bogia. If it had not been for the letter probably he would have been killed.

In Bogia, Mambu claimed that he knew the secret of white men, and that they, being jealous, were preventing Kanakas from obtaining it. Kanakas, said Mambu, should not submit to this. They should be strong and throw the white men out of New Guinea into the sea. And to make themselves strong Kanakas needed money. To this end Mambu travelled around the countryside collecting pennies and shillings. But for doing so Mambu was reported to the administration by a missionary and then gaoled. He was dangerous to white men and might destroy their over-lordship.

When the policemen came to arrest him, Mambu said to them: "You can hit me — never mind! You can maltreat me — never mind! Later, you will understand!"

The policemen were awed, but took him to gaol. That night, though supposedly behind bars, Mambu was seen chewing betel in a nearby village. In some mystical way he had slipped out of his chains. The policemen knew of this escape but were too frightened to report the nocturnal excursion — and some informants say that there were several such forays — lest they be accused of neglect of duty. Nevertheless, Mambu could not escape his fate, and he was taken away to Madang. Before he left, however, he prophesied the coming war.

Mambu also performed another kind of "miracle." He produced for an informant, who had gone to "try" him, a banker's packet or "stick" of money out of thin air — money, moreover, that was actually used to buy an axe and some beads. He said to my astounded informant: "You do not understand. You are like a child who has yet to learn much. You do not understand the things that I know." Mambu then went on to claim that he was able to get more [money] whenever he wanted to.

When Tangu tell the story of Mambu their faces are serious. Bystanders do not interrupt, giggle, or explode into hoots of laughter as they are wont to do when other stories are told. The story of Mambu ends silently. Afterwards there may be embellishments: the number of times Mambu escaped from gaol to talk and chew betel with his friends. Unlike their traditional myths — which Tangu relate with gusto, handing the tale to another when memory runs short, singing and beating the melodies and rhythms of the dances sanctioned by the stories and incidents in them — the Mambu story is humourless, earnest, part of their own recent past. Like the great sickness, the fighting that followed, the advent of the mission, the administration, and the Japanese war, Mambu is. He happened. And he happened the way Tangu say that he happened. He does not belong to the faraway days when a penis slept between sisters, when a hawk gave suck, and when men climbed to the moon on a betel nut palm. His is the myth in creation, a part of their living eyes' evidence.[16]

I have given these two versions of Mambu's biography for the same reason that Burridge reported them, to wit, to show the difference between reality as history and reality as myth-dream. The historicity and normativeness of the Reverend Father Höltker's account is historical, because his account takes place in an arena where normative categories are unquestioned. He has not experienced, or better, he has not given, an acentric interpretation to the cultural contact with the Kanakas. In a word, his confrontation with the Kanakas and the Tangu is not religious in the sense that a new power has been confronted. His myth, the Western ideology, appears as normative reality, because the cultural contact has not, from his point of view, succeeded in rupturing his myth.

The Tangu version of Mambu's biography takes place within an acentric and marginal arena. In it the past as traditional myths, the rupturing of the myths through cultural contact, and the attempt to create a mythical history within the context of the valences of power produce a biography which is a myth-dream.

What has been appropriated from the biography of Mambu is the mythic element which attempts to synthesize the fragmentary forms of experience and point to a mode of conduct and behavior that will approximate not only the renewal of New Guinea culture but also the total situation of the cultural contact between New Guinea and the Westerners — in short, through the cargo cult, the possibility of creating new human beings, neither New Guineans nor Westerners.

> In bald and oversimplified terms the problem of Cargo, is first how to live in an environment which is neither European nor Kanaka, but something *sui generis* compounded of both; and second how to transcend the division and make the environment an intelligible unity.... For Kanakas on the ground the problem is to find ways of cooperating with white men and to persuade white men to cooperate with them. But a prerequisite is laying the guilt. For if all men are guilty Kanakas feel the present situation demonstrates that they carry more guilt than do white men. Atonement, the passage through conflict to unity, needs the cooperation of both white men and black.[17]

In a sense Burridge implies that the cargo cult is the invitation to the white man to descend into the chaos that is prior to every new creation. The cargo cult represents the attempt to create a new humanity out of the chaos of a cultural disequilibrium.

## *A Concluding Note: Some Hermeneutical Reflections on Cargo Cults*

I have tried to keep two or three threads running through this presentation. I have alluded to the history of the issue of cargo cults in anthropological literature, from Williams to the present, and I have spoken of cultural disequilibrium. In addition, I have stressed the kind of interpretation that Burridge has given to these phenomena. But now I must ask the question that prompted Jarvie to write a book entitled *The Revolution in Anthropology*, which is devoted to the literature of cargo cults.

I think that the revolution in anthropology and in all the human sciences arises around the issue of cargo cults because this phenomenon points not only to an acentric and seemingly anomic situation in other cultures but equally to an acentric and anomic situation in the sciences of humankind. That is to say that in the attempt to understand human life, the prestige of the Western scientific apparatus is no longer an adequate tool. In some way the objects of the study, other cultures, must be participants in the study as subjects and objects. The methodological problem of cultural contact is itself an aspect of a cargo cult.

In methodological terms, Jacques Derrida has described this situation as follows:

> There is no unity or absolute source of the myth. The focus or the source of the myth is always shadows and virtualities which are elusive, unactualizable, and non-existent in the first place. Everything begins with the structure, the configuration, and relationship. The discourse on this acentric structure, the myth, cannot itself have an absolute subject, or an absolute center.... In this context, therefore, it is necessary to forego scientific or philosophical discourse, to renounce the *epistémé* which absolutely requires ... that we go back to the center, the source. In opposition to *epistemic* discourse structural discourse on myth — mythological discourse — must itself become mythomorphic.[18]

There are definite methodological implications for the American Academy of Religion when we look carefully at the phenomenon of cargo cults. This does not mean that the Academy is a cargo cult, but there is in fact something to be learned about ourselves from this kind of religious experience and expression. Just as the study of non-Western and especially primitive religious expressions gave us not only an objective view of the life of others, at the same time this so-called objective view told us something about the inner life and subjectivity of the investigator. It is not by accident that once R. H. Codrington had discovered *mana* and *taboo* in Melanesia, these terms became so popular in Western languages that we have forgotten their derivation. The Melanesians would probably not recognize their own terms given present-day usage by Westerners. The same is true of *totem* and several other similar terms and phrases.

The attention now given to cargo cults is of the same order, but with one significant difference. The cargo cult, in the words of Jarvie, defines the locus of a revolution in anthropology, for it raises the fundamental question of the disruption of cultural and religious forms. It points to the "order of disorder"; it describes the anomic and acentric nature of the religious virtuoso and the context of this type of cultural experience. I think this is highly instructive for the Academy, for when we look at the history of this organization, it has, over a short period of time, moved from a small company of biblical instructors to the large amorphous milling groups in the halls and meeting rooms. If one looks at the problem very clearly, it is not a logical order, and in fact if there is an order, it is of some *mytho-logic* kind — an order to be discerned only through a modest but careful and precise delineation of mythical structures akin to the procedures of a Claude Lévi-Strauss. But more than this may be discerned: if the cargo cults point to the impact of an alien culture on the religious imagination of an aboriginal culture, then we must at least ask the meaning of this structure in the Academy. There is surely no other imperialistic culture threatening the American Western culture. We may in fact be experiencing the impact of the accretions of the West upon the West, the impact of America on Americans, and this experience defines a situation of alienation. It is an alienation of Westerners from the West and of Americans from America. The center does not hold. There is no longer that privileged position which is the West or America. There is only the bricolage of America and the West, the flotsam and jetsam of bits and pieces of a reality that once was thought to be an order and a unity, possibly dreamed of in an illusory age when these things were thought to be real. Just as the explorations of Westerners from the fifteenth century to the present violently forced millions of human beings and hundreds of cultures into the dangerous and terrifying reality called history, we are experiencing the descent of America into the reality of the myth; for the Westerners, history making reality has lost its effectiveness. As Mircea Eliade has taught, the very nature of reality as history is in part based upon the ability to intimidate through terror; but this terror has lost its effect. The terror of history lost its impact after Hiroshima, after Buchenwald, after My Lai. We live in and have normalized this terror through airport searches and the delicate diplomatic balance of nuclear weapons. And so, when history has lost its terror, what is the nature of its reality? Or better, what is the nature of the dimension of reality called human when history has lost its terror? These are only some of the implications that cargo cultists as *Homo religiosus* and religious phenomena pose for us. The cargo cultist in his strange and bizarre behavior, his Vailala madness, in his myth-dream had probably outlined a modality of modernity, a modern world where the fragility of a new human dimension was making its first gentle gesture.

## Notes

1. F. E. Williams, *The Vailala Madness and the Destruction of Native Ceremonies in the Gulf District*, Papuan Anthropology Reports, no. 4 (Port Moresby, 1923). Vailala is a district of Papua, New Guinea. Williams was a colonial officer and amateur anthropologist.
2. Ralph Linton, "Nativistic Movements," *American Anthropologist* 45 (1943): 230-40.
3. Peter Worsley, *The Trumpet Shall Sound*, 2d ed. (New York: Schocken Books, 1970); Kenelm Burridge, *Mambu, A Melanesian Millennium* (New York: Harper & Row, 1970); and Kenelm Burridge, *New Heaven, New Earth: A Study of Millenarian Activities* (New York: Schocken Books, 1969). Both Worsley and Burridge (in *New Heaven, New Earth*) have excellent bibliographies of this phenomenon.
4. I. C. Jarvie, *The Revolution in Anthropology* (Chicago: Henry Regnery & Co., 1969).
5. For the most extensive critical bibliography, see Weston La Barre, "Materials for a History of Studies of Crisis Cults: A Bibliographic Essay," *Current Anthropology* 12 (February 1971): 3-44.
6. Williams, *The Vailala Madness*, 1.
7. Ibid., 14.
8. Ibid., 15.
9. Burridge, *Mambu*, xv-xvi.
10. Norman Cohn, *The Pursuit of the Millennium*, rev. and expanded ed. (New York: Oxford University Press, 1970).
11. Gerardus van der Leeuw, *Religion in Essence and Manifestation*, trans. J. E. Turner (London: George Allen & Unwin, 1938), 23. It is significant to note that the interpretation of religion as power was given impetus by a work from the same area from which cargo cults have developed. I speak of R. H. Codrington's *The Melanesians*, the work in which he discusses the meaning of *mana*.
12. Quoted by Jean Guiart, "The Millenarian Aspect of Conversion to Christianity in the South Pacific," in *Millennial Dreams in Action: Studies in Revolutionary Religious Movements*, ed. Sylvia L. Thrupp (New York: Schocken Books, 1970).
13. Claude Lévi-Strauss, *The Savage Mind* (Chicago: University of Chicago Press, 1970), 236.
14. See Godfrey Lienhardt, *Divinity and Experience: The Religion of the Dinka* (Oxford: Clarendon Press, 1961), 170.
15. Burridge, *Mambu*, 184-85.
16. Ibid., 188-89.
17. Ibid., 41.
18. Jacques Derrida, "Structure, Sign and Play in the Discourse of the Human Sciences," in *The Structuralist Controversy*, ed. Richard A. Macksey and Eugenio Donato (Baltimore: Johns Hopkins Press, 1970).

*Part Three*

*Shadow and Symbols of American Religion*

*Part Three*

*Shadow and Symbols of American Religion*

The essays in this section are devoted to reflections on a specific situation of conquest and cultural contact. The United States of America is the classical example of the meaning of cultural contact; it equally demonstrates the dynamics of concealment and the creation of discourses of power that prevent the meaning of *what really happened* from becoming a part of the cultural languages of the national community. In the case of the United States, we do not have to become ethnologists and anthropologists to understand these meanings and dynamics. The facts of the case are the facts of history and the contemporary normality of the American citizen.

The substance of the first essay, "The Black Reality: Toward a Theology of Freedom," was delivered as an address to my colleagues at the Divinity School of the University of Chicago in 1968. While almost all of my colleagues voiced a liberal and sympathetic voice regarding the racial situation and crisis that had come to the fore at that time, I was attempting to persuade them to reflect with the tools of intellectual scholarship upon the issues that had brought forth the crisis. In response to this request, many of them replied that they did not know very much about the history and traditions of Afro-Americans. I will not deal with that response, for that was not what I had in mind in posing the question. They knew something about the history of European and American thought, and it was this area of their competence that I wanted them to explore. What about Hegel's master/ slave dialectic? What relationship is there between various modes of thought that find expression in the same person? For example, are there any continuities between Hume the philosopher, Hume the historian, and Hume the colonial officer? Why, for example, did we not have a full account of the Puritan archives, which related a great deal about the Puritans' descriptions and understanding of the American aborigines, until the publication of Francis Jennings's work, *The Invasion of America,* in 1975? Similar issues of this kind could have been posed to almost every field of the Divinity School faculty. Almost any honest response to questions of this kind might have brought forth a new and different form of scholarship — a scholarship commensurate with the crisis that was being discussed. In another statement, which forms the third part of that essay, I raise the issue of the experience and traditions of Afro-Americans within the context of the problematical context of civil religion in America. The present formulations of that meaning as an authentic structure of American religion will not, in my estimation, make headway until it comes to terms with the several traditions of the American peoples. But this cannot be simply and only an additive dimension of the status quo; a new historiography must appear, and thus methodological and intellectual issues remain to the fore. The second part of this essay is from a response I made to Thomas J. J. Altizer. Altizer, during the phase of his career when he spoke of himself as a "theologian of the death of God," had undertaken a decipherment of the American reality through a theological analysis of William Blake's poem *America* and Herman Melville's *Moby Dick*. In response I presented an alternate critical mode of interpretation. Much has been made of the innocence of America and the Americans; this theme was present in Altizer's address and I thought this issue might be understood in another manner.

The essay "The Oppressive Elements in Religion and the Religion of the Oppressed" was the substance of the William James lecture delivered at Harvard University in 1976. Again I raised the issue of the Afro-American religious tradition within the context of American thought and traditions. I began with Ernst Troeltsch, not only because of his brilliant critical article on William James and the philosophy of religion but equally because Troeltsch's attention to the social forces as the context of religious expression point to an absence in James's orientation to the issue of religious experience and knowledge within the American context. The fact that James was a professor of W. E. B. DuBois makes the point in a much more effective way.

I also wanted to set forth other dynamics of the meaning of religious experience among oppressed peoples. I think that religious categories must always form part of any psychological analysis of the religious experience of oppressed peoples, for in many respects so many of the power valences, the concealments, and the dynamics of repression are correlates of the social political situation. The oppressed person or community must deal with this and at the same time adjudicate the issue of ultimacy in existence, given the valences of oppressive power on societal levels.

In "Perspectives for a Study of Afro-American Religion in the United States," I outline the factors that one must take into account for what I consider to be an adequate rendering of the religious realities of Afro-Americans in the

United States. While the Christian faith and church are not to be excluded, I would expand the meaning of religion in America in general and among Afro-Americans in particular.

The last essay, "Freedom, Otherness, and Religion: Theologies Opaque," is an interpretive essay on "theologies of color," or "theologies of matter." I use the former designation because of the prominence of black theologies and the theological writing of persons such as Vine Deloria, who titled one of his books *God Is Red*. And though I have not spoken about women's theologies, I would include them within this general structure. Theologies of this kind express a very concrete pole, and to the extent that they are effective, call forth new modes of thinking that may not be able to be included within the structures of theology as we know it today. In other words, the issue is not just a change of content but a change of structure and style.

# Chapter 9

## Interpretations of Black Religion in America

A. THE BLACK REALITY: TOWARD A THEOLOGY OF FREEDOM

### The American Experience

Let me begin with some statements from a contemporary theologian and some common elements of the American tradition and the tradition of the University of Chicago Divinity School.

During his visit to our campus a few years ago I had the pleasure of meeting Karl Barth privately and talking with him for some two hours. "How do you like this strange place called the United States?" I asked him. Barth acknowledged this statement in his foreword to the American edition of *Evangelical Theology: An Introduction.* He continued by way of explanation. "This," he said, "is what I was asked by a dusky theological colleague (not a Roman Catholic this time, but a literally black colleague) with a subtle smile, soon after my arrival in Chicago."[1]

I mention this statement of Barth's because in putting this question to him I was at the same time echoing for myself the constant enigma of my native land — the fact that my native land has always been for me a strange place. Barth's description of me as a "dusky theological colleague...a literally black colleague" is an important locus for this strangeness.

But there is another meaning from Barth's lectures that I should like to mention. At the close of his visit, he added the following remarks to his final lecture:

> Now a concluding word: If I myself were an American citizen and a Christian and a theologian, then I would try to elaborate a theology of freedom — a theology of freedom, let us say, from any inferiority complex over against good old Europe from whence you all came, or your fathers. You do not need to have such an inferiority complex. That is what I have learned these weeks. You may also have freedom from a superiority complex, let us say, over against Asia and Africa. That's a complex without reason. Then may I add — your theology should also be marked by a freedom from fear of communism, Russia, inevitable

nuclear warfare and generally speaking, from all the aforementioned principalities and powers. Freedom for which you would stand would be freedom for — I like to say a single word — humanity. Being an American theologian, I would then look at the Statue of Liberty in the New York Harbor. I have not seen that lady, except in pictures. Next week I shall see her in person. That lady needs a little, or perhaps, a good bit of demythologization.

Nevertheless, maybe she may also be seen and interpreted and understood as a symbol of a true theology, not of liberty, but of freedom. Well, it would be necessarily, a theology of freedom. Of that freedom, to which the Son frees us, and which as His gift, is the one real human freedom.

My last question for this evening is this: Will such a specific American theology one day arise?

I hope so.[2]

This is indeed a large order, but I think we have come to a juncture in the life of this university, this Divinity School, and in the culture at large where we must soberly assess our situation and plan for a future that is at least as audacious as Barth's theology of freedom. We may be more prepared for this task than other comparable schools, for in a peculiar manner our school (which was never fully convinced of Barth's theology) has been more open to the tasks of a distinctively American theology. Professor Bernard Meland in his article of 1962, "A Long Look at the Divinity School and Its Present Crisis," stated among other things that the normal impulse of the Divinity School has been to be itself, or perhaps, more truly, to be itself in exemplifying the "American experience." He warns us that this tendency is related to the lay and separatist tradition in our background, but that it should not be interpreted as merely a reflection of this tendency. "It is," he says, "…to be laid more directly, I think, to its sense of an immediate, rather than mediated, experience of Christian faith." He continues, "And this sense of immediacy has issued fully as much from its focus upon American experience as being the cultural matrix out of which issues to be addressed theologically have taken form, as from any inherited bias which may have colored its thought and effort."

This same issue of "American experience" was the subject of an interchange between Professors Joseph Haroutunian and Meland at the fall retreat of the Divinity School faculty in 1964. Haroutunian explicated the implications of a kind of pragmatism as the key to the American experience, and in this interpretation he is close to Meland's notion of the immediacy of experience in America. He, like Meland, also makes the proper distinctions between European and American cultures, and, again in a similar vein, he emphasizes the notion of freedom as paramount in the American experience.

The American feeling for freedom which is in a sense the American soul or life, must be understood as an expression of American experience. Its peculiarly American quality arises from work together, and public and private well-being which have come out of it.[4]

These statements and meanings of our colleagues and teachers are not entirely original, but they do afford a clarity when they are focused on the particularity of our situation. Barth's statement assigned the task of creating an authentic American theology — a theology of freedom. By implication this had not been done, for Americans were either suffering from a superiority complex *vis-à-vis* Africa and Asia or an inferiority complex *vis-à-vis* Europe, or then again they were preoccupied with their fears. Meland in his article, which carries the word "crisis" in its title, hopes that a review of the heritage of the Divinity School might enable us to transcend divisive elements within the school, and Haroutunian's article ends with an admonition and a hope — an admonition to Americans to cease concentrating on particulars and see the cosmos as a whole, and a hope that such a vision might enable Americans to "explicate the logic of communion in America."

Since the publication of these statements, events in the world and in America have brought to the fore another aspect of American experience. How many are dead? Medgar Evers, John F. Kennedy, Martin Luther King, Jr., Robert F. Kennedy. These assassinations are shocking, but they have only brought to the fore that murder, relentless and impassive, has been a perennial trait of the American experience — an aspect seldom spoken of when one speaks of the American experience. The political parties are ineffective or in disarray; there is a rising tide of fascism; cities are being burned; students feel and are expressing the general unrest, and the war in Vietnam drags on.

This is the other side of the American experience, the demonic side, and its heritage has as long or even longer a tradition than those aspects of our heritage which are positive and beneficent. The locus of these congeries of the American experience is now situated in the black community in this land, and no American theology or theology of freedom can come about without dealing with the existence of this community. To be sure, the recognition of the visibility of the black community in America will prompt many to confront the new situation as simply an ethical-moral problem. It is certainly this; but it is much more. The visibility of this community raises critical and constructive issues on the intellectual and theological levels of our work.

Many among us, black and white, will undoubtedly feel uneasy when the issue is put this way. They feel that such an orientation is a handicap, and while commiserating with what is negative in this situation and attempting to bring about positive change, they are taken aback at the suggestion that more than this is required. Some white persons in this country and some Europeans have recognized this fact, however. Doris Lessing, the English novelist, referred to this issue in her preface to *African Stories*, when she said:

> And while the cruelties of the white man towards the black man are among the heaviest counts in the indictment against humanity, *colour prejudice is not our original fault, but only one aspect of the atrophy of the imagination* that prevents us from seeing ourselves in every creature that breathes under the sun.[5] (Italics added)

W. E. B. DuBois spoke to this point more directly when in 1935 he wrote:

> The most magnificent drama in the last thousand years of human history is the transportation of ten million human beings out of the dark beauty of their mother continent into the new-found Eldorado of the West. They descended into Hell; and in the third century they arose from the dead, in the finest effort to achieve democracy for the working millions which this world has ever seen. It was a tragedy that beggared the Greek; it was an upheaval of humanity like the Reformation and the French Revolution. *Yet we are blind and led by the blind. We discern in it no part of our labor movement; no part of our industrial triumph; no part of our religious experience. Before the dumb eyes of ten generations of ten million children, it is made mockery of and spit upon; a degradation of the eternal mother; a sneer at human effort; with aspiration and art deliberately and elaborately distorted. And why? Because in a day when the human mind aspired to a science of human action, a history and psychology of the mighty effort of the mightiest century, we fell under the leadership of those who would compromise with truth in the past in order to make peace in the present and guide policy in the future.*[6] (Italics added)

This atrophy of the imagination, this blindness before the obvious, this concealment, is nothing other than a description of the loss of soul, a lack of concern for the human matter. New and fundamental interpretations must take place before we can arrive at the central issues posed by the black community in America.

### *America: A Hermeneutical Situation*

Friedrich Schleiermacher once remarked that every hermeneutical task must begin with the misinterpretations.[7] This is the critical principle in every hermeneutic. And so we can do no better than to call to mind those misinterpretations which have brought us to this impasse. These misinterpretations are as much a product of a "false consciousness" as they are the result of the atrophy of the imagination — the inability of the interpreter to come to terms with the reality of the obvious. For example, Haroutunian's statement in the article referred to above that

> Americans have been in the main peoples of European extraction who have found themselves in "a land of opportunity." They have been occupied in building a human habitat where they might pursue life, liberty, and happiness.[8]

There are some crucial terms in this statement that should be clarified. What does one mean by the phrase "in the main"? What is a "human habitat," and how are we to construe the terms "life," "liberty," and "happiness"? From the perspective of any non-European who is at the same time an American, the statement consciously overlooks this reality or it tends to conceal an important dimension of American experience which cannot be grasped by any of these terms.

This tendency of Americans "in the main" to "conceal even from themselves," as Sidney Mead puts it, the tragic dimensions of their cultural experience constitutes a critical area of misinterpretation. In the same manner we may point to the fact that this Divinity School pioneered in the area of church history, specifically, American church history, but no major work or courses have ever been devoted to the churches of the black community. We might continue these misinterpretations in several other areas.

These misinterpretations have been noted by the popularity of the "death of God" and "secular" theologians of a few years ago. A certain kind of radicality and feverish dilettantism is a mark of their style. While they are aware of the misinterpretations, they have no particular touchstone, no specific understanding of any reality as ultimate from which to launch a truly radical attack on these issues. They suffer from a linguistic confusion — an inability to assign the proper words to reality. They are like that religious figure, the trickster, who has the power to create but no sense of what or how to create. And thus their works burst above and around us as the ephemeral balloons that they are.

When, for example, Thomas J. J. Altizer speaks of the "death of God," is he not in fact trying to refer to the decline of the West, or the death and end of the American dream? Why assign the category of death to God when you really mean something else?

## Religion, Theology, and Freedom

We might well ponder the coincidence of the visibility of the black man in America with the pronouncement of the "death of God." James Baldwin once remarked:

> That is why the darkness of my skin so intimidates them. And this is also why the presence of the Negro in this country can bring about its destruction. It is the responsibility of free men to trust and celebrate what is constant; birth, struggle, and death are constant, and so is love, though we may not always think so — and to apprehend the nature of change not on the surface but in the depths — change in the sense of renewal.

This sobering sense of death and renewal is a far cry from the futuristic pronouncements of Altizer. What strikes us as authentic and profound in Baldwin's statement may be due to his skill as a brilliant essayist, but I suggest that the impact of his words may equally be attributed to his ability to manifest the *arche* of the American experience. Americans, "in the main" (to make use of Haroutunian's apt phrase), hardly if ever refer to that which is archaic in their experience. As Meland once remarked, they have a sense of immediacy of experience, and in a religious sense it is the experience of *mysterium fascinans*. Rudolf Otto describes this experience as follows:

> [The Wholly Other is]...something that allures with a potent charm, and the creature who trembles before it utterly cowed and cast down, has always at the same time the impulse to turn to it, nay, even make it his own. The mystery is for him not merely something to be wondered at but something that entrances him; and beside that in it which bewilders and confounds, he feels something that captivates and transports him with a strange nourishment, rising often enough to the pitch of dizzy intoxication; it is the *Dionysian element* in the numen.[10] (Italics added)

This quality of the religious experience has been portrayed over and over again in American culture. Alexis de Tocqueville noted it in the nineteenth century when he said, "Up to the present, I don't see a trace of what we generally consider faiths, such as customs, ancient traditions, and the power of memories."[11] And Karl Barth, as late as the earlier part of the 1960s, used one word again and again to describe America — fantastic![12]

American culture, through its concealment of the blacks and the destruction of Indians, has at the same time concealed from itself its inner primordial experience and a definition of the human mode of being which includes richness and variety.

The visibility of the blacks in American cultural experience at this time constitutes a mythology of memory — a cultural and religious attempt to rehearse as a total cultural reality the primordial depths and intention of American culture. The arche of America is its depth and resource, so that in touching it the opportunity for a new beginning is evoked. This depth is often hidden (concealed), but when it manifests itself, it is a response to an evocation of exhaustion on the ordinary levels of cultural experience. Its appearance is synonymous with cultural crisis.

In American experience, the blacks were dealt with at the founding of the republic when they were designated as some fraction of a human being; scarcely a century later the country erupted in Civil War largely over the question of the blacks, and now in the sixth decade of the twentieth century the black reality remains the central issue of American culture.

The knowledge of these facts, indeed the dramatic actions that presuppose these facts, means that America can never be the same. As Eldridge Cleaver put it:

> The rebellion of the oppressed people of the world, along with the Negro revolution in America, have opened the way to a new evaluation of history, a re-examination of the role played by the white race since the beginning of European expansion.[13]

American culture has yet to come to terms with its "native sons" — and this is just another way of saying that America has yet to come to terms with itself. Religiously speaking, America must be afforded the religious possibility for the experience of the *mysterium tremendum*, that experience which establishes the *otherness* and mystery of the holy. It is this element of holiness which is so familiar in my background.

The community from which I come expressed *an-other* attitude, an attitude that confronted the reality of America, not as plastic and flexible, amenable to the will of the human being through hard work and moral fortitude, but a reality, impenetrable, definite, subtle, and *other* — a reality so agonizing that it forced us to give up our innocence while at the same time it sustained us in humor, joy, and promise. I am speaking of a quality of the American experience which through its harsh discipline destroyed forever a naive innocence, revealing a god of creation — a god of our silent tears — a god of our weary years. This may be called "nitty-gritty" pragmatism. It is from this kind of history and involvement with nature, humanity, and God that the dense richness germinates out of which profound religious awareness emerges.

There are indeed some practical inferences that we may draw from these remarks. For sometimes, I suspect, the distance and the otherness of the black experience must remain just that in our culture. While this may cause tensions, these tensions are necessary if we are to accomplish the task of understanding. These tensions are the marks of intellectual honesty and humility. But more than this, the distance and otherness evoked by the racial situation might give both sides the possibility for a kind of humility — the humility to reflect on their common creaturehood, and, I may add, an invitation to participate in both the tragedy and the comedy of human existence.

## Concluding Remarks

What is called for is a common orientation that authentically expresses the necessary concerns for both aspects of our work, theoretically and practically. It may be that the issue with which we are dealing provides an opportunity for discussing some of these problems. I am not proposing that the Divinity School transform itself into an "Institute for Black Studies" with black faculty (though that may not be the worst thing to happen here); I am saying that the visibility of the black community in America opens us to a range of cultural materials and methodological positions that would not be possible if this were not the case. I am saying that the hegemony of Western Christian categories and thought models has come to an end. Notice that I did not say that they were invalid or useless; I am here making the relativity argument. I am saying that the kind of provincialism stemming from the aforementioned hegemony might be overcome if we take seriously the otherness manifested through and in the visibility of the black community. The visibility of the black community in America is our opening to a wider humanity, historically and contemporaneously.

There are already methodological trends in this direction. Of course, this has been present in the history of religions field for a long time. But I am here speaking of the greater interest in the phenomenological approach in ethics and in the psychology of religion. The phenomenological epoche is the restraint we exercise on the level of thought — a restraint that allows the phenomenon, the other, to appear. It is that exercise of thought which is at the same time a critique of a purely westernizing semantic hegemony.

Our colleague Mircea Eliade said long ago that the West was in danger of provincialism through a lack of attention to the orientations and solutions of non-Western cultures. It would be difficult, if not impossible, to make the case for the non-Western identity of the black community in America, though several make this claim. The element of truth in this claim is that though we are Westerners, we are not Western in the same way as our compatriots, and thus we afford within America an entree to the *otherness* of humankind. When DuBois stated in the earlier part of this century that the problem of the twentieth century was the problem of color, he was referring to the political and economic implications of colonialism and neocolonialism. His prediction has come true, but other dimensions — moral, aesthetic, and religious — may also be discerned here.

We can no longer overlook the empirical participatory reality of this issue; neither can we overlook its theological and constructive aspects. We might find an authentic orientation around which both aspects of our task cohere if we took a note from Barth's proposal for a theology of freedom, freedom from fear, yes; but also freedom from a superiority complex in the face of the rising tide of color in the modern world. And again freedom from an inferiority complex *vis-à-vis* Europe. A freedom for humanity, says Barth.

We are at a critical moment in history — a moment in which America might come to terms with itself. The reorientation of America is contingent upon a recognition of the otherness within and the otherness without. America is a hermeneutical situation.

You know my own biases regarding this issue. I think that it is in the religious life of humankind that we are best able to discern the human mode of being. I think that the exemplary "logic of this mode of being" is present here in a distinctive manner, and I also think that the religious life of humanity is the locus of those primordial and perennial patterns that define us as a species. It is at this level that we may orient ourselves through thought, action, and passion to carry out our common task. The visibility of the black community in America is our challenge and our opportunity to develop a theology of freedom — a freedom for humanity — a new humanity.

### B. THE AMBIGUITIES OF INNOCENCE

The first sentence of Thomas J. J. Altizer's essay "Theology and the Contemporary Sensibility" speaks of the image of America which now threatens to pass into the opposite of its original promise. I am not quite clear about what he means by *the* image of America. It seems to me that America has never been defined by any one image; rather, as a culture, it has always been in the process of becoming an image. The problem of what or who is an American has for this reason always evoked the most intense response from Americans.

However, in spite of this qualification, the question of the American image is one way of raising an important issue, for America from its very beginnings has defined a hermeneutical situation — a situation in which *Homo Americanus* was continually trying to discover and decipher the meaning of existence in the context of the most intense new and radical experience of Western humanity. It is the problem of understanding and identity which lies at the heart of America's problematic culture.

If the meaning of America constitutes a hermeneutical awareness, whatever deciphering is done must itself be rooted in the very problematic character of American culture. I can understand why William Blake's poem *America* attracted Altizer, for it is a poetic-mythological deciphering of America as a peculiar structure of human experience. I would rather follow another course in my deciphering, a course more modest and nonpoetic, but nevertheless more akin to my hermeneutical talents.

Friedrich Schleiermacher once remarked that every hermeneutic begins with or presupposes a misinterpretation. This statement has far-reaching implications for the hermeneutical task. Altizer shows an awareness of some of these implications when he speaks of the original promise of America which is now threatened. He continues his discussion of the misinterpretations of America through his analysis of Blake's *America* and Melville's *Moby Dick*. It is, however, necessary for us to know in a manner less impressionistic and poetical the nature of this misinterpretation, for it is the misinterpretations which constitute the problem of interpretation and it is by going through the misinterpretations that a new awareness of the problem will take shape. Any new interpretation will possess not only clarity but depth insofar as it struggles seriously with the misinterpretations. I am suggesting that if America presents in 1965 the possibility of a new interpretation of human reality, then we must at this moment in our history raise to awareness the misinterpretations that have prompted this new hermeneutical situation.

From a religious point of view, the American experience expresses what Rudolf Otto described as *mysterium fascinosum*. Otto describes by this term the quality of the religious object which attracts and evokes the desire for comfort, unification, and identification with the religious object. The contrasting quality, *mysterium tremendum,* which describes the distance of the object of religion from the worshiper, has been relegated to a residual category in the American experience. The deistic orientation of the founders of our country already presents us with a *deus otiosus,* a god who has removed himself from the center of this new world. His distance from the world of humanity does not inspire a sense of awe, majesty, or power, but indifference. The attention of the citizens of this new nation is focused on the more immediate realities which expressed themselves immanently in nature and human society. The statement of Benjamin Rush, one of Thomas Jefferson's scientific colleagues, concerning the connection between religion and nature is a case in point.

> The necessary and immutable connection between the texture of the human mind, and the worship of an object of some kind, has lately been demonstrated by the atheists of Europe, who, after rejecting the true God, have instituted the worship of nature, of fortune, and of human reason; and, in some instances, with ceremonies of the most expensive and splendid kind. Religions are friendly to animal life, in proportion as they elevate the understanding, and act upon the passions of hope and love. It will readily occur to you, that Christianity, when believed and obeyed, according to its original consistency with itself, and with the divine attributes, is more calculated to produce those effects than any other religion in the world. Such is the salutary operation of its doctrines and precepts upon no other argument, this alone would be sufficient to recommend it to our belief.[2]

It has been this direct relationship to the sacred, the *mysterium fascinosum*, the understanding of the sacred as immediately present through the forms of nature and the moral conscience which constitutes a basic theme in the American experience.

This theme is so elemental in American experience that Perry Miller was able to interpret figures as dissimilar as Jonathan Edwards and Ralph Waldo Emerson as instances of the same religious sensibility. Miller states:

> The real difference between Edwards and Emerson, if they can be viewed as variants within their culture, lies not in the fact that Edwards was a Calvinist while Emerson rejected all systematic theologies, but in the quite other fact that Emerson went to nature, in all passionate love, convinced that man could receive from it impressions which he must then interpret, whereas Emerson went to Nature, no less in love with it, convinced that in man there is a spontaneous correlation with the received impressions.... Edwards sought the images or divine things in nature but could not trust his discoveries...but Emerson having decided that man was unfallen announced no inherent gap between mind and thing, that in reality they leap to embrace each other.[3]

The important fact discerned here is the reliance on nature as the mediator of the divine. It is this theme which has been definitive for Americans. When it is stated that Americans have no historical sense, the allusion is to this fact.

It was that perceptive observer of American culture, Alexis de Tocqueville, who noted that "up to the present I don't see a trace of what we generally consider faiths, such as customs, ancient traditions, and the power of memories." The modality through which Americans have experienced the ultimate has been that of nature rather than history. Anyone who would understand America, says Sidney Mead, "must understand that through all the formative years, space has overshadowed time."[5]

If Americans have exploited their world, it has been an exploitation of nature; if they have suffered, it has been through the forms of nature. It was precisely through theories of nature that the destruction of the Indian cultures took place, and a nation which at its inception proclaimed the equality of all human beings was able to continue the institution of slavery under the guise of nature. A rather long but almost lyrical quote from Sidney Mead, continues this line of thought

> Americans during their formative years were a people in movement through space — a people exploring the obvious highways and the many unexplored byways of practically unlimited geographical and social space. The quality of their minds and hearts and spirits was formed in that great crucible — *and in a short time*. Their great and obvious achievement was the mastery of a vast, stubborn and oft-times brutal continent. This is the "epic of America" written with cosmic quill dipped in the blood, sweat and tears of innumerable little men and women.... This is the mighty saga of the outward acts, told and retold until it has overshadowed and suppressed the equally vital, but more somber story of the inner experience. *Americans have so presented to view and celebrated the external and material side of their pilgrim's progress that they have tended to conceal even from themselves the inner experience, with its more subtle dimensions and profound depths.*[6] (italics added).

It is from this concealment that the innocence and naiveté of the American emerges. The American has for one reason or another never taken time to contemplate the ambiguity of act and value, the horror and the evil which is synonymous with the conquest of this new land. But this innocence of the American is not a natural innocence, that innocence which is prior to experience; rather, this innocence is gained only through an intense suppression of the deeper and more subtle dimension of American *experience.* Americans never had or took the time to contemplate the depth of their deeds. It is Mead again who in a poignant manner speaks of this characteristic. He tells of a cultivated New Englander who went to Oregon, and who after shooting an antelope one day was given to this reflection: "When I stood by his side, the antelope turned his expiring eye upward. It was like a beautiful woman's dark and bright. Fortunate that I am in a hurry, thought I, I might be troubled with remorse, *if I had time for it.*[7] (italics added).

Again in reference to Bernard De Voto's historical writing, Mead sees the same theme. "Perhaps," says De Voto, "the Indians might have been adapted to the nineteenth-century order and might have saved enough roots from their own order to grow in dignity and health in a changed world — *if there had been time.*"[8] (italics added).

If Americans are not conscious of history, it is not because they are innocent. It is due to the fact that the depth of the American experience lies in a relationship with nature as a model of ultimate reality. The tendency of Americans to emphasize history and the modality of time — the saga of the mighty outward acts — represents a suppression, and the god of American history results as an image of this suppression. In having a god in this image, Americans are able to repress the profound and agonizing relationship which has defined their being in space and nature. There may indeed be an authentic god of time and history in the American experience, but such a god is, in the words of James Weldon Johnson, a "God of our weary years" and a "God of our silent tears."[9]

This theme of innocence is not merely an intuitive or impressionistic characterization of American culture; it has played an important role in American historiography. A recently published work, David Noble's *Historians Against History*,[10] is based on the thesis that the major American historians since 1830 — George Bancroft, Frederick Jackson Turner, Charles A. Beard, Vernon L. Parrington, and Daniel Boorstin — resist the very notion of history as a meaningful category for the interpretation of American experience. Noble states that these historians

> asserted that the reality of the American experience was the Puritan convenant translated into the material form of the Jeffersonian republic. Americans, they wrote, live not as members of a historical community with its inevitable structure of institutions and traditions, but as children of nature who are given earthly definition by the virgin land that had redeemed their ancestors when they stepped out of the shifting sands of European history.[11]

Noble exempts only Carl Becker from this judgment. Becker, according to Noble, reluctantly gave up the naturalistic interpretation and sought a historical structure that would relate the American experience to its roots in the past of Western culture. Charles Sanford,[12] another American historian, notes the same tendency when he analyzes the paradise myth in American culture. He concludes his work with the hope that Americans might in their contemporary experience learn to accept and live with a tragic view of life.

Altizer puts his finger on this theme of innocence when, in his essay, he discusses Melville's *Moby Dick*. Of Captain Ahab he says, "Ahab is at once an embodiment of the dark altar of America — he has made the full transition from Innocence to Experience." Altizer's discussion of Ahab is accurate, vivid, and convincing. Ahab is willing to launch his ship into the deeper shark-infested waters of life — life beyond innocence.

At this point I need to clarify and summarize my reaction to this problem of innocence, nature and history in American experience. Those historians referred to by Noble, from Bancroft to Boorstin, may have become convinced of the categories of the nature-history dichotomy as methodological principles by the content of the documents with which they dealt. In my opinion, and I tried to bring this out earlier in my citations from the work of Sidney Mead, Americans have in fact thought of themselves in this manner. However, like Noble, Sanford, and Altizer, I am convinced that innocence and nature are not enough and, I add, not a true rendering of American experience. Noble and Sanford leave us with only a hope that contemporary Americans will accept a tragic view of life, thus moving us beyond innocence. If I read Altizer's paper correctly, he presents to us the radical eschatological movement of a Captain Ahab. "As a tragic hero," Altizer says, "Ahab has no choice, he must seek out and kill Moby Dick.... His tragic conflict with the white whale brings upon himself the death that he would inflict upon the whale, and by dying while lashed upon the whale's back he plunges into the sea of chaos and is swallowed up by the sepulcher of God."

Are our only choices for a movement beyond innocence to be defined by the vague hope of our historians and the eschatological and apocalyptic vision of Ahab? The hopes are too vague and, in my opinion, whatever is profound and true in the figure of Ahab is undercut by Ahab's inability to communicate and to be understood by his crew. His is the lonely and heroic stance of a Faustian man and while he presents us with a vision of life on the far side of innocence, his vision is, in the last analysis, demonic, incommunicable, and escapist.

But more than this, I object to what I consider to be the call for an abrupt and radical movement beyond nature and innocence into history and experience. I object because such a movement fails to take account of the evil inflicted on nature during this so-called period of innocence. America in a certain sense has not been a virgin land since the establishment of the first colonies. To view American culture as if it has been some kind of Polynesia of Western culture is hermeneutically unsound, because such a view fails to understand that through this modality of nature America was exploited, through innocence and repression. Any movement to experience and history must in the end reconcile itself with nature, not in innocence but in redemption. I am saying that America cannot affirm the future until it affirms its past. An eschatology which does not redeem the body of nature as well as announce a consummation to history can easily turn into just another ideology of power.

I discern hints, as I follow Altizer's dialectic, that he is concerned about this same issue. But, one can never be sure with a dialectic, and especially with Altizer's.

There is, finally, another point to be raised here with Altizer. One might refer to it as the issue of tone or style — I am trying to speak of the mood evoked by his essay. In reading it, I caught a sense of great passion, urgency, radicality — and, I must add paradoxically, naiveté and innocence. On this level, which may ultimately be the most important, I felt that Altizer was portraying exactly the kind of innocence which he himself has set out to conquer. Like Mead's New Englander who killed an antelope but who is afraid to be confronted by the gaze of its great and beautiful dying eyes, Altizer has not the time. He is a man who speaks of death as glibly as if he has never experienced, or is afraid to experience, the dying and the killing itself. He wishes for us to plunge on, or, to put it in Frederick Jackson Turner's language, to move on to a new frontier. There is no patience, no meditative attitude, no attentiveness in his proposal.

The eschatological mythology which Altizer proposes is not rooted in that basic contact with reality which is the touchstone of every myth. It presents us with a rich exterior and a glorious future, but it has no interiority, no depth — a gnostic dialectic substitutes for the depth of primary appearances of reality.

What has been forgotten in all of this talk about death is the humanity of death or, to put it another way, the religious meaning of death. It is a characteristic of human perception and imagination that any form of the world may signify meaning — even the dead continue to signify; if God is dead, the signification is even greater. Altizer, I suspect, has for this very reason not taken account of the fact that there might very well be another attitude in the American experience, an attitude that has confronted the reality of America, not as a plastic and flexible reality, amenable to the human will through hard work and moral fortitude, but a reality impenetrable, definite, subtle, a reality so agonizing that it forced the American to give up innocence while at the same time sustaining as joy and promise. I am speaking of a quality of the American experience which through its harsh discipline destroyed forever the naive innocence, simultaneously revealing a God of both nature and time — a God of our silent tears and a God of our weary years. This is indeed a tragic vision of life and nature. It is not unique to the Negro community in America, for it is present as a theme in American literature. It is a portrayal of the subtle and profound depths that lie at the heart of American culture.

Precisely at this time in American history, when we see our symbols, language, and behaviors in danger of being emptied of their meaning, we at the same time see the possibility of a renewal of our language, symbols, and behaviors. But can this task be accomplished by the exorcistic and heavy-handed style of "the death of God" rhetoric? Such a style is related to the power symbolism of an inauthentic god of repression, a god which Altizer ostensibly seeks to destroy. I propose a more modest orientation — one that might be able to affirm nature as a non-innocent reality and at the same time open up the possibility of a true historical future.

It may be true that America has the best possibility for setting the style for the future, but America must come to terms with its own depth in reality before it can move authentically into a future. It is not a coincidence that the basic problems that confront us as a nation today result from the fact that we have not taken the integrity of nature seriously. The exploitation of our natural resources and of blacks and other racial minorities stems from this fact. Until we come to terms with these dimensions of our experiences and the meanings resulting from them, any future will be an escapism sustained only by the physical and psychological repression. America is the youngest of the nations of the West, but it is the oldest of the new democracies. Its future lies in its ability to live with, support, and understand the new worlds of Asia and Africa. While America is related in a special manner to Europe, European culture cannot become an absolute cultural norm for the American.

The challenge before America is not so much eschatological as it is reflective. Let us take the time for this reflection on who we are.

## C. CIVIL RIGHTS — CIVIL RELIGION: VISIBLE PEOPLE AND INVISIBLE RELIGION

American religion is usually understood as the religion of European immigrants transplanted into the American soil. Most general texts that deal with this topic begin with the coming of the Puritans, continue through to the breakdown of the Puritan theocratic ideal and on to the new light, old light debate of the Presbyterians. We are then treated to a description of the great awakenings and the religion of the pioneers as they moved across the American landscape.

Other texts pay equal attention to the different religious communities of the thirteen original colonies and their histories. More precise and detailed work in the area of American religious history has shown that certain themes tend to run through much of this history, becoming the threads with which American religious life weaves its fabric of meanings. Thus the notions of wilderness, new land, errands, and so on, form the symbolic threads of the American religious tradition.

In this vein some historians have more recently become interested in what is now called American civil religion. "Civil religion" is an exceedingly vague phrase, and attempts to define it have often led to more ambiguity. However, some basic notions are involved in the phrase. Greater clarity might be forthcoming if the phrase is placed in the context of the French sociological tradition from Denis Fustel Coulange's *The Ancient City* to Émile Durkheim's *The Elementary Forms of the Religious Life*. Works in this tradition define and locate religion as either a projection of the image of society into objective and sacred symbols or as a correlate of the structure of society. If notions such as these are applied to American religion, the emphasis falls on the religious meanings implicit in the founding documents of the American Republic: the Declaration of Independence and the Constitution. As such, the religious vision stemming from this orientation differs from that of the revealed religion, Christianity; for the revealed religion offers salvation to all human beings regardless of circumstance whereas, in the civil religion, salvation is seen within the context of belonging to the American national community. But the American national community in its ideals and history also offers salvation to all, since it has defined itself as a community that includes peoples from all over the world who seek the forms of freedom and order enunciated in the founding documents.

Civil Religion emerges as a parallel structure alongside revealed religion and its institutions, or it may find expression through revealed religion, or again it may borrow symbols from the revealed religion. Issues of this kind are exhaustively discussed in H. Richard Niebuhr's *Christ and Culture*, where a typology of the possible range of relationships is described in detail.

If American religion is dealt with in either of these two ways or in a combination of these ways, we must note some glaring omissions. Let me raise the issue by asking a simple question, the answer to which will raise a serious issue of method and description. What is meant by "American" and by "religion" in the phrase "American religion"? If by "American" we mean European Christian immigrants and their progeny, then we have overlooked American Indians and Afro-Americans. And if religion is defined as revealed Christianity and its institutions, we have overlooked much of the religion of Afro-Americans, American aborigines, Asian Americans, the Jewish communities, and others. Even from the point of view of civil religion it is not clear, from the perspective of the various national and ethnic communities, there has ever been a consistent meaning of the national symbols and their meanings. In short, a great many of the writings and discussions on the topic of American religion have been consciously or unconsciously ideological, serving to enhance, justify, and render sacred the history of European immigrants in this land.

Indeed, this approach to American religion has rendered the religious reality of non-Europeans to a state of invisibility, and thus the invisibility of the non-European in America arises as a fundamental issue of American history at this juncture. How are we to understand this invisibility and how are we to deal with it as a creative methodological issue? It is no longer possible for us to add the "invisible ones" as addenda to a European-dominated historical method, for such a procedure fails to take into account the relationships of the ones omitted throughout the history of religion in America. Nor is it possible for us, simply in imitation of the historical method and historiography we are criticizing, to begin the project of writing history in which the ideological values of blacks or American Indians dominate. This procedure has no merit, for it could not make sense of that problem of invisibility which allowed us to raise the issue of our discussion. The issue raised here is a subtle one, and questions must be asked concerning the nature of historical method. Reference has already been made to the issue of concealment as described by Sidney Mead in his *The Lively Experiment*. Allow me to add another statement in regard to this same matter. Ralph Ellison, in his prologue to his novel *Invisible Man*, writes:

I am an invisible man. No, I am not a spook like those who haunted Edgar Allan Poe; nor am I one of your Hollywood-movie ectoplasms. I am a man of substance, of flesh and bone, fiber, and liquids — and I might even be said to possess a mind. I am invisible, understand, simply because people refuse to see me. Like the bodiless heads you sometimes see in circus side-shows, it is as though I have been surrounded by mirrors of hard distorting glass. When they approach me they see only my surroundings, themselves, or figments of their imagination — indeed, everything and anything except me.

Nor is my invisibility exactly a matter of a biochemical accident of my epidermis. That inevitability to which I refer occurs because of a peculiar disposition of the eyes of those with whom I come in contact. A matter of construction of the inner eyes, those eyes with which they look through their physical eyes upon reality.... You wonder whether you aren't simply a phantom in other people's minds.

Mead's statement and this one by Ellison deal with the issues of concealment and invisibility. From the point of view of a religious historian, these statements carry great import, for they refer to definitive and fundamental modes of orientation of the American tradition of history and religious history. The statements have to do with the American cultural language, the American mode of perception, and the American religion. "The mighty saga of the outward acts" is a description of the origins not simply of an American language rooted in the physical conquest of space but equally of a language which is the expression of a hermeneutics of conquest and suppression. It is a cultural language that conceals the inner depths, the archaic dimensions of the dominant peoples in the country, while at the same time it renders invisible all those who fail to partake of this language and its underlying cultural experience. The religion of the American people centers around the telling and retelling of the mighty deeds of the white conquerors. This story hides the true experience of Americans from their very eyes. The invisibility of Indians and blacks is matched by a void or a deeper invisibility within the consciousness of white Americans. The inordinate fear they have of minorities is an expression of the fear they have when they contemplate the possibility of seeing themselves as they really are.

This American cultural language is not a recent creation. It is a cosmogonic language, a language of beginnings; it structures the American myth of the beginnings, and has continued to express the synchronic dimensions of American cultural life since that time. It is a language forged by the Puritans and the Jeffersonians and carried on by succeeding generations. The Puritan "errand in the wilderness" was undertaken in the name of religious freedom, a freedom that would allow the colonists from Europe to divine the Word of God in a manner appropriate to their dispositions and knowledge, and a freedom to show this light of the gospel to all human beings, both far and near. This wilderness was, in following the biblical paradigm, a place of retreat from the world for prayer and reflection upon divine meanings. And again, this wilderness was paradise, a space overflowing with the bounty of creation. These meanings of the wilderness are undercut when they confront the American aborigines. The aborigines do not partake of these Puritan understandings of their culture and lands. Even when the aborigines become the teachers of the Puritans, the Puritan cultural languages fail to take cognizance through an alteration of their own language; or even when they are treated benignly by the aborigines, the shift in language and thus in cultural perception does not take place. The aborigine is a wilderness creature who, like the wilderness itself, must be conquered. The conquest of the aborigine began in the seventeenth century and continues into the present. The linking of the aboriginal cultures with the wilderness and the subsequent conquest of both raise issues of race and ecology. These are issues that point up an inherent hermeneutical structure in American historical and religious interpretation.

The Jeffersonian language is equally ambiguous, and this ambiguity is made more intense by the factor of self-consciousness. Unlike the Puritans who wished to be a light unto Europe, the Jeffersonians were thrilled by the possibilities of creating a free society in a new land. They were enlightened people who had thought about the meaning of freedom as an essential ingredient of human societies. Around the issue of slavery was to be played the poignant and commiserating drama of the Jeffersonian conscience; Jefferson is the archetype of the sophisticated liberal. But this issue is deeper than the biography of Jefferson; Jefferson is the hand behind the Declaration of Independence and one of the moving spirits of the Constitution; these are the founding documents, the structures of cosmogony. Through these documents the character of the Jeffersonians and the structure of American cultural language gain a definitive form.

The compromise over slavery at the beginning, in the formation and promulgation of the Constitution, is the archetype of that long series of compromises concerning the freedom of black Americans within the American national community. This first compromise sets the tone for what is almost a ritual of language concerning the nature of black freedom and, consequently, the meaning of freedom in the American Republic. Indeed, we are able to discern almost precisely the one-hundred-year periods in which the Jeffersonian cultural and linguistic compromises rise to an intense and violent level; where the antinomies of its inner structure are exposed. These are cycles of American history. From 1776 to the 1860s is almost a hundred years, and from the Civil War to the 1960s and 1970s is another hundred-year period. These cycles represent dramatic rituals of the archetypes of American history and religion.

At each of these mythical cycles the opportunity is presented for a change of the ritual, for a break in the repetition of this kind of eternal return. It was present in 1776, and then again in the bloody Civil War, and then again in the 1960s with the Kennedys and Martin Luther King, Jr., and Malcolm X; but at each of these junctures the American revolution is aborted and clever priests of our national language and apparatus, skillful in the ways of ritual purity and manipulation, come upon the scene to ensure the repetition of the American ritual.

It is from this perspective that we must understand the meaning of religion in America from the point of view of one who is not a part of the heritage of European immigrants. In this sense, the distinction between civil religion and church religion is not one that looms large for us. In the first place, it is the overwhelming reality of the white presence in any of its various forms that becomes the crucial issue. Whether this presence was legitimated by power executed illegally, or whether in institution or custom, its reality, as far as blacks were concerned through most of their history, carried the force of legal sanction enforced by power. The black response to this cultural reality is part of the civil rights struggle in the history of American blacks.

The fact that black churches have been the locus of the civil rights struggle is not incidental, for the civil rights struggle represented the black confrontation with an American myth that dehumanized the black person's being. The struggle was a mode of affirmation on the part of blacks and a protest in the name of human rights and freedom. The location of this struggle in the church enabled the civil rights movement to take on the resources of black cultural life in the form of organization, music, and artistic expression, and in the gathering of limited economic resources. The civil rights movement has been one of protest and exposition — a protest in the name of freedom and an exposition of the hypocrisy of the American cultural language. But more than hypocrisy was being exposed in this movement, for at points the American system was seen as a gross irrationality or a rationalized demonism. This is religious language and the expression of religious experience. The vicissitudes of the black struggle against the American myth can be traced from recalcitrant slaves through persons symbolized by the names of Nat Turner,

Denmark Vesey, David Walker, Marcus Garvey, W. E. B. DuBois, Martin Luther King, Jr., and others.

To the extent that the struggle for black freedom was carried on through the seeking of legal redress and petition, it participated in and made use of the American cultural language; for in this affirmation there is the tacit acceptance of the American language as adequate for the expression of human freedom for all the American people. But something more is at work here within the black communities. First of all, the very organization of black people meant that they were not invisible to each other; their humanity was affirmed within their communities. Second, they came to know the meaning of the American cultural language in all of its subtleties and antinomies, or, to use a colloquial expression, they came to know the Man. Third, and probably more important, they came to a knowledge and experienced *another reality*, a reality not created or given by the Man. This otherness is expressed in the spirituals as God, or as a mode of perception that is not under the judgment of the oppressors. It is equally expressed in the practical and concrete proposals that speak of *another space*, whether Africa or another geographical location, or heaven. This sense of otherness, or the sense of the other that has arisen out of the black experience, is present when the black communities contemplate the meaning of America as a free society; for if blacks are to be free in American society, this society will indeed have to become a radically different one, *an-other* place.

In the light of this perspective on American religion, let us ask our second question: How is it possible to do justice to the facts of American religious history and at the same time overcome the concealment of peoples? How might it be possible to make visible those who have been rendered invisible religiously and historically? The issue has to do with the network, the nexus, onto which and out of which the facts are generated and interpreted. I am raising a question that is close to the problem of myth.

If we take myth as defined by Mircea Eliade — namely, that myth is a *true* story — then it is the question of a rendering of American religion as a story that does justice to the inner-life meanings and vitalities of those who were made invisible in the old interpretive schema, and it should be a true story that can halt the repressive concealment that has characterized so much of American history.

As in all hermeneutical procedures, one must take account of the misunderstandings and misinterpretations; only by going through these can we arrive at meanings that are substantive. I have stated above that I wish to be faithful to the facts of American history and religion; my problem, or better, the problematical issue, centers around the matrix or pattern onto which these facts are spread. The issue is one of the relationship between authenticity and truth as involving both the facts and the interpretations of these facts. Myth emerges as a category at this point, because I am interested in telling a story of America that is both true and authentic — a story that can respond to an objective and felt meaning of all Americans, a *true story* of the American peoples that moves beyond concealment and invisibilities.

In the telling of the story of America and American cultural reality, we have been dominated by one tradition, the tradition of "the mighty saga of the outward acts," told and retold in such a manner, "until it overshadowed and suppressed the equally vital but more somber story of the *inner experience.*"

The telling and the retelling of the American experience in this mode have created a normative historical judgment and ideology of the American experience. The *historical* telling of this story has in the form of historiography relegated itself to a position of objectivity in terms of the canons of scholarship; it has become identified with truth and legitimacy. Those identified with this approach have not openly asked the question of why they wish the facts to conform to this conception of the truth of the American reality, or better, why certain facts were chosen as the sinew of this truth.

Most interpretations of American religion, whether from the point of view of the revealed tradition or the civil tradition, have been involved with an ideological concealment of the reality of the inner dynamics of their own religio-cultural psychic reality and a correlative repression and concealment of the reality of others. This procedure has been undertaken to give American reality a normative mode of interpretation centered in one tradition. This mode of interpretation has a hallowed position in Western intellectual thought. It constitutes the problematic and resolution of the issue of the episteme. The notion of the episteme constitutes a problem for any form of coherence, and as understood in this context it is the issue of the normative center of interpretation of American religion.

The invocation of the notion of the episteme is an indication of the seriousness of this problem at the level of method. While the notion of the episteme as a pre-methodological meaning allowed for an organizing principle of coherence and provided a normative structure for the organization of data, it simultaneously operated as a center, a presence, making possible the permutation or transformation of other data. "The mighty saga of the outward acts" represents the data produced from the unknown, suppressed, never revealed "inner depths." It is this ideological construct that forces all other traditions to remain in their places — places allocated to them by the centering of this "great tradition."

The concealment and correlative invisibility of various and sundry American peoples result from this methodological centeredness of the American episteme. But even when this tradition is the normative center, we observe that it cannot be known in itself. It is known only through the data that it generates about itself and others. Once this is revealed, we are able to see the contradiction; it constitutes a coherence encompassed by a contradiction, and from a hermeneutical point of view this issues into a problem of desire. It is precisely this desire to uncover, reveal, make visible, the truth of the American reality that explains the violent centennial outbreaks of the American antinomies.

On the practical level, a method must be found whereby we deal with the religious history of all the American peoples. I suggest that we might begin by defining this culture as an Aboriginal-Euro-African culture. The terms should not be seen as simply additive or descriptive. The terms are relational. This means that these meanings should always form the background for any discussion of American religion at any historical period. They are not simply additive, that is, I am not suggesting them because I wish to include all the peoples in America in this methodological paradigm. I am saying that once the singularity of a normative tradition is overcome, the problem of inclusion of all peoples will no longer be at issue. The notion of equality which is part and parcel of the American cultural language must express itself in theoretical terms also; we must work for a meaning of this notion that has relevance for historical method. The question of the meaning of American religion in its revealed or civil forms calls for new theoretical considerations.

In this short essay I have attempted to raise certain theoretical problems in relationship to historical method and historiography of American religion. New understandings of this history will be forthcoming with a change of consciousness; with this I agree, but my emphasis has been directed toward changes on the levels of the intellectual and theoretical expressions of human consciousness.

## Notes to A

1. Karl Barth, *Evangelical Theology: An Introduction* (New York and Chicago: Holt, Rinehart & Winston, 1963), v.
2. "Introduction to Theology," Questions to and discussion with Karl Barth, *Criterion* 2, no. 1 (Winter 1963).
3. *Criterion* 1, no. 2 (Summer 1962), 23.
4. Joseph Haroutunian, "Theology and American Experience," *Criterion* 3, no. 1 (Winter 1964), 4.
5. Doris Lessing, *African Stories* (New York: Ballantine Books, 1966), vii.
6. W. E. B. DuBois, *Black Reconstruction in America* (New York: S. A. Russell Co., 1935), 727.
7. See Friedrich Schleiermacher, *Hermeneutics: The Handwritten Manuscripts*, ed. Heinz Kimmerle and trans. James Duke and Jack Forstman (Missoula, MT: Scholars Press, 1977), 110 and 153ff.
8. Haroutunian, "Theology and American Experience," 3.
9. James Baldwin, *The Fire Next Time* (New York: Dial Press, 1963), 106.
10. Rudolf Otto, *The Idea of the Holy*, trans. John Harvey, 2d ed. (Oxford: Oxford University Press, 1958).
11. Quoted in G. W. Pierson, *Tocqueville and Beaumont in America* (New York: Oxford University Press, 1938), 153.
12. Barth, *Evangelical Theology* vi.
13. Eldridge Cleaver, *Soul on Ice* (New York: McGraw-Hill Book Co., 1968), 70.

## Notes to B

1. Rudolf Otto, *The Idea of the Holy*, trans. John W. Harvey, 2d ed., (Oxford: Oxford University Press, 1958), chap. 6.
2. Quoted in Daniel Boorstin, *The Lost World of Thomas Jefferson* (Boston: Beacon Press, 1960), 154.
3. Perry Miller, *Errand Into the Wilderness* (New York: Harper & Row, Harper Torchbooks, 1964), 185.
4. Quoted in G. W. Pierson, *Tocqueville and Beaumont in America* (New York: Oxford University Press, 1938), 153.
5. Sidney Mead, *The Lively Experiment: The Shaping of Christianity in America* (New York: Harper & Row, 1963), 11.
6. Ibid., 8.
7. Ibid., 4.
8. Ibid., 5.
9. Words from the song "Lift Every Voice and Sing," by James Weldon Johnson, Negro poet and writer. This song was, until the middle of the 1950s, referred to quite seriously in the Negro community as "The Negro National Anthem."

10. David Noble, *Historians Against History* (Minneapolis: University of Minnesota Press, 1965).
11. Ibid., 176.
12. Charles L. Sanford, *The Quest for Paradise: Europe and the American Moral Imagination* (Urbana: University of Illinois Press, 1961).

## *Note to C*

One sees again the influence of Sidney Mead's work *The Lively Experiment: The Shaping of Christianity in America* (New York: Harper & Row, 1963).

I am indebted to works that have come from the history of religions methods and from what has come to be known as the "structural schools." In the former, Mircea Eliade's *The Myth of the Eternal Return*, trans. Millard R. Trask (New York, Pantheon Books, 1954), and in the latter Claude Lévi-Strauss's *The Savage Mind* (Chicago: University of Chicago Press, 1970), and Jacques Derrida's programmatic essay, "Structure, Sign, and Play in the Discourse of the Human Sciences," in *The Structuralist Controversy*, ed. Richard A. Macksey and Eugenio Donato (Baltimore: Johns Hopkins Press, 1970), have been of particular importance to me.

# Chapter 10

## The Oppressive Elements in Religion and the Religions of the Oppressed

### I

In 1912, Ernst Troeltsch published a memorial review article for William James entitled "Empiricism and Platonism in the Philosophy of Religion."[1] This article, which deals with James's *The Varieties of Religious Experience*, is still the clearest succinct statement of James's position within the context of the general problems of Western philosophies of religion.

After defending James from spurious charges, Troeltsch points out the fundamental departure taken by James in his philosophy of religion. Troeltsch rightly states that all European philosophies of religion are Platonic in their derivation, and he lays out what he considers to be five major characteristics of this tradition. The last summarizing *nota* must suffice here.

> All these investigations have set out from the fact of consciousness, which, however, as already said, is more than mere fact, being a compound of both the necessary and the contingent. Such a way of thinking gains its final security only when it firmly anchors the individual consciousness, of itself always contingent, in the holding-ground of "consciousness in general," and then, on that basis, makes the compound somehow comprehensible, so that in it the elements of necessity are plainly seen to derive their origin from the absolute consciousness, and the direction of evolution is understood as a movement toward that goal. In the background here stands the problem of the connection of finite and infinite consciousness.[2]

In contrast to this Platonic orientation to the nature of religion, Troeltsch sees James rejecting the notion of an "essence" of religion: "James takes the religious experiences in a purely empirical way and gives a purely empirical, approximate characterization, which accumulates its marks indefinitely, and leaves the question wholly open whether religious experiences are really unitary and specific experiences."[3] Or again, he says:

---

William James Lecture on Religious Experience delivered at the Harvard Divinity School, 19 November 1975. Originally published in the *Harvard Theological Review* 69, nos. 3-4 (1976): 397-410.

So, while the European philosophy of religion, from its premise of a unitary essence, seeks to comprehend the historical stages of evolution as teleological, James knows the varieties only as *psychological* variations, in every case dependent on general psychical condition and on nervous constitution. The great historical complexes, taken by and large, are merely accidental differences in name and external historical location. In truth, he holds, analogies and psychically conditioned varieties run through all religious systems, and are to be understood by psychological and psychophysical interpretation, not by any dialectic of self-evolving thought.[4]

It would seem, therefore, that though Troeltsch makes a claim for the authenticity of James's *The Varieties of Religious Experience* as a genuine philosophy of religion, such claim has the salutary effect of placing the European and James's positions at unbridgeable distances. Troeltsch's adjudication of this polarity consists of a concluding statement of mutual critique — the points of agreement in the face of the difference:

> One observation must be made which will again diminish the practical difference between the two types. On each theory the result for the conception of religion *is very much the same*. In both cases the result is a complete reaction from dogmatic theology, church, ecclesiastical worship, ritual, sacrament, and canonical law to the element of purely *personal religious attitude*. The marrow of religious phenomena is understood, on both sides, in a mystical and spiritual sense; only with the Platonists the contemplative mysticism of the vision of the Absolute and Eternal preponderates, with the empiricists the practical mysticism of experience of the mystical state, saintliness, and love of humanity. In both cases the theory emphasizes the immediateness of the religious life, in contrast to historical authorities and traditions and to sociological constructions.[5]

And finally Troeltsch states:

> In neither case does the philosophy of religion substitute a "pure religion" for the dominant religions; it simply furnishes a solid foundation and justification for the religious life in general, leaving free its living course, which it essays to regulate only for those to whom reflective thought is a necessity. This naturally brings about a difference between the esoteric religion of the thinker and the exoteric religion of the masses. On either hand, the freedom which is secured to the heart of religion to create its own form involves a complete mutual tolerance between the religious groups and between believers within each group. This means that in the end both views see on the whole the highest, or most valuable, evolutionary form in an individualized and spiritualized Protestantism, such as has resulted from a great part of Protestant history, and itself, indeed, stands under the influence of such theories.

What are we to make of this theoretical analysis of religious experience from dialectically different points of view? In spite of different philosophical points of view and processes, Troeltsch's sense of the commonality of positions is neither gratuitous nor accidental; I attribute the commonality to an epistemological oversight which might be defined and located in different places in the two traditions, but conclude that its commonness lies in what I shall define as the Western ideology of religion. Given this, let us first of all deal with the two Western pseudo-protagonists *of* religious experience — James and Troeltsch.

First James. Let us pose the question: How radical is James's *radical empiricism*? To what extent has James's demolition of all religious absolutes prevented him from seeing and understanding what is radical in experience? The case in point is the singular recording of Henry James Sr.'s most depressive state of consciousness from his *Society: The Redeemed Form of Man*.

> One day, however, towards the close of May, having eaten a comfortable dinner, I remained sitting at the table after the family had dispersed, idly gazing at the embers in the grate, thinking of nothing, and feeling only the exhilaration incident to a good digestion, when suddenly — in a lightning-flash as it were — "fear came upon me, and trembling, which made all my bones to shake." To all appearance it was a perfectly insane and abject terror, without ostensible cause, and only to be accounted for, to my perplexed imagination, by some damned shape squatting invisible to me within the precincts of the room, and raying out from his fetid personality influences fatal to life. The thing had not lasted ten seconds before I felt myself a wreck, that is, reduced from a state of firm, vigorous, joyful manhood to one of almost helpless infancy. The only self-control I was capable of exerting was to keep my seat. I felt the greatest desire to run incontinently to the foot of the stairs and shout for help to my wife — to run to the roadside even, and appeal to the public to protect me, but by an immense effort I controlled these frenzied impulses, and determined not to budge from my chair till I had recovered my lost self-possession.[7]

A similar statement from William James is recorded in *The Varieties Of Religious Experience* and it describes almost word for word the same kind of experience.

> Whilst in this state of philosophic pessimism and general depression of spirits about my prospects, I went one evening into a dressing-room in the twilight to procure some article that was there; when suddenly there fell upon me without any warning, just as if it came out of the darkness, a horrible fear of my own existence. Simultaneously there arose in my mind the image of

an epileptic patient whom I had seen in the asylum, a black-haired youth with greenish skin, entirely idiotic, who used to sit all day on one of the benches, or rather shelves against the wall, with his knees drawn up against his chin, and the coarse gray undershirt, which was his only garment, drawn over them enclosing his entire figure. He sat there like a sort of sculptured Egyptian cat or Peruvian mummy, moving nothing but his black eyes and looking absolutely non-human. This image and my fear entered into a species of combination with each other. *That shape am I,* I felt, potentially. Nothing that I possess can defend me against that fate, if the hour for it should strike for me as it struck for him. There was such a horror of him, and such a perception of my own merely momentary discrepancy from him, that it was as if something hitherto solid within my breast gave way entirely, and I became a mass of quivering fear.[8]

As far as we know, the psychologically inclined, neurologically and biologically oriented James did not understand the relationship between his experience and that of his father. Given his radical empiricism and his paradigm of the individual as the locus of such experience, he had no mode of relating the two experiences within the general orientation of his philosophical presuppositions.

The same problem arises in a different manner in the philosophical orientations of Ralph Waldo Emerson and Josiah Royce. They, like William James, represented attempts to come to terms with the radicality of the American experience even as did William James's father Henry. William Clebsch, in a work that is in part devoted to James, characterizes the general style of Jonathan Edwards, Ralph Waldo Emerson, and William James as an aesthetic spirituality.[9] If this is correct, then following F. S. C. Northrup's theoretical analysis[10] of culture, we would have to say that James embodied a *differentiated* aesthetic component.

William James's recourse to neurological-biological and individualistic categories was in lieu of a clearly articulated notion of American society and culture as the transmitter of tendencies, meanings, and values. Was he in fact searching for community in America? His notions regarding religious experience sound true, but somehow constructions such as "once born" and "twice born" do not seem capable of bearing the weight of the cultural experiences of Americans, much less the experience of humankind. But what does ring true is the protest against the canceling of the issue through spurious general categories.

One would expect Ernst Troeltsch, the European intellectual, the author of *Die Soziallehren,* to have challenged James at precisely this point, for if anyone had the data of strange, contingent religious forms, it was Troeltsch; but Troeltsch's Platonism, the absolute that moves through and is present in all modes of consciousness, prevents him even in *Die Soziallehren* from coming to terms with the radical contingency present in James's proposal. Even in the introduction to *The Social Teaching of the Christian Churches* he is at pains to state the relationship between Christianity and society in disjunctive terms.

> To put it quite plainly: Christianity was not the product of a class struggle of any kind; it was not shaped, when it did arise, in order to fit into any such situation.... The fact, however, remains that Jesus addressed Himself primarily to the oppressed, and to the "little ones" of the human family, that He considered wealth a danger to the soul, and He opposed the Jewish priestly aristocracy which represented the dominant ecclesiastical forces of His day. It is also clear that the Early Church sought and won her new adherents chiefly among the lower classes in the cities.[11]

The question that must be raised in regard to both James and Troeltsch has to do with that experience of religion which accounts for the inner reality of religion as negative as it finds expression in the individual and the community. Can there not be another source for the "twice born" soul? As noted above, James and his father, Henry James, Sr., had experienced what Rudolf Otto a few years later would refer to as "daemonic dread." Baron von Hügel reports that after 1912, and especially after the outbreak of the First World War, Troeltsch himself felt more and more alone and despairing.[12]

So neither James nor Troeltsch is able to come to terms in a fundamental manner with that oppressive dread in the religious experience, albeit on the surface for quite different reasons. For James this experience can be explained in terms of individual psychology, and for Troeltsch the experience is expressive of the relative historical situation in which Christians find themselves. But common to both positions is a kind of Protestant individualism that cannot at heart face up to this mode of the divine.

It is only later in the work of Otto that this characteristic of the meaning of religion is enunciated, and it is significant to note that Otto's analysis denies both the psychological and the neurological reduction of James, on the one hand, and the ideational essentialistic notion of the Troeltschian Absolute, on the other.

Otto's discussion moves at a level that allows us to understand how that which evokes the religious experience within us, this numinous, as he says, "has its wild and demonic forms and can sink to an almost grisly horror and shuddering."[13] Otto is telling us that it is possible to experience apart from the categorical schema; this is precisely the meaning he is giving to the notion of the nonrational. It is this experience of reality as *a priori*, as a datum that has not yet become a structure of the human project, that evokes in us the feeling of *mysterium tremendum et fascinosum*.

It is especially the *mysterium tremendum* that evokes our feelings of creatureliness, of the diminution of our plans and hopes; it is this feeling that leads to a sense of unworthiness — a sense of the overpowering reality of that which stands over against us, and the fundamental distinction between the human and the divine. This is a moment in the religious experience, and Otto claims that this ambiguously negative oppressive and overwhelming sense of the divine is present in all religious traditions. Such feelings lead on to a sense of absolute dependence and humility in the sight of the divine and one's fellow human beings. In other words, it may lead to a specifically religious community. It is from these notions that the internal meaning of oppression in religion arises. It is the oppressive sense evoked by the power and majesty of the divine, the belittling of the creature and the human project itself.

Gerardus van der Leeuw later was to express this same meaning in a more precise manner.

> Religious experience, in other terms, is connected with a "Somewhat." . . . In order that man may be able to make more significant statements about this "Somewhat," it must force itself upon him, must oppose itself to him as being Something Other."[14]

## II

But let us now make a transition through a return to William James. In the latter part of the 1880s, W. E. B. DuBois was one of James's students. DuBois remarks that it was James who urged him to continue in his philosophical approach to the issues of life but advised him also to find something else to do, since it was hard to make a living as a philosopher.[15] It is strange to note the conjuncture of these two men, James and DuBois" — James, the psychologist and philosopher of religion, and DuBois, who became one of the earliest, if not the first, of the American social scientists.

DuBois had come to Harvard from Fisk University in Nashville, Tennessee. It was at Fisk that DuBois first experienced and participated in the communities of the oppressed blacks in the United States; that is to say, this was his introduction to the religion of the oppressed. DuBois himself describes this experience in that half-autobiographical, half- historical/sociological and poignant text, *The Souls of Black Folk,* a text that James had read. The quote below occurs in that section which William had asked Henry, his brother, to read "for local color etc."

> It was out in the country, far from my foster home, on a dark Sunday night. The road wandered from our rambling log-house up the stormy bed of a creek, past wheat and corn until we could hear dimly across the fields a rhythmic cadence of song — soft, thrilling, powerful, that swelled and died sorrowfully in our ears. I was a country school-teacher then, fresh from the East, and had never seen a Southern Negro revival.... And so most striking to me as I approached the village and the little plain church perched aloft, was the air of intense excitement that possessed that mass of black folk. *A sort of suppressed terror hung in the air and seemed to seize us ,— a pythian madness, a demonic possession, that lent terrible reality to song and word. The black and massive form of the preacher swayed and quivered as the words crowded to his lips and flew at us in singular eloquence.*[17]

We should note the language here; in some particulars it sounds very similar to the kind of dread described by both Henry James, Sr., and William James himself. The setting for the Jameses' experiences is solitude; the setting for DuBois's experience is community, indeed the discovery of community. William James, in *The Varieties of Religious Experience,* had already described religion in just this manner. "Religion," he said, "therefore, as I now ask you arbitrarily to take it, shall mean for us *the feelings, acts, and experiences of individual men in their solitude, so far as they apprehend themselves to stand in relation to whatever they may consider the divine.*"[18]

William James's response to the *mysterium tremendum* was through will and belief in action. Much the same is true of DuBois, for in the discovery of this community a career of intellectual and practical activity is defined for the young scholar. But there is a reflective moment of a historical kind in DuBois. He is given to reflect not in the abstract manner of the philosopher but in the concrete manner of memory and historical imagination. He ponders the beauty and sorrow of his community, and these ruminations rush his consciousness back to the African forest, to the sense of a *primordium* of history and imagination.

I am not trying to make a case that DuBois was defining his life in sociological terms, whereas the Jameses saw things from an individualistic point of view. Those who knew DuBois describe him as a most idiosyncratic person, not given to gregariousness; William James was probably the more sociable and easily met of the two. Rather, I am attempting to locate and provide a context for the meaning of community as a dimension of the religious experience itself. But then, again, I am not saying that in James we have a definition of religion as solitude and in DuBois such a definition would be sociological. I have said above that within every genuine religious experience there is an element of the ambiguously negative, what Otto called the *mysterium tremendum*. It arises out of the experience of otherness as divine and cannot be reduced to any other categories, though it may be schematized into other meanings and notions, for example, sin. We know this to be present in the religious experiences of blacks. One has only to read the accounts of the conversion experiences of blacks to see how this *mysterium tremendum,* in the life of slaves and ex-slaves, is never identified with the sociological situation or with the oppression of slavery itself; it is, in fact, a manner in which these human beings recognize their creatureliness and their humanity, shall we say, before God, and it is this essential humanity which is not given by the slave system or the master.[19]

The situation of external oppression, oppression in history, however, colors and, as it were, creates a screen, or, as DuBois would have it, gives a sense of being "born with a veil." "The Negro is sort of a seventh son, born with a veil, and gifted with second-sight in this American world — a world which yields no true self-consciousness, but only lets one see oneself through the revelation of the other world. It is a peculiar sensation, this double consciousness, this sense of always looking at one's self through the eyes of another, measuring one's soul by the type of a world that looks on in amused contempt and pity ... two souls, two thoughts, two unreconciled strivings; two warring ideals in one dark body, whose dogged strength alone keeps it from being torn asunder."[20]

This is at least a critical statement; it points to the ambiguity of community and religious experience at the very moment of perception. It conveys in a sober manner the overtones of the same sense of demonic terror and excitement that DuBois describes when he visits the black church. The same experience may lie behind the Jameses, both father and son. William James made an attempt to come to terms with this character of the religious experience as a philosopher of religion by giving meaning to the religious sentiment through the categories of psychic states; and his father's attraction to Swedenborgian thought is the mystical counterpoint. Henry, the younger, became an expatriate. All three Jameses express a form of radicalism in their actions, but none had to come to terms with the more radical contingency expressed by DuBois. Wherein lay their concrete memory and primordium? To be sure, this illustrious American family had memories, and whether they expressed these concrete memories or not, they were indeed there — much as Faulkner describes in a scene in *Intruder in the Dust*, when the young adolescent white Mississippian asks his elder why, after the white community had realized that they were about to lynch an innocent black man, Lucas Tanner, they did not seek him out to apologize and admit their error. The answer of the elder is that even though they do not make public and concrete amends, they know and they remember. But it is a memory that is concealed, for to make this memory concrete and public would be to plunge the community into a radically contingent state.

It is this conundrum which lies at the heart of the religions of the oppressed. Their religious experience and the forms of its expression reveal a critique of community and a fascination with the possibility and hope of intimacy. The veil, the double consciousness, is a critical stance, and they speak of primordial experiences and histories as the locus of new resources not yet categorized and rationalized by the communities under criticism.

Since the later part of the nineteenth century there have appeared with increasing momentum new religious phenomena. In the language of the scholarly disciplines they have been called cargo cults, millenarian movements, religions of the oppressed. Once noted on the modern scene, these movements have been likened to earlier movements in the older strata of world religions. Weston La Barre has referred to them as crisis cults,[21] and has seen some characteristics of the crisis cult in the beginnings of all soteriologically oriented religions. While analogies to earlier movements in Judaism, Christianity, and Buddhism might be noted, it is not enough to explain these modern movements as simply perennial forms of the religious life. These movements have become one of the loci for serious study in the disciplines of anthropology and the history of religions — we have only to mention Vittorio Lanternari's *The Religions of the Oppressed*, Kenelm Burridge's *Mambu*, Bryan Wilson's *Magic and the Millennium*, Walter J. Hollenweger's *The Pentecostals*, Weston La Barre's *The Ghost Dance*, or F. C. Wallace's *Religion: An Anthropological View*. Indeed, I. C. Jarvie notes that the data of these movements provide the basis for a methodological revolution in the discipline of anthropology.[22]

These movements of the oppressed cannot be understood in the terms of the older movements of the world, for they presuppose the specific nature of modernity, and modernity itself is a form of critique; these movements thus constitute a critique of the critique. We must understand that it was the modern Western world that created the categories of civilization, such as the primitives, the races, and so on. These terms are part and parcel of the universalizing and critical structures of the modern Western consciousness. In many respects, most of those cultures which have given rise to the religions of the oppressed were "created" for the second time by the critical categories of the West. This is the source of the double consciousness referred to by DuBois. The source of DuBois's demonic dread occurs when he touches the possible source of a new critique of this second creation. Prior to oppressed peoples' own meanings, as expressed in the "crisis cults," their only access to meanings within the Western experience was under the control of the Western hegemony of language. They were peoples created out of the theoretical disciplines stemming from the Enlightenment. The first true word about them in this "second creation" was from a knowledge *about* rather than a knowledge *of* them. No intimacy of language was to be found in this second creation. Their second creation within the context of their experience was characterized by a spurious *mysterium tremendum*; "the other" was only the other culture and not the divine. "The other" of religious experience, with its impenetrable majesty, was replaced by the quixotic manipulation of a fascinating trickster whose rationality was only a veneer for control.

It is only in some such manner that we are able to understand the seemingly strange rituals and orientations of these cults. Whether they are the American Indian Ghost Dance of the 1890s, the Vailala Madness, the Rastafarians, or even aspects of the black power movement, all of these movements have come face to face with radical contingency, the critique of the critique, and this critique takes place not just directly but behind the veil. The response is not simply intellectual; it is experiential and total. It is a religious response. The fear and shuddering common to the experience of James *père* and James *fils* and also of DuBois are worked through in very different ways, DuBois forming the transition, for he was both intellectual and man of action.

I turn now to the only philosophical paradigm in modern Western philosophy that might serve as a bridge in our discussion, Hegel's master-slave dialectic.[23] David Brion Davis argues quite cogently that early modern philosophers had almost abolished the grounds for any philosophical defense of the institution of slavery and in so doing had removed slavery from its context and supposed protections of an organic and hierarchical social order.[24] Davis cites three modern philosophical discussions of slavery, Thomas Hobbes, John Locke, and G. W. F. Hegel. For Hobbes, slavery was the context for a struggle between two combatants:

The loser, in order to save his life, finally promises absolute obedience to the victor, in return for subsistence and corporal liberty. By terms of the "compact," the slave can only will what his master wills. The master can be guilty of no injustice, since he has spared the slave's life.[25]

In contradiction to this position, Locke expressed the notion that slavery could arise only outside the social contract. All individuals, according to him, held an original and absolute ownership of their own persons, and the products of their labor. The voluntary social contract should thus protect every individual from the inconstant, uncertain, unknown, arbitrary will of another person. Yet, according to Davis's understanding of Locke, "any man may by an act of violence, forfeit his life to another. Nor can such a criminal complain of injustice if his captor spares his life." For Locke, then, slavery always stood outside the bounds of a peaceful and rational order: "The perfect condition of *Slavery* is nothing else, but the *state of War continued, between a lawful Conqueror and a Captive*. The elemental struggle between two enemies defined slavery's essential and the inconstant, uncertain, unknown, arbitrary will of another person. Yet, according to Davis's understanding of Locke, "any man may by an act of violence, forfeit his life to another. Nor can such a criminal complain of injustice if his captor spares his life." For Locke, then, slavery always stood outside the bounds of a peaceful and rational order: "The perfect condition of *Slavery* is nothing else, but the *state of War continued, between a lawful Conqueror and a Captive*. The elemental struggle between two enemies defined slavery's essential and continuing character."[26] Hegel also sees slavery as the scene of primal combat, but the locus of this combat is human consciousness itself. "Whereas Locke had seen slavery as peripheral to society and history, Hegel saw it as the natal core of men's condition."[27] This point is especially pertinent when we place it within the context of modernity, for the religions of the oppressed manifest tendencies that are attempts to create new forms of human consciousness. The problem of identity for colonized and neocolonized societies is the same issue of consciousness, but it is not simply an attempt to create a new consciousness among the oppressed but a new form of human consciousness and thus a new historical community.

But let us continue Davis's summary of Hegel's master-slave dialectic. The master, following Aristotle's definition of slavery, sees the slave as an instrument of his own will and demands absolute obedience:

> Yet every day he must contradict this Aristotelian definition since he is now dependent on another human life (having spared the life), and since he has found that the "slavish consciousness" is the object "which embodies the

truth of his certainty of himself." The act of enslavement has created two opposed forms or modes of consciousness.[28]

The master is the consciousness that exists for *itself*, but no longer merely the general notion of existence for self. Rather, it is a consciousness existing on its own account which is mediated with itself through another consciousness whose very nature implies that it is bound up with an independent being or with thinghood in general.[29]

The master is trapped by his own power, which he can only seek to maintain. He cannot achieve the true autonomy that can come only from the recognition by another consciousness that he regards as worthy of such recognition. The condition of omnipotent lordship, then, becomes the reverse of what it wants to be: dependent, static, and unessential.[30]

The slaves, out of fear and for the sake of self-preservation (survival), assimilate themselves to the master's definition of their role and function, immersing themselves in nature and work. The labor of the slaves places them in contact with nature, and through the transformation of nature they create an objective reality that confirms and shapes their own consciousness of self independent of the master's definition. Thus, in their labor, the slaves become aware through this rediscovery of themselves by themselves of having and being a consciousness of their own.

Unlike the master, the slaves are not consumers who look upon the products of their works as satisfying historical desires.

The products which the slave creates become an objective reality that validates the emerging consciousness of his own subjective reality. Through coerced labor, the slave alone acquires the qualities of fortitude, patience, and endurance.... Only the slave, therefore, has the potentiality for escaping an imbalanced reciprocity and for becoming truly free.[31]

Let us now recall the situations of demonic dread of Henry James, Sr., William James, and W. E. B. DuBois. There is no need to doubt the authenticity of the Jameses' experiences. What is most telling about their experiences is their mode of expression. In the case of Henry James, Sr., the objective element that is the *other* in the experience is vague, ill-defined, abstract. He reports:

To all appearance it was a perfectly insane and abject terror, without ostensible cause, and only to be accounted for, to my perplexed imagination, by some *damned shape* squatting invisible to me within the precincts of the room, and raying out from his fetid personality influences fatal to life.[32]

In the case of William James the report is similar:

> Suddenly there fell upon me…a horrible fear of my own existence. Simultaneously there arose in my mind the image of an epileptic patient whom I had seen in the asylum, a black-haired youth with greenish skin, entirely idiotic…. This image and my fear entered into a species of combination with each other. *That shape am I,* I felt, potentially.[33]

For the Jameses, the objective form of the otherness in the experience bears the form of the fantastic and the psychologically oriented rhetoric of that which is totally unrelated to existence.

For W. E. B. DuBois, the experience of *mysterium tremendum* is more precise:

> A sort of suppressed terror hung in the air and seemed to seize us, — a pythian madness, demonic possession, that lent terrible reality to song and word. The black and massive form of the preacher swayed and quivered as the words crowded to his lips and flew at us in singular eloquence.[34]

Here we are speaking not of fantasies but of community, a community listening to the sounds and words of each other, and if there is something fantastic about this experience, such must obviously be present, for this experience was the occasion of demonic dread for DuBois — it is DuBois's experience of the products of this ex-slave community. For in this one moment of experience the immediacy of experiencing outside of veil and double consciousness is afforded; it is his first experience of the autonomous creation of the slave community.

Hegel's speculative dialectic of master-slave is most insightful as a philosophic guide in our attempt to understand the religions of the oppressed, but the more specific meaning of this dialectic may be expressed by W. E. B. DuBois' notion of the double consciousness. Even when slaves, ex-slaves, or colonized persons become aware of the autonomy and independence of their consciousness, they find that, because of the economic, political, and linguistic hegemony of the master, there is no space for the legitimate expression for such a human form. The desire for an authentic place for the expression of this reality is the source of the revolutionary tendencies in these religions. But on the level of human consciousness, religions of the oppressed create in another manner. The hegemony of the oppressors is understood as a myth — myth in the two major senses, as true and as fictive. It is true as a structure with which one must deal in a day-by-day manner if one is to persevere, but it is fictive as far as any ontological significance is concerned.

But such a procedure does not define a simple dichotomy, for the day-to-day existence is in fact the oppressed's labor — labor from which their autonomy arises; therefore their own autonomy takes on a fictive character. The truth of their existence must necessarily involve not only the change of their consciousness but the realization of the true and fictive consciousness of the oppressors. This drama is carried out again and again in the religion of the oppressed.[35] But the basic structure of such meanings approximates the myth, for only the consciousness as myth can express the full range of this dialectical mode of being.

The oppressed must deal with both the fictive truth of their status as expressed by the oppressors, that is, their second creation, and the discovery of their own autonomy and truth — their first creation. The locus for this structure is the mythic consciousness which dehistorizes the relationship for the sake of creating a new form of humanity — a form of humanity that is no longer based on the master-slave dialectic. The utopian and eschatological dimensions of the religions of the oppressed stem from this modality.

The oppressive element in the religions of the oppressed is the negation of the image of the oppressor and the discovery of the first creation. It is thus the negation that is found in community and seeks its expression in more authentic forms of community, those forms of community which are based upon the first creation, the original authenticity of all persons which precedes the master-slave dichotomy. There is thus a primordial structure to this consciousness, for in seeking a new beginning in the future, it must perforce imagine an original beginning.

I have attempted to make sense of two kinds of paradigms of religious experience. I have tried to show how common structural elements of the religious experience bear the weight of their histories and situations. Unlike James, I have tried to account for religious experiences in historical rather than psychological terms and I have seen history as the arena for the constitution of consciousness rather than the temporal-spatial arena in which the powerful overcome powerlessness with justifying ideology. The differentiation of consciousness is a reality, and we owe James a debt of gratitude for making this clear, but if indeed James expressed, in the words of William Clebsch, an aesthetic spirituality, his research did not lead him far enough to understand the grotesque and bizarre convolutions of human consciousness which emerge when the constitution of the religious consciousness faces historical memory.

## Notes

1. *Harvard Theological Review* 5 (1912): 401-22.
2. Ibid., 408-9 (my italics).
3. Ibid., 413.
4. Ibid., 414 (my italics).
5. Ibid., 417-18.
6. Ibid., 418.
7. From Henry James, Sr., *Society: The Redeemed Form of Man* (Cambridge: Houghton, Osgood & Co., 1879), 44-49, quoted in *The Writings of William James,* ed. John J. McDermott (New York: Modern Library, 1968), 3.
8. William James, *The Varieties o Religious Experience* (New York: Modern Library edition; facsimile of the 1902 edition), 157.
9. See William A. Clebsch, *American Religious Thought: A History* (Chicago: University of Chicago Press, 1973), xvi.
10. See F. S. C. Northrup, *The Meeting of East and West* (New York: Macmillan Co., 1952), esp. chap. 12.
11. Ernst Troeltsch, *The Social Teaching of the Christian Churches* (London: George Allen & Unwin, 1950), 39.
12. See Ernst Troeltsch, *Christian Thought: Its History and Application,* ed. and intr, Baron von Hügel (New York: Meridian Books, 1957), 12; and Ernst Troeltsch, *Briefe an Friedrich von Hügel, 1901-1923.*
13. Rudolf Otto, *The Idea of the Holy,* trans. John W. Harvey (London: Oxford University Press, 1950), 13.
14. Gerardus van der Leeuw, *Religion in Essence and Manifestation*, trans. J. E. Turner (London: George Allen & Unwin, 1938), 23.
15. See W. E. B. DuBois, *Dusk of Dawn: An Essay Toward an Autobiography of a Race Concept* (New York: Schocken Books, 1968), 39.
16. William James mentions W. E. B. DuBois in a letter to his brother, Henry. "I am sending you a decidedly moving book by a mulatto ex-student of mine, DuBois, professor of history at Atlanta (Georgia) Negro College. Read Chapters VII to XI for local color, etc." (The book was DuBois, *The Souls of Black Folk.*) Henry James, ed., *The Letters of William James* (Boston: Atlantic Monthly, 1920), 2, 196.
17. W. E. B. DuBois, *The Souls of Black Folk* (Basic Afro-American Reprint Library, Johnson reprint; originally published in Chicago: A. C. McClurg, 1903), 189-90 (my italics).
18. William James, *The Varieties of Religious Experience,* 31.
19. See Clifton H. Johnson, ed., *God Struck Me Dead: Religious Conversion Experience and Autobiographies of Ex-Slaves* (Boston: Pilgrim Press, 1969).
20. DuBois, *The Souls of Black Folk,* 3.
21. Weston La Barre, "Materials for a History of Studies of Crisis Cults: A Bibliographic Essay," *Current Anthropology* 12 (February 1971): 3-44.
22. Vittorio Lanternari, *The Religions of the Oppressed* (New York: Alfred A. Knopf, 1963); Kenelm Burridge, *Mambu, A Melanesian Millennium* (New York: Harper & Row, 1970); Bryan R. Wilson, *Magic and the Millennium* (New York: Harper &

Row, 1973); Walter J. Hollenweger, *The Pentecostals* (London: SCM Press, 1972); Weston La Barre, *The Ghost Dance: Origins of Religion* (New York: Doubleday & Co., 1970); F. C. Wallace, *Religion: An Anthropological View* (New York: Random House, 1966); I. C. Jarvie, *The Revolution in Anthropology* (Chicago: Henry Regnery & Co., 1969).
23. I am indebted to Richard J. Bernstein, *Praxis and Action* (Philadelphia: University of Pennsylvania Press, 1971) and especially to David Brion Davis, *The Problem of Slavery in the Age of Revolution* (Ithaca, N.Y.: Cornell University Press, 1975). My discussion follows closely Davis's epilogue, 557-64.
24. For a thorough discussion of the ideology of hierarchical societies, see Louis Dumont, *Homo Hierarchicus* (Chicago and London: University of Chicago Press, 1970).
25. Davis, *The Problem of Slavery,* 559.
26. Ibid., 559-60.
27. Ibid., 560.
28. Ibid., 561.
29. G. W. F. Hegel, *The Phenomenology of Mind,* trans. J. B. Baille, 2d ed. (London: George Allen & Unwin, 1949), 234-35.
30. Davis, *The Problem of Slavery,* 561-62.
31. Ibid., 562.
32. McDermott, *The Writings of William James,* 3.
33. William James, *The Varieties of Religious Experience,* 157.
34. DuBois, *The Souls of Black Folk,* 190.
35. See my article "Cargo Cults as Cultural Historical Phenomena," *Journal of the American Academy of Religion* 42, no. 3 (September 1974): 403-14, chap. 8 in this volume.

# Chapter 11

## Perspectives for a Study of Afro-American Religion in the United States

Americans of African descent have for some time been the subject of countless studies and research projects — projects extending from the physical through the social sciences. The religion of this culture has not been overlooked.[1]

Most of the studies of religion have employed the methodology of the social sciences; hardly any of the studies have come to terms with the specifically religious elements in the religion of black Americans. We have not yet seen anything on the order of Pierre Verger's[2] study of African religion in South America or of Alfred Métraux's[3] study of the same phenomenon in the Atlantic islands.

On the contemporary scene, a group of black scholars have been about the task of writing a distinctively "black theology." I refer here to the works of Joseph Washington (*Black Religion* [Boston, 1961]) and James Cone (*Black Theology and Black Power* [New York, 1969]), and to Albert Cleage's sermons (*The Black Messiah* [New York, 1968]). In this enterprise these men place themselves in the religious tradition of David Walker, Henry Garnett, Martin Delaney, and W. E. B. DuBois. They are essentially apologetic theologians working implicitly and explicitly from the Christian theological tradition.

What we have, in fact, are two kinds of studies: those arising from the social sciences, and an explicitly theological apologetic tradition. This limitation of methodological perspectives has led to a narrowness of understanding and the failure to perceive certain creative possibilities in the black community in America.

One of the most telling examples of this limitation of perspectives in the study of black religion is to be found in Joseph Washington's work cited above. Washington has correctly seen that black religion is not to be understood as a black imitation of the religion of the majority population. His religious norm is Christianity, and the internal norm for Christianity is faith expressing itself in theology. From his analysis he concludes that black religion is not Christian,

---

Originally published in *History of Religions* 11, no. 1 (August 1971): 54–66.

thus does not embody faith, and therefore has produced no theology. Black religion has, in his view, been more concerned with civil rights and protest, and hardly, if ever, concerned with genuine Christian faith.

I do not wish to take issue with Washington regarding his understanding of Christian faith and theology, for this lies outside the scope of the concerns in this essay. However, a word or two must be said in passing. Washington seems to conceive of Christianity and theology in static terms unrelated to historical experience. He seems to be unaware of the historical situations that were correlative to European and American theology, and he seems equally unaware that Americans have produced few theologians of the variety that would meet his norm. In short, his critique of black religion from the stance of Christian theology is blunted by the lack of his historical understanding of theology.

But now, to the point that is most relevant for this discussion: the distinctive nature of black religion. Washington's insights here are very accurate, for he shows in his work how folkloric materials, social protest, and Negro fraternalism, along with biblical imagery, are all aspects of black religion. He experiences a difficulty here, for he is unable to deal with religion outside the normative framework of Christian theology. But even if one is to have a theology, it must arise from religion, something that is prior to theology.

For some time I have felt the need to present a systematic study of black religion — a kind of initial ordering of the religious experiences and expressions of the black communities in America. Such a study should not be equated with Christianity, or any other religion for that matter. It is, rather, an attempt to see what kinds of images and meanings lie behind the religious experiences of the black communities in America. While recognizing the uniqueness of this community, I am also working as a historian of religions. These perspectives constitute symbolic images as well as methodological principles. They are:

1. Africa as historical reality and religious image
2. The involuntary presence of the black community in America
3. The experience and symbol of God in the religious experience of blacks.

## *Africa as Historical Reality and Religious Image*

It is a historical fact that the existence of the black communities in America is due to the slave trade of numerous European countries from the seventeenth to the nineteenth century (slaves were still being illegally smuggled into the

United States as late as the 1880s). The issue of the persistence of African elements in the black community is a hotly debated issue. On the one hand, we have the positions of E. Franklin Frazier and W. E. B. DuBois, emphasizing the lack of any significant persisting elements of Africanism in America. Melville Herskovits held this same position but reversed his position in the *Myth of the Negro Past* (Boston, 1958), where he places a greater emphasis on the persistence of African elements among the descendants of the slaves in North America. One of the issues in this discussion had to do with the comparative level of the studies. Invariably, the norm for comparison was the black communities in the Atlantic islands and in South America. In the latter, the African elements are very distinctive, and, in the case of Brazil, Africans have gone back and forth between Africa and Brazil.[5] African languages are still spoken by blacks in Brazil. Indeed, Pierre Verger first became interested in Yoruba religion when he saw it being practiced in South America!

It is obvious that nothing of this sort has existed in the United States. The slave system of the United States systematically broke down the linguistic and cultural patterns of the slaves, but even a protagonist for the loss of all Africanisms, such as E. Franklin Frazier, acknowledges the persistence of "shout songs," African rhythm, and dance in American culture. Frazier, and in this matter DuBois, while acknowledging such elements, did not see these elements of ultimate significance, for they could not see these forms playing an important role in the social cohesion of the black community. Without resolving this discussion, we need to raise another issue. The persistence of elements of what some anthropologists have called "soft culture" means that, given even the systematic breakdowns of cultural forms in the history of North American slavery, the slaves did not confront America with a religious *tabula rasa*. If not the content of culture, a characteristic mode of orienting and perceiving reality has probably persisted. We know, for example, that a great majority of the slaves came from West Africa, and we also know from the studies of Daryll Forde that West Africa is a cultural as well as a geographical unit.[6] Underlying the empirical diversity of languages, religions and social forms, there is, according to Forde, a structural unity discernible in language and religious forms.[7] With the breakdown of the empirical forms of language and religion as determinants for the social group, this persisting structural mode and the common situation as slaves in America may be the basis for the persistence of an African style among the descendants of the Africans.

In addition to this, in the accounts of the slaves and their owners we read of "meetings" which took place secretly in the woods. It is obvious that these "meetings" were not devoted to the practice of the masters' religion. They were related to what the slaves themselves called "conjuring," and the connotation reminds one of voodoo rites in Haiti.

Added to this is the precise manner in which slaves, by being slaves, black persons, were isolated from any self-determined legitimacy in the society of which they were a part and were recognized by their physiological characteristics. This constituted a complexity of experience revolving around the relationship between their physical being and their origins. So even if they had no conscious memory of Africa, the image of Africa played an enormous part in the religion of the blacks. The image of Africa, an image related to historical beginnings, has been one of the primordial religious images of great significance. It constitutes the religious revalorization of the land, a place where the natural and ordinary gestures of the blacks were and could be authenticated. In this connection, one can trace almost every nationalistic movement among the blacks and find Africa to be the dominating and guiding image. Even among religious groups not strongly nationalistic, the image of Africa or Ethiopia still has relevance.[8] This is present in such diverse figures as Richard Allen, who organized the African Methodist Episcopal Church in the late eighteenth century, through Martin Delaney in the late nineteenth century, and then again in Marcus Garvey's,[9] "back to Africa movement" of the immediate post-World War I period, and finally in the taking up of this issue again among black leaders of the present time.

The image of Africa as it appears in black religion is unique, for the black community in America is a landless people. Unlike the American Indian, the land was not taken from them, and unlike the black Africans in South Africa or Zimbabwe (Rhodesia), the land is not occupied by groups whom they consider aliens. Their image of the land points to the religious meaning of land even in the absence of these forms of authentication. It thus emerges as an image that is always invested with historical and religious possibilities.

### *The Involuntary Presence of the Black Community in America*

Implied in the discussion concerning the land and the physiological characteristics of the blacks is the significance attributed to this meaning in America. The stance has, on the one hand, been necessitated by historical conditions and, on the other hand, been grasped as creative possibility. From the very beginning, the presence of slaves in the country has been involuntary; they were brought to America in chains, and this country has attempted to keep them in this condition in one way or another. Their very presence as *human beings* in the United States has always constituted a threat to the majority population. From the point of view of the majority population, they have been simply and purely legal entities, first as slaves defined in terms of property, and then, after the abolition of chattel property, as citizens who had to seek legal redress before they could use the common facilities of the country — water fountains, public accommodations, restaurants, schools, and so on. There is no need to repeat this history; it is too well known, and the point I wish to make is more subtle than these specific issues, important as they may be.

In addition to the image and historical reality of Africa, one must add, as another persisting datum, the involuntary presence and orientation as a religious meaning. I have stated elsewhere the importance of the involuntary structure of the religious consciousness in the terms of oppugnancy.[10] In the case of the slaves, America presented a bizarre reality, not simply because of the novelty of a radical change of status and culture but equally because their presence as slaves pointed to a radical contradiction within the dominant culture itself. The impact of America was a discovery, but one had little ability to move from the bizarre reality of discovery to the level of general social rules of conduct, which happens in the case of other communities presented with an ultimate discovery. In addition to this, to normalize the condition of slavery would be to deny the existence of the slaves as human beings.

The slaves had to come to terms with the opaqueness of their condition and at the same time oppose it. They had to experience the truth of their negativity and at the same time transform and create *an-other* reality. Given the limitations imposed upon them, they created on the level of the religious consciousness. Not only did this transformation produce new cultural forms but its significance must be understood from the point of view of the creativity of the transforming process itself.

Three short illustrations of this phenomenon must suffice at this point. Listen to the words of this spiritual:

> He's so high, you can't get over him,
> He's so low, you can't get under him,
> So round, you can't get around him,
> You got to go right through the door.

Or this poem by a black poet:

> Yet do I marvel at this curious thing,
> To make a poet black and bid him sing.

Or a folk aphorism:

> What do you mean I gotta do that?
> Ain't but two things I got to do — Be black and die.

The musical phenomenon called the blues is another expression of the same consciousness. What is portrayed here is a religious consciousness that has experienced the "hardness" of life, whether the form of that reality is the slave system, God, or simply life itself. It is from such a consciousness that the power to resist and yet maintain one's humanity has emerged. Though the worship and religious life of blacks have often been referred to as forms of escapism, one must always remember that there has always been an integral relationship between the "hardness" of life and the ecstasy of religious worship. It is, in my opinion, an example of what Gaston Bachelard described in Hegelian language as the lithic imagination. Bachelard had reference to the imaginary structure of consciousness that arises in relationship to the natural form of the stone and the manner in which the volitional character of human consciousness is related to this imaginary form.[11] The black community in America has confronted the reality of the historical situation as immutable, impenetrable, but this experience has not produced passivity; it has, rather, found expression as forms of the involuntary and transformative nature of the religious consciousness. In connection with this point, I shall illustrate by returning to the meaning of the image and historical reality of Africa.

Over and over again this image has ebbed and flowed in the religious consciousness. It has found expression in music, dance, and political theorizing. There has been an equally persistent war against the image in the religion of black folk. This war against the image of Africa and blackness can be seen in the political and social movements connected with the stratagems of segregation and integration. Even more telling is the history of the names by which the community has chosen to call itself. From African to colored, to Negro, Afro-American, and, presently, black. The history of these designations can be seen as a religious history through which this community was coming to terms with a primary symbol of opacity.

Recall the words of Gerardus van der Leeuw. He said, "Religious experience, in other terms, is concerned with a 'Somewhat.' But this assertion often means no more than this 'Somewhat' is merely a vague 'something,' and in order that man may be able to make more significant statements about this 'Somewhat,' it must force itself upon him, oppose it to him as being Something Other. Thus the first statement we can make about religion is that it is a highly exceptional and extremely impressive 'Other.'"[12] From the point of view of religious history, one could say that this community in its own self-interpretation has moved from a vague "Somewhat" to the religious experience of a highly exceptional and *extremely impressive* "Other." The contemporary expressions of black power attest to this fact, and the universalizing of this notion in terms of pan-Africanism, negritude, or neo-Marxian and Christian conceptions must equally be noted.

The meaning of the involuntary structure or the opacity of the religious symbol has within this community held together eschatological hopes and the archaic religious consciousness. In both secular and religious groups, new expressions such as Moorish Temple, Black Jews, and Black Muslims retain an archaic structure in their religious consciousness, and this structure is never quite settled, for it is there as a datum to be deciphered in the context of their present experience.

## *The Experience and Symbol of God*

The sources for my interpretation of the experience of the holy in this community are from the folkloric tradition. By this, I mean an oral tradition that exists in its integrity as an oral tradition, the writing down of which is a concession to scholarship.

These sources are slave narratives, sermons, the words and music of spirituals and the blues, the cycles of Brer Rabbit and High John, the Conqueror, stories. These materials reveal a range of religious meanings extending from trickster-transformer hero to High God.

To be sure, the imagery of the Bible plays a large role in the symbolic presentations, but to move from this fact to any simplistic notion of blacks as slaves or former slaves converted to Christianity would, I think, miss several important religious meanings.

The biblical imagery was used because it was at hand; it was adapted to and invested with the experience of the slave. Strangely enough, it was the slave who gave a religious meaning to the notions of freedom and land. The deliverance of the Children of Israel from the Egyptians became an archetype which enabled the slave to live with promise.

God for this community appears as an all-powerful and moral deity, though one hardly ever knows why he has willed this or that. God is never, or hardly ever, blamed for the situation of humanity, for somehow in an inscrutable manner there is a reason for all of this. By and large, a fundamental distinction is made between God and Jesus Christ. To the extent that the language of Christianity is used, black Americans have held to the Trinitarian distinction, but adherence to this distinction has been for experiential rather than dogmatic reasons. Historians of religions have known for a long time that the Supreme Being appears in differing forms. To be sure, God, the first person of the Trinity, is a powerful creator deity.

It is not so much the dogma of the Trinity as it is the modalities of experience of the Trinity which is most important. The experience of God is thus placed within the context of the other images and experiences of black religion. God, as first person of the Trinity, is, of course, a powerful Creator and Supreme deity. Though biblical language is used to speak of his historical presence and intervention in history, we have neither a clear Hebraic nor what has become a Christian interpretation of history. I am not implying that the deity is a *deus otiosus*, for there is an acceptance of historical reality, but in neither its Hebraic nor its traditional Christian mode. We must remember that the historicity of these two traditions was related to the possession of a land, and this has not been the case for blacks in America. In one sense, it is possible to say that their history in America has always presented to them a situation of crisis. The intervention of the deity into their community has not been synonymous with the confirmation of the reality of their being within the structures of America. God has been more often a transformer of their consciousness, the basis for a resource that enabled them to maintain the human image without completely acquiescing to the norms of the majority population. He provided a norm of self-criticism that was not derivative from those who enslaved them. I cite two examples as illustrations:

> When I was very small my people thought I was going to die. Mama used to tell my sister that I was puny and that she didn't think that she would be able to raise me. I used to dream nearly all the time and see all kinds of wild-looking animals. I would nearly always get scared and nervous.
>
> Some time later I got heavy one day and began to die. For days I couldn't eat, I couldn't sleep; even the water I drank seemed to swell in my mouth. A voice said to me one day, "Nora you haven't done what you promised." And again it said, "You saw the sun rise, but you shall die before it goes down." I began to pray. I was making up my bed. A light seemed to come down from heaven, and it looked like it just split me open from my head to my feet. A voice said to me, "Ye are freed and free indeed. My son set you free. Behold, I give you everlasting life."
>
> During all this time I was just dumb. I couldn't speak or move. I heard a moaning sound, and a voice said, "Follow me, my little one, and I will show you the marvelous works of God." I got up it seems, and started to traveling.

I was not my natural self but a little angel. We went and came to a sea of glass, and it was mingled with fire. I opened my mouth and began to pray, "Lord, I will perish in there." Then I saw a path that led through the fire, I journeyed in this path and came to a green pasture where there were a lot of sheep. They were all of the same size and bleated in a mournful tone. A voice spoke to me, and it sounded like a roar of thunder: "Ye are my workmanship and the creation of my hand. I will drive all fears away. Go, and I go with you. You have a deed to your name, and you shall never perish."[13]

Everybody seemed to be getting along well but poor me. I told him so. I said, "Lord, it looks like you come to everybody's house but mine. I never bother my neighbors or cause any disturbance. I have lived as it is becoming a poor widow woman to live and yet, Lord, it looks like I have a harder time than anybody." When I said this, something told me to turn around and look. I put my bundle down and looked towards the east part of the world. A voice spoke to me as plain as day, but it was inward and said, "I am a time-God working after the counsel of my own will. In due time I will bring all things to you. Remember and cause your heart to sing."

When God struck me dead with his power I was living on Fourteenth Avenue. It was the year of the Centennial. I was in my house alone, and I declare to you, when his power struck me I died. I fell out on the floor flat on my back. I could neither speak nor move, for my tongue stuck to the roof of my mouth; my jaws were locked and my limbs were stiff.[14]

These two narratives are illustrative of the inner dynamics of the conversion experience. The narratives combine and interweave the ordinary events with the transformation of the religious consciousness. It is not merely a case of God acting in history, for the historical events are not the locus of the activity but then neither do we have a complete lack of concern for historical events in favor of a mystification of consciousness. It is the combination of these two structures that is distinctive in these narratives; clues such as these might help us to understand the specific nature of the black religious consciousness.

But this structure of the deity is present in non-Christian movements among the blacks; the transforming power of the deity may be seen among the Black Muslims and the Black Jews. This quality of the presence of the deity has enabled blacks to affirm the historical mode by seeing it more in terms of an initiatory structure than in terms of a progressive or evolutionary understanding of temporality.

Continuing with the Christian language of the Trinity, Jesus has been experienced more in the form of a dema-deity[15] than as conquering hero. One could make the case that this understanding of Jesus Christ has always been present in the history of the Western church, but it is clear that this image of the Christ has not been experienced as a symbol of Western culture as a whole since the seventeenth century. Christ as fellow sufferer, as the little child, as the companion, as the man who understands — these symbols of Christ have been dominant. Consider, for example, the spirituals:

> I told Jesus it would be all right if he changed my name,
> Jesus told me that the world would hate me if he changed my name.

Or:

> Poor little Jesus boy, made him to be born in a manger.
> World treated him so mean,
> Treats me mean too ...

But there is more than biblical imagery as a datum. In the folklore we see what appears as the trickster-transformer hero. More than often he appears in the Brer Rabbit cycle of stories, which seem related to similar West African stories ofAnanse, the Spider.

This is one of the cycles of the Brer Rabbit stories.[16] Brer Rabbit, Brer Fox, and Brer Wolf were experiencing a season of drought. They met to decide the proper action to take. It was decided that they should dig a well so that they would have a plenteous supply of water. Brer Rabbit said that he thought this was a very good plan, although he did not wish to participate in the digging of the well, because, he said, he arose early in the morning and drank the dew from the grass and thus did not wish to participate in the arduous task of digging. Brer Fox and Brer Wolf proceeded with their task and completed the digging of the deep well. After the well was dug, Brer Rabbit arose early each morning and went to the well and drank his fill, pretending all the time that he was drinking the morning dew. After a while, Brer Fox and Brer Wolf became suspicious of Brer Rabbit and set about to spy upon him. Sure enough, they caught him one morning drinking from their well. They subjected him to some punishment, which we need not go into, for the point of the story has been made.

Brer Rabbit is not simply lazy and clever; it is clear that he feels that he has something else to do — that life cannot be dealt with in purely conventional terms and committee meetings. In many respects the preacher in the black community exhibits many of the traits of Brer Rabbit, and it was often the preacher who kept alive the possibility of another life, or who protested and affirmed by doing nothing.

One other instance should be mentioned: High John, the Conqueror. It is stated explicitly in the folklore that High John came dancing over the waves from Africa, or that he was in the hold of the slave ship. High John is a flamboyant character. He possesses great physical strength and conquers more by an audacious display of his power than through any subtlety or cunning. He is the folkloric side of a conquering Christ, though with less definite goals.

The essential element in the expression and experience of God is his transforming ability. This is true in the case of God as absolute moral ruler as well as in Brer Rabbit or High John, the Conqueror. Insofar as society at large was not an agent of transformation, the inner resources of consciousness and the internal structures of the blacks' own history and community became not simply the locus for new symbols but the basis for a new consciousness for the blacks.

It is therefore the religious consciousness of the blacks in America which is the repository of who they are, where they have been, and where they are going. A purely existential analysis cannot do justice to this religious experience. A new interpretation of American religion would come about if careful attention were given to the religious history of this strange American.

## Notes

1. W. E. B. DuBois, ed., *The Negro Church* (Atlanta: Atlanta University Press, 1903); Carter G. Woodson, *The History of the Negro Church* (Washington, D.C.: Associated Publishers, 1921); Benjamin E. Mays and Joseph W. Nicholson, *The Negro's Church* (New York: Russell & Russell, 1969); Arthur Fauset, *Black Gods in the Metropolis* (Philadelphia: University of Pennsylvania Press, 1944; London: Oxford University Press, 1944); E. Franklin Frazier, *The Negro Church in America* (New York: Schocken Books, 1962); Howard Brotz, *The Black Jews of Harlem* (New York: Schocken Books, 1970); C. Eric Lincoln, *The Black Muslims in America* (New York: Beacon Press, 1961); and E. U. Essien-Udom, *Black Nationalism: The Search for an Identity in America* (Chicago and London: University of Chicago Press, 1962).

2. Pierre Verger, *Notes sur la culte des Orisa at Vodun à Bahia la Baie de tous les saints au Bresil et à l'ancienne Côte des esclaves en Afrique* (Dakar, 1957).
3. Alfred Métraux, *Le Vaudou haitien* (Paris, 1958).
4. See W. E. B. DuBois, *The Souls of Black Folk* (Basic Afro-American Reprint Library, Johnson reprint; originally published in Chicago: A. C. McClurg, 1903).
5. See Verger, *Notes sur le cults des Orisa*.
6. Daryll Forde, "The Cultural Map of West Africa: Successive Adaptations to Tropical Forests and Grassland," in *Cultures and Societies of Africa*, ed. Simon Ottenberg and Phoebe Ottenberg (New York: Random House, 1960).
7. Joseph Greenberg makes a similar argument for the structural similarity of West African languages in his *Studies in African Linguistic Classification* (New Haven: Yale University Press, 1955).
8. See especially Edward W. Blyden, *Christianity, Islam and the Negro Race* (London, 1887). Blyden, though born in the Virgin Islands and ordained as a Presbyterian minister, was one of the early leaders in pan-Africanism. It is interesting to note that he set the problem within a religious context. The publication of his work is directly related to the problems created in the 1840s by the passage of the Fugitive Slave Law and the Dred Scott decision of the United States Supreme Court.
9. See E. David Cronon, *Black Moses* (Madison: University of Wisconsin Press, 1962).
10. See Charles H. Long, "Prolegomenon to a Religious Hermeneutic," *History of Religion* 6, no. 3 (February 1967): 254-64; chap. 2 in this volume.
11. See Gaston Bachelard, *La terre et les rêveries de la volonté* (Paris, 1948).
12. Gerardus van der Leeuw, *Religion in Essence and Manifestation*, trans. J. E. Turner (London: George Allen & Unwin, 1938), 23.
13. Clifton H. Johnson, ed., *God Struck Me Dead*, Religious Conversion Experiences and Autobiographies of Ex-Slaves (Boston: Pilgrim Press, 1969), 62-63.
14. Ibid., 58-59.
15. Adolf E. Jensen defined this religious structure as a result of his researches in Ceram. See his *Hainuwele* (Frankfurt, 1939) and *Myth and Cult Among Primitive Peoples* (Chicago and London: University of Chicago Press, 1963). I do not wish to say that Jesus Christ is understood in any complete sense as a dema-deity in black religion; I am saying that it is from this religious structure that one should begin the deciphering of the meaning of Jesus. Essential to this structure is the notion of the deity as companion and creator, a diety related more to the human condition than deities of the sky, and the subjection of this deity in the hands of human beings.
16. See T. F. Crane, "Plantation Folklore," in *The Negro and His Folklore*, ed. Bruce Jackson (Austin: University of Texas Press, 1967), 157-67.

## Chapter 12

## *Freedom, Otherness, and Religion: Theologies Opaque*

In this essay I should like to deal with four major topics. First, I wish to provide a religious and intellectual background for the meaning of "theologies of color;" second, I intend to give an analysis of two of the American versions of this theology, that of James Cone and that of Vine Deloria; third, on the basis of this analysis I will attempt to point to a reorientation in the intention of these kinds of theologies; and last, I will venture a constructive position in relationship to what has gone before.

### *The Religious and the Intellectual*

Before we discuss the content and analyze the structure of the theologies under question, I shall provide a context for the appearance of these types of theology. For our purposes I shall have recourse to two articles published in the Spring 1967 edition of *Daedalus*. This particular edition of *Daedalus* was devoted to the problem of race. The articles I have in mind are Edward Shils's "Color, the Universal Intellectual Community and the Afro-Asian Intellectual" and Roger Bastide's "Color, Racism, and Christianity." One might wonder why these articles have the respective authors, but that wonderment itself is part of the problematic that I wish to address through the course of this essay. I have chosen these two articles because they deal in a precise manner with the two issues that are at the heart of the black theologies, the wedding of intellectual intention with a religious valorization of color — this is the well-spring of their novelty.

Let us begin with Shils's analysis. The article begins with a philosophical approach to the meaning of color. As a matter of fact, Shils says, color in itself is meaningless. Unlike religion or kinship, color does not implicate the semantic range that is a precondition for any meaning. Color exists, but it has no significance beyond its existence. "Color," says Shils, "is just color."

> It is a physical spectroscopic fact. It carries no compellingly deducible conclusions regarding a person's belief or his position in any social structure. It is like height or weight — the mind is not involved. Yet it attracts the mind; it is the focus of passionate sentiments and beliefs. The sentiments

color evokes are not sentiments of aesthetic appreciation. Nor does color have any moral significance; color is not acquired or possessed by leading a good moral life. No intentions are expressed by color, no interpretations of the world are inherent in it. The mind is not at work in it and it is not a social relationship. It is inherently meaningless.

If this is indeed the case, why has color assumed such a significance in human history and especially in the modern period? Why has such an eminent scholar and prophet as W. E. B. DuBois defined an entire history as focused on the issue of color? DuBois said early in this century that the problem of the twentieth century was the problem of the *color line*. But we need not look to such highly placed authorities. The issue of race still lies at the heart of many of the issues confronting us in our common life. From the entrance of students of color into the educational process, to the problem of oil, to the quotidian mundacity of big-time sports whether on the college or university levels — race is always with us. It may be that the very neutrality and meaninglessness of race has made it the most meaningful item in a meaningless world. But this disparity of meaningfulness and meaninglessness has not escaped Shils. He offers two explanations for the inordinate and intense meaning of the meaningless. The first explanation is historical. During the period of Western modernity the conquest and exploitation of the World by the West created a geographical and historical context in which the white races formed the centers from which the exploitation and exercise of hegemonous power took place. These centers defined the structures of authentic human existence. The distances from these centers were adjudicated by varying degrees of humanity, so that at the outermost periphery, where color or blackness coincided with distance, the centrist position held that these were lesser human beings. But geography is relative; centers and peripheries change and thus new human relationships might ensue. This has not been the case with the issue of race, and thus Shils has recourse to another and ancillary proposition.

> There is truth also in the proposition that color identification arises in part from the assimilation by the colored periphery of the dominant white center's use of the categories, "whiteness" and "coloredness." But these hypotheses, valuable though they are, do not provide an exhaustive alternative explanation. Another element should be mentioned, not as an exhaustive explanation, but as a complementary one that deals with a vital phenomenon otherwise excluded from consideration. It is this: "Self-identification by color has its origins in the sense of primordial connection with which human beings find it difficult to dispense."[2]

So Shils now has recourse to an additional explanation, one of another order, an explanation that supplements but is not identical with the geographical-historical significance of color. He links the meaning of color to a primordial sense of identity, and it is at this point that he interjects the religious and sacred significance of color into the discussion.

This primordial sense of self-identification through color may ally itself with other nonprimordial forms, as a matter of fact, forms antithetical to the significations of the primordiality of color — for example, nationalism. In nationality, according to Shils, the primordial element begins to recede. "It yields to an 'ideal' or 'ideational' element — a 'spirit,' an 'essence' — that is recognized as involving the mind."[3]

The international scientific community exists in spite of, and not because of, the racial or nationalistic modes of self-identification. While the primordial and peripheral are elements in the formation of Afro-Asian intellectuals, it is nevertheless possible for them to become members of the international scientific community — a community in which the geographical-historical and primordial give way to a universal belongingness within the intellectual community.

There are several problems related to this rather ideal analysis of the Afro-Asian intellectual and the international community of scholars. First of all, the peripheral and primordial elements have more often than not served as the basis of their exclusion from the international intellectual community, not from the point of view of the "coloreds," but from those at the center who are the definers and arbiters of knowledge.

Second, a great deal of the "knowledge" held by the centrist, especially in the areas of the human sciences, is knowledge about these primordial peripheral "others" — a knowledge that does not correspond to what these others wish to know, nor does it reflect a meaning of truth in method that is consistent with their understanding of human possibilities.

And third, there is the issue of power — power of an economic and military character that continues to be the correlate of center/periphery distinction as well as a paradigm for a model of knowledge. I shall return to these issues in another context. Let us proceed to a discussion of that primordiality of color — which, you may remember, was invested with the meaning of sacrality by Shils — by way of some comments of Roger Bastide concerning "Color, Racism, and Christianity."

Bastide begins his discussion with a statement that agrees with and is almost identical with one made by Shils. "Color is neutral; it is the mind that gives it meaning."[4] This statement occurs at the end of a paragraph in which he relates how blind persons are able in a racist culture to recognize immediately the race of a person whom they meet. Racism thus has several registers for its ranges of perception; it is the symbolic meaning or the power of color to signify that underlies this phenomenon.

In a very general manner Bastide surveys the meaning of color symbolism within the Christian West. There has been an attitude toward almost all color, but the most important distinction has been the white/black distinction. This distinction is the paradigm and equation for several other meanings — Christ/Satan, good/bad, and so forth. "Whiteness brings to mind the light, ascension into the bright realm, the immaculateness of virgin snow, the white dove of the Holy Spirit, the transparency of limpid air; blackness suggests the infernal streams of the bowels of the earth, the pit of hell, the devil's color."

The history of the interpretation of color in Roman Catholicism has ebbed and flowed with the rhythms of its history and geographical spread. The three wise men will change from a symbolism of time to one of space. Sainthood was conferred upon those who were blacks, and Africans and Indians respond and react in an iconography that portrays their physical features. But in all of these changes, the Christ remains white and is more and more Aryanized.

Bastide notes the changes in the meaning of the symbolism of color among Protestants, especially in Calvin and the New England Puritans. Calvin believed that the knowledge of God was deeply rooted in all human beings. This knowledge could be stifled by superstition — a superstition that blinded the intelligence — or by sin, which corrupted the senses. The perseverance of the Indian in diabolical and sinful ways was to the Puritan, therefore, an infallible sign of negative predestination, and the unavoidable damning of the Indian's soul.

Bastide is particularly perceptive when he relates some specific elements of Calvin's Institutes to the meaning of election, land, the frontier thesis, and racism. In Bastide's interpretation of Calvin,

> ...man is assailed from all sides by temptations and living in a doubtful world; Calvin includes in the dangers that threaten man life among the savages and the pitfalls of country life. Although he condemns racism, he maintains that the precept of salvation must be limited to those who have some alliance or affinity with Christians. He adds in his commentary on Matthew that God esteems more highly the small company of his own than all the rest of the world.[6]

These ideas, the danger of pagan contagion and the priceless value of the small flock, constitute the religious basis for the "frontier complex" or restricted group sentiment, present as much in North America as among the Boers in Africa.

> The "frontier complex" or restricted-group feeling rests, therefore, in the final analysis upon the Calvinist idea of predestination and visible signs of divine election. In this way, dark skin came to symbolize, both in Africa and in America, the voluntary and stubborn abandonment of a race in sin. Contact with this race endangered the white person's soul and the whiteness of his spirit. The symbolism of color thus took on one of the most complicated and subtle forms, in both Protestantism and Catholicism, through the various steps through which darkness of color became associated with evil itself.[7]

I have gone through this short discussion of Shils and Bastide to show how the intellectual and the religious relate to the problem of race in the contemporary world. The issue of race is raised within structures of academic theology. This issue has not so much to do with the particular statements regarding race enunciated within a theology or by a particular theologian. The issue has more to do with the historical, religious, and philosophical structures of the intellectual task itself as this task implicates the meaning of race. What is the stance of a theology or a theologian when the very intellectual religious task is framed within a racist context?

The fact that black theologians accuse mainline theology of being "white theology" is to the point when seen from this perspective. How did the meanings of color assume such proportions in the post-Enlightenment secular and religious worlds? What significations have operated to produce the semiotics of racism?

The nonwhite color symbolizes and its significations have been acted upon within the modern Western world as signs of defilement and uncleanness. Paul Ricoeur's analysis of the originary form of the primary symbolism of evil would aptly apply to the historical-cultural formation of the symbolism of blackness in the history of the modern West. The significations of stain, pollution, and guilt accompany the archaic level of the modern Western consciousness in its confrontation with the "meaninglessness" and neutrality of color.

Ricoeur puts it thusly:

> In truth, defilement was never literally a stain; impurity was never literally filthiness, dirtiness, (and we might add that black was never literally dirty or unclean).... The representation of defilement dwells in the half-light of a quasi-physical infection that points towards a quasi-moral unworthiness.[8]

That "thing" (the blackness) must be suppressed, but the very act of suppression introduces the thing suppressed into the symbolic universe that it stakes out.

> Now, defilement enters into the universe of man through speech, or the word (parole); its anguish is communicated through speech...the opposition of the pure and the impure is spoken...a stain is a stain because it is there, mute; the impure is taught in the words that institute the taboo.

Blacks, the colored races, caught up into this net of the imaginary and symbolic consciousness of the West, rendered mute through the words of military, economic, and intellectual power, assimilated as if by osmosis structures of this consciousness of oppression. This is the source of the doubleness of consciousness made famous by W. E. B. DuBois. But even in these symbolic structures there remained the inexhaustibility of the opaqueness of this symbol for those who constituted the "things" upon which the significations of the West deployed its meanings. This doubleness of consciousness, this existence in half-lights and within the quasi fields of human infection, is the context for the communities of color, the opaque ones of the modern world.

These twilight zones of half-light and quasi-physical infection were inhabited by the semirealities of the modern Western world. Octavio Paz tells us that they were filled with poets, proletarians, colonized peoples, the colored races. "All these purgatories and hells lived in a state of clandestine ferment. One day in the twentieth century, the subterranean world blew up. This explosion hasn't yet ended and its splendor has illumined the agony of the age."[10] This is why W. E. B. DuBois announced that the problem of the twentieth century is that of the color line, and this is equally why there have appeared theologies opaque.

## *Theologies Opaque*

James Cone's first book of 1969, *Black Theology and Black Power,* was the signal for a new mode of theological writing. It does not, however, represent the first time that blacks have raised the issue of theology within the context of the black experience. The venerable Howard Thurman's several works over a span of half a century drew heavily upon the black experience for content and method. Benjamin E. Mays and Joseph W. Nicholson's work on the Negroes' God is as explicit as its title. And Joseph Washington and Eric Lincoln have made major contributions. There is, nevertheless, a novelty in the work of Cone. Its style is evocative and prophetic; its focus is the meaning of the oppressed as the focus of Christian theology. It appears within the historical context of the civil rights movement, and its avowed aim is to explicate the theological meaning of black power.

The programmatic intent of Cone's work has found further expression in his *The Spirituals and the Blues, A Black Theology of Liberation,* several major articles, and his influence as a professor at Union Theological Seminary in New York where he has guided several students, as well as his influence and relationships with Third World and liberation theologians throughout the world. While rooted in the black American experience, his work and career seem destined to have catholic implications.

Published in the same year as Cone's *Black Theology and Black Power* was the work of Vine Deloria, Jr., *Custer Died for Your Sins: An Indian Manifesto.* This work was followed by *We Talk, You Listen* (reminiscent of Richard Wright's *White Man, Listen*) and then in 1973, *God Is Red.* Like Cone's work, Deloria's point of departure is the history of the oppression, suffering, and exploitation of the aborigines. Because the two histories, that of the red and that of the black, are different, the narrative structures differ, but the common themes of exploitation and oppression, the desire and necessity to initiate thought and action for themselves, are present in both. We are in some sense revisiting that arena and range of thought raised by Alexis de Tocqueville's *Democracy in America.* Chapter 10 of volume 1, part 2, is entitled "Some Considerations Concerning the Probable Future of the Three Races That Inhabit the Territory of the United States." The works by Cone and Deloria adumbrate and explicate that wise Frenchman's musings and are stark reminders that American theology has consistently avoided serious attention to the meaning of de Tocqueville's considerations.

To the extent that American theology has shown an awareness of this issue, it has more often than not been expressed in the terms of what has come to be called the civil religion or theology. Cultural or church theology has rarely faced the issue at all. It may very well be that civil religion is indeed the proper locus for the institutional and majority theology in America for such considerations. Civil religion is almost the common ground for institutional majority theologies and the theologies of Cone and Deloria. This common basis is admitted by Cone and Deloria just long enough for it to become a point of departure and accusation.

The civil rights movement of the 1960s is the context in which Cone and Deloria present their work; it would be difficult to imagine these works apart from this context. It is at this point and upon this ground that they seize the initiative. They make it clear that though their works appear within the civil rights movement, their efforts should not be seen as a continuation of the American reformist apologetics of the perennial American dilemma. Neither have they attempted to conform to scholarly or popular stereotypes of their images on the American scene.

Cone states explicitly in *Black Theology and Black Power* that his work is an effort made in order to investigate the meaning of black power, placing primary emphasis on its relationship to Christianity, the church, and contemporary American theology. Later on, he defines black power. It is, "in short, an attitude, an inward affirmation of the essential worth of blackness.... This is Black Power, the power of the black man to say YES to his black being and to make the others accept him or be prepared for a struggle."[11]

In *Custer Died for Your Sins,* Deloria's first comment puts his finger on a singular problem. He says:

> One of the finest things about being an Indian is that people are always interested in you and your "plight." Other groups have difficulties, predicaments, quandaries, problems, or troubles. Traditionally we Indians have had a "plight."
>
> Our foremost plight is our transparency. People can just tell by looking at us what we want, what should be done to help us, how we feel, and what a "real" Indian is really like. Indian life, as it relates to the real world, is a continuous attempt not to disappoint people who know us.[12]

In his second book, *We Talk, You Listen,* Deloria devotes an entire chapter (chap. 5) to the notion of Others. A few of the comments from this chapter should be heard.

> Sometimes when people ask me what tribe I belong to, I am tempted to say Others.
>
> Housing becomes an OTHERS when superhighways are discussed. Pollution becomes an OTHERS when industrial development is discussed. Land becomes an OTHERS when suburbs are planned or a jetport is needed. Religion is an OTHERS when wars are planned.... Another way of describing this process is that American society has so functionalized itself that it is unable to function as a society. Things are used and not experienced and tribalism becomes quite important, because Indians are always experienced.[13]
>
> Obviously the most important thing that people can do today in the field of race relations is to develop additional understanding of groups that used

to compose the category of OTHERS. On the one hand, this means that the OTHERS will have to develop political power within the structure and defend the new intellectual territory they are able to forge out.[14]

Cone exhorts his reader to understand the black affirmation of being. Deloria accuses the language of American culture for relegating the aboriginal to the category of a functional otherness and to a state of transparency. These themes of affirmation and accusation are not in themselves new. Ralph Ellison made explicit the case of transparency as regards blacks in his *Invisible Man*, and a host of blacks, including Bishop Henry McNeil Turner and Marcus Garvey, have enunciated the blackness of being.

What is novel in this case is the context for these statements and the programmatic intent. Cone's *Black Theology and Black Power* is the first in a series of works that go on to explicate the meaning of blackness and power within the structures of American theology and culture, while Deloria follows through with two additional works of construction. The civil rights movement of the 1960s in the United States is a postcolonial situation. The old clichés of the "white man's burden" are no longer lying around in the background as valid rhetorical fuel. Colonialism is at an end, and if we are to believe Paul Tillich, we have also come to the end of the Protestant Era. And further, a few years ago a group of American theologians announced "the death of God," and Daniel Bell's book of the mid-1950s announced the end of ideology. So it is in the midst of all these endings and deaths that the "theologies opaque" appear. The people of the quasi-zones and the twilights, of subterranean regions, emerge or are revealed. But it is as Ralph Ellison replied to Irving Howe, "Hey Man, there's real people down here," or as Claude Lévi-Strauss pointed out to Jean-Paul Sartre, the colonized cultures are human, and have always been human. Deloria and Cone join a group of intellectuals all over the world who have undertaken the issue of what I call the *opacity of reality*. Black is beautiful; God is red! These pronouncements by the opaque ones deny the authority of the white world to define their reality, and deny the methodological and philosophical meaning of transparency as a metaphor for a theory of knowledge. Paul Tillich in his *Systematic Theology* made explicit the meaning of transparency in his Christological formulation. In the crucifixion, Tillich affirms that Jesus became transparent so that through him the believer could see God. The theologians of opacity with their emphasis on suffering and oppression force one to deal with the actuality of the suffering itself, and with that human act whereby one human being or community forces another person or community to undergo an ordeal for the salvation of one or both.

## *Power and Passivity*

What is the meaning of the opaque theologies, or can there really be theologies of the opaque? What is one to make of these theologies of redness, blackness, and blueness of deity and being? We are, after all, still within the cultural arena of Western religious meanings; we are not Hindus or Africans who have never made a great fuss about the color of their deities. And of course, any good historian of religions knows that deities come in different colors. Protestant Christianity in implicit and unconscious ways has thought of deity as either white or transparent, so that the issue of color has been obscured.

It may also be that after a decade we have normalized the meaning of the opaque. The "coloreds" can now be placed within the category of the ethnic resurgence, with every group having the right to portray the godhead in their own image. Or even at a more sophisticated mode, these theologies are part and parcel of the new liberation theologies — theologies that carry a familiar Enlightenment ring with their emphasis on liberation and their open consorting with Marxism.

There is an internal ambiguity within the theologies opaque. They grow out of the realization of the primordial meaning of color and they push this signification into the critical and constructive arena of intellectual construction, yet they do not wish to claim simple ethnic goals or superiority; they do not wish to be another and obverse example of racism and exclusiveness. In every case, the claim of these theologies is more than an accusation regarding the actions and behavior of the oppressive cultures; it goes to the heart of the issue. It is an accusation regarding the world view, thought structures, theory of knowledge, and so on, of the oppressors. The accusation is not simply of bad acts but, more important, of bad faith and bad knowledge. It is indeed a battle of theology. The polemics, rhetoric, and intellectual resources of the debate remind one of the Lutheran Reformation.

But do the protagonists wish only to win a theological debate? While this may be salutary, it is not their basic intent. They wish to claim or prepare a place and a time for the full expression of those who have suffered alterity and oppression. Such a place and time would by implication free all human beings, even the oppressors, for it is their consciousness and acts of oppression that constitute their unfreedom and inhumanity. Is theological discourse appropriate for this intention? Theologies are specific modes of religious discourse that have become overwhelmingly predominant within the Christian church. Theologies are about power, the power of God, but equally about the power of specific forms of discourse about power. These discourses are about the hegemony of power — the distribution and economy of this power in heaven and on earth-whether in the ecclesiastical locus of a pope or, more generally since the modern period, the center of this power in the modern Western world. It is this kind of power which is attacked in the opaque theologies, for this power has justified and sanctified the oppression rendering vast numbers of persons and several cultures subject to economic-military oppression and transparent to the knowledge of the West. It is clear that the opaque theologians do not wish to extend either this meaning or this structure. It is the intent and structure of theology as a mode of discourse that is at stake at this point.

Running as a thread through the theologies of Cone and Deloria is a leitmotif whose significance they may have overlooked. Cone's book *The Spiritual and the Blues* and several chapters in Deloria's *God Is Red* make reference to their respective cultures during the period of oppression. Their references are to a structure of human meaning and value achieved in the past and during the period of oppression. These are narratives about the beauty and meaning of these communities throughout their histories. Heroic persons are mentioned, but the narratives are not built around heroic themes. The narratives are filled with ordinary persons with anonymous creations that emerge from the self-definitional intimacy of all human communities. It is the sheer power of being of these communities —a power they expressed even when they had to be passive in the situation of historical oppression.

But passive power is still power. It is the power to be, to understand, to know even in the worst historical circumstances, and it may often reveal a clearer insight into significant meaning of the human venture than the power possessed by the oppressors.

If God is red, if black is beautiful, then this modality of the godhead has always been the case and there are those who have lived this testimony. The opacity of God forms a discontinuity with the bad faith of the other theological modes. There is a theology of accusation and opposition which is to the fore in the theologies opaque. But it is precisely at this point that these theologies should not move forward to possess the theological battlefield wrested from their foes. It is at this point that theologies opaque must become deconstructive theologies —that is to say, theologies that undertake the destruction of theology as a powerful mode of discourse.

The resources for this kind of deconstructive theology are present in the histories and traditions of those who have undergone the oppressive cultures of the modern period. It means that attention must be given in a precise manner to the modes of experience and expression that formed these communities in their inner and intimate lives. I don't have in mind here a romantic return to an earlier period. I am speaking of the resources that might enable us to generate another kind of meaning for the temporal-spatial existence of human beings on this globe. The designations post-Enlightenment, death of God, end of the Protestant Era, the end of ideology, which we referred to earlier, are pronouncements that have come from the intellectual orders of the sophisticated West, and they may well be the most authentic statement about their intellectual resources for the definition of the human venture.

But what would be a history stemming from the oppressed? Are they destined to imitate and repeat a destructive cycle of events? The appearance of theologies of the opaque might promise another alternative of a structural sort, but only if these theologies move beyond the structural power of theology as the normative mode of discourse and contemplate a narrative of meaning that is commensurate with the quality of beauty that was fired in the crucible of oppression. Those who have lived in the cultures of the oppressed know something about freedom that the oppressors will never know. Opaque theologies in their deconstructive tasks will be able to make common cause with folklorists, novelists, poets, and many other nontheological types who are involved in the discernment of these meanings.

### *Reality, Oppugnancy, and Freedom*

David Brion Davis ends his work *The Problem of Slavery in the Age of Revolution* with a statement spelling out the significance of Hegel's master-slave dialectic for modern thought. He says:

> It was Hegel's genius to endow lordship and bondage with such a rich resonance of meanings that the model could be applied to every form of physical and psychological domination. And the argument precluded the simple and sentimental solution that all bondsmen should become masters, and all masters the bondsmen. Above all, Hegel bequeathed a message that would have a profound impact on future thought, especially as Marx and Freud deepened the meaning of the message: that we can expect nothing from the mercy of God or from the mercy of those who exercise worldly lordship

in His or other names; that man's true emancipation, whether physical or spiritual, must always depend on those who have endured and overcome some form of slavery."[15]

The thought of Freud and Marx forms part of the liberating thought structures of the Enlightenment heritage. As ideological structures, they undertake a devastating critique of the Western theological foundation. The transcendent meaning in the notion of God is dethroned in favor of definable human structures; the worker and the economic order in the case of Marx, and the authority principle that lies behind the pulsations of desire within the social context for Freud. A new primordium that is universal within the actualities of history rather than mind is brought to the fore. These ideologies not only counter the older Western theological notions but serve as well to deconstruct the Enlightenment primordium of reason and rationality. Growing out of Enlightenment thought, they make a juncture and discontinuity with its basic presuppositions. As ideologies, they form part of the late European debate about the meaning of freedom.

But what expression would a freedom deriving from people who had indeed endured and overcome oppression make? If this freedom is not to be simply the sentimental imitation of the lordship-bondage structure with a new set of actors, it would have to be a new form of freedom. As stepchildren of Western culture, the oppressed have affirmed and opposed the ideal of the Enlightenment and post-Enlightenment worlds. But in the midst of this ambiguity, for better or for worse, their experiences were rooted in the absurd meaning of their bodies, and it was for these bodies that they were regarded not only as valuable works but also as the locus of the ideologies that justified their enslavement. These bodies of opacity, these loci of meaninglessness, in the words of Shils and Bastide, were paradoxically loci of a surplus of meaning, meanings incapable of universal expression during the period of oppression. These opaque ones were centers from which gods were made. They were the concrete embodiments of matter made significant in the modern world. They formed new rhythms in time and space; these bodies of opacity were facts of history and symbols of a new religious depth. The totalization of all the great ideals of Western universalization met with the factual symbol of these oppressed ones. Opaque theologies emerge because the strategies of obscuring these peoples and cultures within the taxonomies of the disciplines of anthropology as primitives or the classification of them as sociological pathologies is no longer possible.

The oppressed have faced the hardness of life. The world has often appeared as a stone. As I stated in "Perspectives for a Study of Afro-American Religion in the United States" (see p. 173), Hegel spoke of a form of consciousness as the lithic imagination, that mode of consciousness which in confronting reality in this mode formed a will *in opposition*. This hardness of life was not the oppressor; the oppressor was the occasion for the experience but not the datum of the experience itself. The hardness of life or of reality was the experience of the meaning of the oppressed's own identity as opaque. Reality itself was opaque and seemed opposed to them. The affirmations "black is beautiful" or "God is Red" are more than mere slogans. They are shorthand for the agonizing history of communities that have had to face the ultimacy of reality as a daily experience in the modern world. The matter of God is what is being experienced. This may be an old god (but all old gods are new gods). The expression of this god cannot be in the older theological languages. This god has evoked a new beat, a new rhythm, a new movement. It is a god that must be commensurate with both the agony of oppression and the freedom of all persons. One of the best expressions of this reality is by a black poet:

> Lift every voice and sing
> Till earth and heaven ring,
> Ring with the harmonies of Liberty;
> Let our rejoicing rise
> High as the listening skies,
> Let it resound loud as the rolling sea.
> Sing a song full of the faith that the dark past has taught us,
> Sing a song full of the hope that the present has brought us,
> Facing the rising sun of our new day begun
> Let us march on till victory is won.
>
> Stony the road we trod,
> Bitter the chastening rod,
> Felt in the days when hope unborn had died;
> Yet with a steady beat,
> Have not our weary feet
> Come to the place for which our fathers sighed?
> We have come over a way that with tears has been watered,
> We have come, treading our path through the blood of the slaughtered,
> Out from the gloomy past,
> Till now we stand at last
> Where the white gleam of our bright star is cast
> God of our weary years,
> God of our silent tears,

Thou who has brought us thus far on the way;
Thou who has by Thy might
Led us into the light,
Keep us forever in the path, we pray.

Lest our feet stray from the places, our God, where we met Thee,
Lest, our hearts drunk with the wine of the world, we forget Thee;
Shadowed beneath Thy hand,
May we forever stand,
True to our God,
True to our native land.

(James Weldon Johnson, "Lift Every Voice and Sing," in *American Negro Poetry*)

## Notes

1. Edward Shils, "Color, the Universal Intellectual Community and the Afro-Asian Intellectual," *Daedalus* (Spring 1967): 279.
2. Ibid., 282.
3. Ibid.
4. Roger Bastide, "Color, Racism, and Christianity," *Daedalus* (Spring 1967): 312.
5. Ibid., 315.
6. Ibid., 321-22.
7. Ibid., 323.
8. Paul Ricoeur, *The Symbolism of Evil* (Boston: Beacon Press, 1969), 35.
9. Ibid., 36.
10. Octavio Paz, *The New Analogy,* The Third Herbert Read Lecture, 25.
11. James Cone, *Black Theology and Black Power* (New York: Seabury Press, 1969), 8.
12. Vine Deloria Jr., *Custer Died for Your Sins* (New York: Avon Books, 1970), 1.
13. Vine Deloria Jr., *We Talk, You Listen* (New York: Dell Press, 1972), 92.
14. Ibid., 98.
15. David B. Davis, *The Problem of Slavery in the Age of Revolution* (Ithaca, NY: Cornell University Press, 1975), 564.

# Index

**A**

*A priori*, the...14, 40, 43, 176
Aborigines...103
   (*see also* Archaic; Origins; Other;
     Primitives)
   American...97, 99, 103-04, 141, 161,
     164
   Australian...32, 35-36
   culture of the...136-37
Adams, Charles J....89
Adams, Robert McCormick...79, 108
Africa...34, 73, 97, 166, 189, 192, 196,
   203
   Asia and...108, 145, 160-61
   myth of inferior races of...116
   peoples of...7, 126
   slaves from...115, 119, 189-90
   West, art forms used by Picasso...6
Afro-Americans...8, 141-42, 192
   (*see also* Black Americans)
   religion of...6-7, 143, 162
Allen, Richard...190
Altizer, Thomas J. J....142, 149-50,
   141-42, 145-47
America...25, 66, 152-55, 160-61
   (*see also* Black Americans; Bricolage;
     Indians; Innocence; Invisibility)
   arche of...151
   cultural languages of... 7, 162-66,
     168, 1206
   discovery of... 97-98, 114
   epic of, the "mighty saga of the out-
     ward acts" (Mead)...156,163,
     166-68
   experience of...146-47, 149-50,
     154-58, 167, 174
   impact of, on...74, 136-37, 151,
     153, 147
   importation of slaves to...115-16,
     177
   inferiority complex of, toward Eu-
     rope...145, 147, 153
   meaning of freedom in...146-47,
     153, 160, 162
   movement of Europeans to...102-04,
     113, 115
   myth of...26, 163-67
   native peoples of...115,119
   North...99, 114-16, 189, 203
   "otherness" of...28, 153, 166
   religion of...142-43, 160-68, 197
   South...98-100, 103, 119, 187-88
   superiority complex of, *vis à vis* Af-
     rica and Asia...146-47, 153
   tragic dimensions of...149, 157-59
   United States of...3, 9, 74, 121, 141,
     145, 189, 191, 207
   (*see also under* Cultural contact;
     Europe; Ideology; Images; Myth)
American Academy of Religion...16,
   28, 64, 135-37
Anthropologists, anthropology...31, 43,
   48, 55, 76, 101, 141, 189, 211
   methodology in...4, 82-83
   of religion...2
   revolution in...126, 135-37, 179
Archaic (forms), archaism...8-9, 54, 56,
   66, 69, 83
   (*see also* Aborigines; Crawling;
     Hermeneutics; Origins; Other;
     Primitives)
   definition of...43
   and primitive religion and religious
     phenomena...43, 82
   return to the beginnings...51-52
   of the subject...48
Archetypes...78, 99, 116, 164, 193
Aristotle...79, 181
Arouet, François Marie
   *see* Voltaire
Aryan myth...22, 24, 26, 85

Auerbach, Erich...25
Australia...132-34
  aborigines of...32, 35-36

**B**
Bachelard, Gaston...192
Bakhtin, M. M....74
Baldwin, James...149-50
Bambara...37-39
Barth, Karl...145-47, 150, 153
Bastide, Roger...199, 201-03
Baudet, Henri...96
Becker, Carl...157
Benveniste, Émile...93
Berlin, Sir Isaiah...25
Bernheimer, Richard...91
Black Americans..679, 149, 151, 189, 192
  (see also Afro-Americans)
  author as a...8, 27, 145
  freedom of...164-66
  religion and religious experience of...9, 151, 167, 177-78, 187-88, 189, 194-97, 205
  (see also Transformation)
  visibility of community of...147-50, 152-54, 160-61
Black, Max...67
Blake, William...142, 154
Boas, George...89-90, 100
Boden, Lieutenant-Colonel Joseph...17
Bopp, Franz...17-21
Boswell, James...93
Bournouf, Émile...17, 81
Braudell, Fernand...84, 87
Brer Rabbit...193, 196
Bricolage, of America and the West
  see Flotsam and jetsam
Burridge, Kenelm...118, 125-26, 130, 134-35, 179

**C**
Calvin...202
Cargo cults...74, 102-04, 117, 179
  cultural-religious dynamics of...127-30, 134-36
  description of...125-26
  Mambu, leader of a...130-35
  methodological implications of...135-37
  problem of, basis for a "revolution in anthropology...125, 135-37, 179-80
Center, the...83, 108, 128, 136, 169, 200
  ceremonial...73, 79, 108
  decentering process...84, 87, 137
  Eliade's notion of, as a religious reality...78-79
  epistemological...76, 80-83
  power of...73, 79, 107-09, 201
Chantepie de la Saussaye, Pierre Daniel... 23, 44
Chaudhuri, Nirad...19
Chicago, University of, Divinity School...  27, 141-42, 145-47, 149, 152-53
Childe, V. Gordon...108
Christianity...18, 21, 23, 47, 155, 174, 208
  in America...161-62
  and black religion...187, 193-94, 206
  and pilgrimage...109-110
Citied traditions...73, 75, 69-72, 83, 108
Civilization
  civilized, the...94, 101-04, 115, 120
  as locus of power...81, 97
  meaning of...90, 93, 101
  opposed to primitives...73, 86, 90, 94-95, 99-101, 103-04, 180
  as a symbol...95-96, 102, 104
Civil religion
  America, in...140, 161-63, 165, 205
Civil rights movement...77, 164-65, 188, 205-07
  (see also Protest)
Cleaver, Eldridge...151
Clebsch, William...174, 184

Clown, unserious, religious studies as a...16
(*see also* Jabberwocky; Patchwork)
Codrington, R. H....136
Cogito (*see* Ego)
Colonialism...3, 65-66, 68, 153, 207
Colonization...19, 98
Colonized peoples...4, 8, 83, 183, 204, 207
(*see also* Oppressed; Other)
Color...4, 116, 143, 201, 208
(*see also* Race)
meanings of...199-204, 208
problem of...152-53
Columbus, Christopher...3, 97-99, 109-110, 112, 113
Comte, Auguste...64
Concealment...141-42, 148-49, 156, 162, 166-68
Cone, James...189, 199, 204-07, 209
Consciousness, double...120, 123 n. 21, 178-80, 184, 204
(*see also* Second creation)
Consciousness, human...23, 35, 83-44, 90, 107, 168, 181, 183, 192
*a priori* religious category of...44
forms of the world apprehended in...27, 32-33
intentionality toward action as a structure of...34, 39, 40 n. 8
ordered and centered intelligence in...676 80-81
phenomenology in...48-49
Cook, Captain...89
Crawling back through history...9
(*see also* Archaic; Hermeneutics; Origins)
Cuddihy, John...85
Cultural contact...103, 108-11, 115, 118, 121
America the classical example of...141
from the point of view of those under going conquest...73-74, 117, 134
issue in the understanding of religion... 3-8, 73, 127, 135-36

D
Daniel, Samuel...116
Darwin, Charles...22-23, 85, 89-90
*Das Heilige*, (*The Idea of the Holy*)
see under Otto
Davis, David Brion...180-81, 210
de Mirabeau, Marquis...93
(*see also* Riqueti, Victor)
de Tocqueville, Alexis...113, 150, 156, 205
Death of God...53, 63, 65-66, 142, 149, 159, 207, 210
Deloria, Vine, Jr....142, 199, 205-07, 209
Derrida, Jacques...9, 103-04, 136
Descartes, René...47, 52
*Deus otiosus*...9, 63, 128, 154, 194
De Voto, Bernard Augustine...157
Dilthey, Wilhelm...22, 25, 47, 84
Dinka...35, 130
Discourse...1-2, 13, 16, 21, 73, 84, 87, 136
destruction of theology as a mode of...209-10
modes of, related to discovery of Indo-European language family... 20-23
new, concerning the meaning of religion...25-27, 85
of power...141, 208-09
DuBois, W. E. B....120-21, 123 n. 21, 142, 148, 153, 166, 176-81, 182-84, 187, 189, 200
Dumezil, Georges...50
Dumont, Louis...7, 26, 85-86
Durkheim, Émile...86, 128, 161

E
Eckhart, Meister...67
Edwards, Jonathan...155, 174
Ego (*cogito*)...46, 49
(*see also* Subject-object relationship)
Cartesian, a false...58 n. 18
Merleau-Ponty's analysis of...58 n. 18
Self as a lonely...53

shadows of, and history...57
Egypt...90
Eliade, Mircea...27, 33, 37, 50, 54-56, 63, 78-79, 82, 84, 86, 89, 104,108, 114, 137, 152
   *The Myth of the Eternal Return*...26-27, 56, 78
   *Patterns in Comparative Religion*...27, 50, 63, 78
Elias, Norbert...94
Ellison, Ralph...162, 1207
Emerson, Ralph Waldo...155, 174
England...17-18, 22, 24, 93-94,
   and the American Indians...115-16
   literary figures of...111, 148
Enlightenment, the...3-4, 8, 61-62, 64-65, 77-78, 101, 210-11
   German...19, 21
   origins of history of religions in...24, 76-77, 80-81, 85
Epistemology...76, 77, 80-83, 104
Epoche, the bracketing of experience... 52, 152
   (*see also* Phenomenology)
Ethiopia...97, 190
Europe...15, 18, 86, 155
   American inferiority complex toward...145, 147, 153
   cannot be an absolute cultural norm for Americans...160
   immigrants from...264, 149, 160-61, 161-62
   impact of New World on consciousness of...90, 92, 94-101, 106 n. 28, 109-114
   languages of...17, 20, 22
   movements of people of, to America... 102-04, 113, 114-15
   myth of wild man in...91-92, 99-100, 116
   response of aboriginal peoples to people and culture of...103, 120, 126, 128, 130
Evolutionary theories...43, 45, 77, 85, 89, 171-72

**F**
Flotsam and jetsam of bits and pieces of a reality that was once thought to be an order, America and the West the... 137
Forde, Daryll...189
Foucault, Michel...91-92
Frazer, James...85-86, 89-90
Frazier, E. Franklin...189
Freedom...110, 146-47, 153, 161, 163-66, 172, 193, 210, 212
   meaning of...164, 111-12
   theology of...141, 145-47, 153
Freud, Sigmund...83-85, 90, 211

**G**
Gadamer, Hans Georg...14, 25
Germany...17-21, 23-24
God...21-22, 38, 81, 127, 164, 166, 188, 192-97
   (*see also* Death of; *Deus otiosus;* High God)
   as a structure of intimacy has disappeared...62, 64
   "Be still and know that I am"...67, 69
   (*see also under* Other; Transformation)
God of our weary years, silent tears... 151, 157, 160, 212-13
Goethe, Johann Wolfgang von...64
Gossen, Gary...103
Greenblatt, Stephen...111-114
Griaule, Marcel...34
Grimm, Jacob and Willhelm (the Brothers Grimm)...21

**H**
Hanselmann, the Reverend R....129
Harnack, Adolf...23
Haroutunian, Joseph...146-47, 149-50
Hegel, G. W. F....26, 55, 141, 180, 210-12
Heidegger, Martin...49, 51
Heiler, Friedrich...24
Herder, Johann Gottfried von...19, 76, 84

Hermeneutics...24-25, 26, 82, 87, 94-95, 163
(*see also* Archaic; Crawling)
  archaism and...43-59 passim
  begins with the misinterpretations...148, 154
  every adequate, is at heart an essay in self-understanding...51-52
  phenomenology and...46-47
  prolegomenon to a religious...31-41 passim
  as a response to intellectual crisis...26-27, 101
  of suspicion...95, 101-02, 105 n. 15
  utopias and...95-101 passim
Herskovits, Melville...189
High God...63-64, 67, 193
High John, the Conqueror...193, 196-97
Historian/history of religions...45-47, 50, 54-56, 63, 68, 80, 85, 179, 194, 208
(*see also Religionswissenschaft*)
  author as a...2, 7, 188
  chairs in...22, 23-25
  Eliade's contribution to...78
  issues that are grist for the mill for...38
  method in...14, 75, 80, 84, 89, 152
  origins of, in the Enlightenment...24, 75-77, 80-81
  problem of origins in...48, 50, 85, 89
  as science of religions...82, 87
  study of archaic and primitive religious phenomena in...48, 89, 101-02
  traced back to a confrontation with an irrationality...83
  at Univ. of Chicago...27
Historiography...86, 98, 142, 157, 162, 167-68
Höltker, the Reverend Fathe Georg...131, 134
*Homo religiosus*...34, 549, 137
Hügel, Baron von...175
Human sciences...9, 46, 75, 77, 80, 83, 86, 102

Hume, David...77, 141
Hunt, Eva...103
Husserl, Edmund...26-27, 46-47, 49, 52
Hyman, Stanley...85
Hysteria, history of...90-91

I
Ideology...27, 86, 159, 184, 207, 210, 211
  of America...162-63, 167
  defined by Dumont...19, 85-86
  German...19-20, 85
  of primitivism...100
  sacred, of conquest and domestication of space...108-09
  of the West...78, 94, 96, 127, 134, 173
Images...194-95
  of Africa...190
  of America...153-54, 156-57
  of black Americans...183-84, 194
  of non-Western peoples and worlds...96-97, 98-99
India...17-18, 20, 22-23, 37, 39, 79
Indians, American...99, 110, 112-13, 114-15, 117, 157, 162-63, 190, 202, 206
  destruction of...150, 156
  invisibility of, and blacks...163
  and Spanish...119
  (*see also under* Aborigines)
Indo-European languages...20, 22-23, 26, 85
Innocence, of America and Americans...142, 156
  beyond...145-46
  destroyed...160
Invisibility, of non-Europeans in America...161-64, 165-68

J
Jabberwocky of loose ends and bad fits, religious studies as a...15
(*see also* Clown; Patchwork)

James, Henry, Sr....172-75, 177-78, 180, 182-83
James, William...142, 171-79, 180, 182-83, 184
Jarvie, I. C....125, 135-36, 179
Jastrow, Morris, Jr....25-26
Jefferson, Thomas...164
Jennings, Francis...103, 141
Jensen, A. E....34
Jewish religious tradition...20, 23, 47, 65, 89, 128
Johnson, James Weldon...157
Jones, William...20

**K**
Kant, Immanuel...19, 22, 26, 28 n. 7, 45, 55, 62, 76-77, 85
Kitagawa, Joseph...27
Kittell, Rudolf...24
Kupperman, Karen...115

**L**
La Barre, Weston...179
Lafaye, Jacques...103
Lang, Andrew...22
Language...51-52, 54, 80, 85, 92, 112, 116, 121
 cultural...6-7, 65-66, 73, 115, 141
  (*see also* under America)
 interrelation of, and silence...67-68
 meanings of...37-38
 origin of...20-23
 as a premonition of human autonomy...34
 of signification...1, 8-9, 73
 of Western cultural creativity...65-66
Leeuw, Gerardus van der...24, 28, 45-46, 48, 53, 89, 127, 129, 176, 192
Lessing, Doris...148
Lévi-Strauss, Claude...14, 55, 82-83, 85, 104, 121, 129, 136, 207
Lévy-Bruhl, Lucien...82, 104
Lienhardt, Godfrey...35-36, 55
Lincoln, Eric...204

Linton, Ralph...125
Little Rock, Arkansas...1
Locke, John...180-81
Lovejoy, Arthur O....89-90, 100

**M**
McCleary, Richard...53
Madness...130, 164-77
 (*see also* Hysteria; Ship of fools; Vailala)
Maine, Sir Henry...18
Malraux, André...52
Mambu (cargo cult leader)...130-35
Marlowe, Christopher...111, 113-14
Marx, Karl...85, 211
Master-slave dialectic...141, 180-84, 210
Mays, Benjamin E....204
Mead, Sidney...149, 156-58, 159, 163
Meland, Bernard...146-47, 150
Melanesia...136
Melville, Herman...142, 154
Merleau-Ponty, Maurice...52, 53, 67
Method, methodology...21, 49, 73-74, 84-85
 as expression of a cultural milieu...2, 4
 of pathology...8
 principles of...31, 158
 problem of, generated by cargo cults...135-37
 in the study of religion...2-3, 13-14, 16, 27, 43-44, 75-76, 80, 82-84, 87, 89, 142, 168, 187-88
 three-fourths of any science...26
Mexico...103
Millar, John...94
Miller, Perry...155
Misinterpretations...148-49, 154, 166
Money...118, 131, 133
 economy of, replaces barter...128
 procreative powers of "How and when does money copulate?"...120
 as a sign of the devil...119
Monier-Williams, Sir Monier...17-18
Müller, F. Max...17-28 passim, 43-44, 48, 53, 78, 80, 85-86

Mumford, Lewis...79
*Mysterium fascinans*...45, 107, 150, 154-55, 176
 (see also *Mysterium tremendum*)
*Mysterium tremendum*...9, 45, 107, 151, 154, 176, 177, 180, 183
 (see also *Mysterium fascinans*)
Myth, mythology...22, 24, 32-33, 85, 96-97, 102, 115-16, 183
 of America...26, 163-67
 creation of a new cultural...129-30, 134
 critique of...79-80
 descent of America into the reality of...141
 discourse on, cannot have a center...136
 as a disease of language...43, 80
 Eliade's study of...78-79
 making of the modern, of the European...114
 rupture between humanity and nature in...34-35, 37-38
 of the wild man...91-92, 99, 116
Myth-dream...118-20, 130, 134, 137

N
Nature...62, 82-83, 99, 155-60, 182
 (see also under Myth)
Neruda, Pablo...121
New Guinea...129-30, 133-34
New world...96, 100, 114, 121
 of Americas and South Pacific...90, 92-93, 98
 of latent creative possibilities...62, 65-66
New World...7, 99, 102, 117
 impact of, on European consciousness...90, 93-94, 106 n. 28, 109-112
 myth of the...114-17
Nicholson, Joseph W....204
Niebuhr, H. Richard...162
Nietzche, Friedrich Wilhelm...63
Noble, David...157
Northrup, F. S.C....174

O
O'Gorman, Edmundo...97-98, 114
Ontology...48, 53, 65-66, 68-69, 83-84, 104-05
 of the sacred...33-39, 41 n. 11
Opacity..117-18, 121-22, 123 n. 14, 192-93, 207, 209, 211
Oppenheimer, Robert, "Thou hast become Death, destroyer of worlds"...64
Oppressed peoples...8, 151, 175-76, 209-10
 (see also Colonized peoples; Other)
 religions of...120, 142, 178-79, 181
Oppression in religion...173-84 passim, 205
Oppugnancy, "hardness" of life...87, 211-12
Origins of human culture, quest for...43-44, 89
 (see also Aborigines; Archaic; Crawling; Other; Primitives)
 language and religion...20-24, 43
 problem of, in history of religions...48, 50, 85
Other, the; otherness...4-5, 37, 53, 80-81, 92, 104, 116, 150-51, 182, 201, 206-07
 (see also Aborigines; Archaic; Colonized peoples; Oppressed; Origins; Primitives)
 of America...27, 153
 empirical...90-91, 96, 99,101-02
 evoked by racial situation...151-53, 166
 methodologies and theories about...26-27, 86
 religious experience of radical...9, 166, 177, 180
 "Something Other"...127, 129, 176, 193
 threatening...111, 114, 118
 to understand the self through mediation of...51
Other World
 see New World

Otto, Rudolf...8, 14, 23, 33, 45, 47-48, 75-78, 82, 84, 86, 107, 150, 154, 175-76
  *The Idea of the Holy*...24-27, 44, 48, 77, 86
  the last stomach ache...45
Oxford University...17

## O

Parry, J. H....114
Pascal, Blaise...61-62, 64, 68
Patchwork of potpourri confused, religious studies as a...15
  (*see also* Clown; Jabberwocky)
Paz, Octavio...121, 204
Pedersen, Holger...20
Peirce, Charles Sanders...14
Pettazzoni, Raffaele...47, 63
Phenomenology...24, 47, 49, 52, 152
  (*see also* Epoche)
  method of...46, 48
  of religion...31, 33, 44, 47, 52, 77, 86
Philology...17-18, 20-23, 26, 52
Philosophy...49, 55, 67, 84-85, 111
  of religion...142, 171-72
Picasso, Pablo...6
Pilgrimage...93, 109-10, 112-13, 115-16, 122 n. 5
Plato...79
Power...2, 33, 67, 81, 120, 141, 159, 182, 201-02, 204, 208-09
  black...121, 180, 193, 204, 206-07
  in and of the ceremonial center...73, 79, 108-09
  civilization as locus of...81, 97
  element of, in naming...4-5
  of established structures...2, 5, 7
  van der Leeuw refers all religious manifestations to...45, 48, 127
  of the sacred...32, 36, 95, 128-29
  will to...95
Primitives, primitive peoples...4, 8, 20, 28, 50, 54, 66, 83
  (*see also* Aborigines; Archaic; Origins; Other)
  assumed to represent an early stage of development...75, 77
  contrasted with civilized...73, 86, 90, 94-95, 99-102, 103-04, 179
  cultures of...75, 89, 127
  definitions of...43
  High God among...63
  religions and religious phenomena of...43, 82, 89-90, 102, 136
Primitivism...89-90, 94, 99-102, 103
Protest movements...5-6, 165-66
  (*see also* Civil rights)
Puritans...103, 141, 161, 163, 201

## R

Race, racial situation, racism...66, 115-16, 120, 141, 151, 163, 199-200, 202-03, 208
  (*see also* Color)
Ranke, Leopold von...19, 84
Religion...7, 31, 65, 107
  departments of (religious studies)...11, 15-16, 74, 76-77, 86
  (*see also* Clown; Jabberwocky; Patchwork)
  meaning and nature of...3-4, 16-17, 39
  as orientation in the ultimate sense...7, 107-08
  as power...45, 48, 127, 138 n. 11
  (*see also* Civil religion; Historian; Jewish religious tradition; Oppression)
  (*see also under* Afro-Americans; America; Anthropologists; Archaic; Black Americans; Christianity; Discourse; Method; Oppressed; Origins; Phenomenology; Philosophy; Primitives; Symbol; Theologians)
*Religionswissenschaft*...17, 24, 76-78
  (*see also* Historian)
Religious experience...34, 45, 84, 107, 126-27, 130, 136, 142, 148, 150, 192-93
  apprehends and discovers sacredness

of forms of the world...32
William James on...171-79, 180, 184
Religious studies
*see under* Religion
Renaissance...96-99, 104, 110, 118
Réville, Albert...23
Ricoeur, Paul...14, 52, 55, 85, 95, 203
Riqueti, Victor (Sibylle-Gabrielle-Marie Antoinette de Comtesse de Martel de Janville Riqueti de Mirabeau)
*see* de Mirabeau, Marquis
Romanticism...19, 22, 76-77, 83
Rush, Benjamin...155

**S**
Sacred, the...50-52, 56, 63, 87, 103, 107-108, 155
  demonic form of...120
  locus of, in the center...78-79
  ontology of...32-39, 41n. 11
  power of...32, 36, 95, 128-29
Sanford, Charles...157
Sanskrit...17-18, 20-21, 80, 85
Sartre, Jean-Paul...83, 207
Saussure, Ferdinand de...1, 2
Savigny, Friedrich Karl von...21
Schelling, Friedrich...17, 76
Schlegel, August Wilhelm von...19
Schlegel, Friedrich...19, 20
Schleiermacher, Friedrich...27, 76, 148, 154
Schmidt, Wilhelm...63
Schumpeter, Joseph...24
Sciences, human
  *see* Human sciences
Second creation...120-21, 180, 184
  (*see also* Consciousness, double)
Shils, Edward...199-204
Ship of fools...92-93
Significations...14, 73, 101, 202, 204
  even the dead continue to signify; if God is dead, the signification is even greater...159
  explanation of the term...1-9
  silence and...62-69
  (*see also under* Symbol)
Silence...38, 63-69

Slavery...156, 164-65, 178, 180-81, 188, 190-91
Smith, Adam...93
Smith, Jonathan...27
Socrates...67
Söderblom, Nathan...23, 89
South Pacific...90, 99, 104
Spenser, Edmund...111-12
Stanner, W. E. H....32, 35-36, 38
Subject-object relationship...54-55, 130
  (*see also* Ego)
  in van der Leeuw...32, 46
Symbol, symbolism...2, 32, 36, 95-96, 102, 119, 130, 161, 204, 211
  of the center...78-79
  civilization as a...95-96, 102, 104
  invites thought, signifies...55
  religious...47, 52, 54-56, 59 n. 21, 84, 86, 102

**T**
Taussig, Michael...119
Terror of history, effect of lost...136-37
Teutonic mythology and religion...21-22
Theologians, theology...56, 61, 110, 143, 145, 155, 203, 208
  American...146-47, 188, 105-07
  black...7, 143, 145, 187, 199, 205-06
  Christian...187, 205
  of color...143, 199
  of the death of God...142, 149
  of freedom...141, 145-47, 153
  opaque...204, 207-09
  study of religion outside of...13-16, 76, 172, 188
Thurman, Howard...204
Tieck, Ludwig...21
Tiele, Cornelius P....22
Tillich, Paul...207
Time...110, 128, 202
  never enough...156, 159
  primordial...33, 53
  space has overshadowed, in America...155-56
  use and killing of...114
Transformation, in black religion...191-92
  God the agent of...194-97

Trickster...149, 180, 193, 196
Troeltsch, Ernst...142, 171-75
Turner, V. W....36
Tylor, E. B....9, 22-23, 43-44, 48, 53, 86, 89-90, 104

**U**
Urban forms
  *see* Citied traditions
Utopias, and hermeneutics...95-102, *passim*

**V**
Vailala Madness...117, 121, 125-26, 130, 137, 180
Valéry, Paul...51
Veith, Ilza...90-91
Vespucci, Amerigo...98-99
Vico, Giambattista...21, 77, 85, 87
Voltaire (assumed name of Francois-Marie Arouet)...62, 64

**W**
Wach, Joachim...23-27, 75-76, 84, 107
  *Sociology of Religion*...23, 33
Wachtel, Nathan...103
Wallerstein, Immanuel...110
Washington, Joseph...187-88, 204
Wheatley, Paul...79, 108
Whitehead, Alfred North...52-53, 84
White men, white races...131-35, 147-48, 151, 163-65, 200, 203, 207
Williams, F. E....117, 125, 135
Wilson, H. H....17
Wittgenstein, Ludwig...67-68
Worsley, Peter...125
Wundt, Willhelm...24

**Z**
Zahan, Dominique...37-38

Made in United States
North Haven, CT
22 January 2025